LIBERATING THE CHURCH

Liberating the Church

The Ecology of Church and Kingdom

Howard A. Snyder

Marshalls

To my sisters and brothers
of the
Irving Park Free Methodist Church
and of
The Olive Branch
Chicago
Partners in the nitty-gritty work
of seeking the Kingdom

Marshall Paperbacks
3 Beggarwood Lane, Basingstoke, Hants, UK.

© Inter-Varsity Christian Fellowship of the United States of America 1983
First published in the UK by Marshall Morgan & Scott 1983

*Scriptural quotations, unless otherwise noted, are from the Holy Bible: New International
Version © 1978 by the New York International Bible Society. Used by permission
of Zondervan Bible Publishers.*

*This book incorporates in substantially revised form the following previously published
material by the author: "Why the Local Church is Becoming More and Less," Christianity
Today 25, no. 13 (July 17, 1981): 66–70; 'The Church and the Language of Sacrament,"
in Kenneth Cain Kinghorn, ed., A Celebration of Ministry (Wilmore, Ky.: Francis
Asbury Publishing Company, 1982), pp. 48–59; "An Evangelistic Lifestyle for the
Congregation," in C. Norman Kraus, ed., Missions, Evangelism, and Church Growth
(Scottdale, Pa.: Herald Press, 1980), pp. 82–108; "Simple Faith, Simple Life," Light and
Life 112, no. 10 (September 1979): 8–10; "Who Shepherds the Shepherds?" Light and
Life 111, no. 11 (July 11, 1978): 8–9; "What Does It Really Mean to Be Spiritual?" Light
and Life 111, no. 4 (March 7, 1978): 6–7; "Woman's Place," Light and Life 114, no. 2
(February 1981): 10–13; "I Couldn't Do Everything—But I Wasn't Supposed To,"
Pastoral Renewal 2, no. 7 (January 1978): 56.*

ISBN 0 551 01041 X

Printed in Great Britain by A. Wheaton & Co. Ltd., Exeter, Devon.

PREFACE

In his most challenging and provocative book to date Howard Snyder here examines the radical questions which Christians have to face when understanding the Church as the advanced guard of God's Kingdom.

Although parallels between Britain and America have to be drawn with care, the author writes at a deeper level than the particular features of Church and Society in the United States. His is a way of thinking about the Church in the late twentieth century. He draws widely from Scripture, Church history and experience of the World Church, but he writes as an American.

We in Britain however cannot dismiss his critique of American values and attitudes, as of no relevance to us. Materialism and its alliance with technology, the industrial–military complex, the prostitution of Christianity as civil religion, baptising an unjust status quo are all featured in Britain if in different forms and to different degrees. We are not wealthy, but we are still rich. We were an imperial power, America now is. Our history is their present experience which may help us to see even more clearly the relevance of his analysis.

Those who are enthusiastic about Church Growth need to take seriously Howard Snyder's critique. So too do those who argue and work for large scale evangelistic crusades. His appraisal of the 'Here's Life' campaign should be weighed carefully by enthusiasts for Mission to London and Mission England. He deals helpfully with Liberation Theology, especially arguing for the distinctiveness of the Church in the world, which is often blurred and sometimes obliterated by some Liberation Theologies.

It's his central message that needs to be heard and acted upon in the U.K. as well as the U.S. The Church is for the Kingdom and the Kingdom is about God's mission in His world. Too readily God's people turn in on themselves, become institutionalised, serve the Church, and maintain the status quo. Our disobedience denies the Good News of the Kingdom to a world desperately needing salvation—wholeness. Each of the Liberating Models of the Church are a call to repentance and action. That of 'sacrament' explores a dimension usually lacking in the protestant tradition. The necessity of being a counter culture is beginning to be recognised. The row over the Falklands Service at St Paul's and the arguments over Nuclear Weapons of mass destruction may be signs that the collective Christian voice in Britain is capable of calling the nation to repentance.

Contemporary hot issues, like doing theology, using the Bible, lifestyle, priesthood, ministry, women's rights, the poor and powerless and discipleship are all covered in ways that prompt fresh thought. The standpoints of ecology and economy give a different perspective to themes that need a fresh look. Our world faces a crisis at the point of impact of the economy on ecology. Unlimited, sustainable economic growth on an over-populated planet is impossible. Our non-renewable resources of energy and raw materials are running out. A new world economic order has to emerge or we all perish, and we in Britain sense, as well as any nation, the disturbing and painful consequences of this. America is only recently facing similar effects so it is easier for British Christians to appreciate the thrust of the author's biblical exposition of ecology and economy than for Americans. He will be even better understood amongst Christians in Third World countries and the 'Fourth World' of the Urban Poor.

Howard Snyder has a wide understanding of *renewal*. His 10 theses in the prologue should be nailed to the doors of every theological Seminary and Bible School in the country. We limit our understanding of the Spirit's work if we confine renewal to the 'Charismatic' or 'house church' or 'community' or 'liturgical' or whatever Movements. God by His Spirit is renewing His people in a variety of ways, but to what purposes? For His own glory, certainly, but also for the sake of the world and ultimately for the whole created order. Any experience of 'renewal' which locks the Good News of the Kingdom into the private experience of self serving and preserving groups of Christians needs seriously to be questioned. Both the older denominations and the newer forms of church in our time will benefit from getting to grips with the uncomfortable thrust of this prophetic book. If obedience follows from our wrestling together with God's word through Howard Snyder, God's world will benefit.

"If you have ears, then, listen to what the Spirit says to the Churches."

Michael Eastman
December 1982.

Michael Eastman serves on the staff of Scripture Union as Secretary and Development Officer of Frontier Youth Trust. He is also currently Secretary of the Evangelical Coalition for Urban Mission of which FYT is one of the founding partners.

CONTENTS

The burden of this book may be summed up in three verses:
The earth is the LORD's, and everything in it,
the world, and all who live in it. (Ps 24:1)
Seek first his kingdom and his righteousness. (Mt 6:33)
He . . . gave some to be apostles, some to be prophets, some to be
evangelists, and some to be pastors and teachers, to prepare God's
people for works of service, so that the body of Christ may be built
up. (Eph 4:11-12)

*I remain convinced that a biblical theology is impossible without a biblical
ecclesiology. This book explores that premise, looking at the church in the
broader framework of the whole Kingdom and economy of God. The argument assumes what I have previously published on the church and therefore
repeats little. It also reflects my conviction that questions of ecology, economics
and international justice are essential, not secondary, to the biblical picture of
the church and the new order for which we yearn and to which biblically faithful churches point.*

*The book leads to the conclusion that the pastoral role—understood as dis-
cipling and equipping people for Kingdom work—is crucial for liberating the
church today. In fact, my own pilgrimage and ministry have come precisely to
this point, and I have recently assumed the role of pastoral coordinator of a
struggling urban congregation.*

I was raised in the Free Methodist Church. After attending Spring Arbor and *Greenville colleges and Asbury Theological Seminary, I served as a pastor in Detroit for two years. This was followed by six years' missionary service in Brazil and five years' work in Winona Lake, Indiana, both in affiliation with my denomination. In 1980 my family and I moved to the Albany Park area of Chicago, where we presently reside.*

The chief value of my writing, as I see it, is in offering an alternative model—a new way of seeing—and not in giving specific blueprints. For me, fulfillment and confirmation come in learning of the growing number of places around the world where more biblically authentic, Kingdom-conscious models of church life and witness are successfully being put into practice.

My aim in this book is to be constructive, not controversial. Yet I know that the range of topics covered, and the comprehensiveness of the perspective proposed, may raise both questions and eyebrows. I have probably managed to offend everyone at some point. But my quest is for the real truth of the Kingdom.

much more clothe you, O you of little faith? So do not worry, saying, "What shall we eat?" or "What shall we drink?" or "What shall we wear?" For the pagans run after all these things, and your heavenly Father knows that you need them. (Mt 6:25-32)

Later Jesus said his disciples should focus on the hungry and thirsty, the refugees, the sick, the naked, the imprisoned, and not on their own self-nourishment and self-protection (Mt 25:31-46). These are the concerns of the Kingdom. My hope is that the church today can become free for such Kingdom concerns.

We must see that *everything* is for the sake of God's Kingdom. The world was created to show forth God's good rule. Jesus' birth was for the sake of the Kingdom. The new birth is entrance into God's Kingdom (Jn 3:3) so that we may live for Kingdom priorities (Mt 6:33). The baptism of the Holy Spirit is for the sake of the Kingdom; "the Spirit knows that the very crux of all truth lies in the Kingdom of God."[1] Sanctification and holiness are for the Kingdom. The gifts of the Spirit are granted so we may do the work of the Kingdom. The church is for the Kingdom; it prays constantly that God's Kingdom may come (Mt 6:10). Evangelism is for the Kingdom; its goal is to win people to God so that they will serve the King. And Jesus' Second Coming, "the time . . . for God to restore everything" (Acts 3:21), will finally establish the Kingdom forever. So we "look forward to the day of God and speed its coming," knowing that "in keeping with his promise we are looking forward to a new heaven and a new earth, the home of righteousness" and justice (2 Pet 3:12-13).

The church in Fortress America, especially, needs to hear such words. Surveys show that most Americans have guns at home and many support more guns in Washington. They have a siege mentality bred of fear, distrust and the breakdown of community. Much of the church is also caught up in this mood. Like the nation, America's churches breathe the atmosphere of self-protection and self-aggrandizement. They run after the same things the world does. The church is not free for the Kingdom. Its sickness is symbolized by the average church budget: eighty or ninety per cent spent on itself, a pittance for the rest of the world.

In North America, many Christians have so mixed free enterprise with Christianity that they can't tell the difference. Like Amway's Richard DeVos, they believe that poor people are poor because that is "the way they choose to live." "Most people I know want a new house, a nice car, a cottage on Lake Michigan," DeVos says, and he thinks these are proper goals for success-minded Christians. The Amway empire and others like it have been built on such self-centered piety. The poor, DeVos believes, should understand that "those who work shall be rewarded, that you should not covet what your neighbor has—it's none of your business." Everyone has access to employment and success, so if anyone really is poor (which is questionable), then it's his own fault. And this philosophy is safely insulated from any larger accountability to society or even the church because "accountability to God is very personal" (read "private"). The gospel concerns only one's individual relationship to God, and the church's mission is simply "to reach the unchurched and support each other in the body of believers."[2] The church's mission, in this view, is not to show any concern about social justice; that smacks of socialism. Church business and commercial business operate in different worlds. Kingdom business is shrunken to church business, which means business as usual.

If there is one charge to be made against the church today, it is the charge of worldliness. Evangelical churches protest the world's values at some points (sexual morality, family life, abortion) but have been seduced by the world at others (materialism; personal and institutionalized self-interest; styles of leadership, motivation and organization; the uses of power). Many Christians are convinced that technology changes things, even if they are unsure that prayer does. Technique works better than grace in the technological society.

Perhaps it's true that what's good for General Motors is good for the church. But at what price? Certainly the church can powerfully use the ways of the world. But is it then still the church of *God's* Kingdom? Take a Madison Avenue approach, and you get a Madison Avenue church.

Liberating Models Because of the morass the church is in today, I have chosen the themes of liberation and ecology in organizing this book. These provide a usefully unsettling way of looking at the church in our day. This is certainly not the only way to look at the church. But these themes pinpoint where the church is weak and how it may become more faithful. Using them is like saying, "Let's walk over here a ways and look at the church from a different angle. Maybe we'll see some things we hadn't noticed before."

Despite thousands of books and the speculation of scholars, the church remains a mystery. Perhaps as time passes and more is said about the church, its true reality becomes even more clouded. In any case, since there is truly "something of God" in the life and course of the church, even in its most institutionalized form, it always eludes our full explanation.

It is becoming increasingly clear that the best way to deal with this strange phenomenon called "church" is the way Scripture itself does —through various figures, word pictures and images. Formally, this means understanding the church through the use of models.[3] Models and mystery. Precisely because we can't fully grasp the meaning of the church, we resort to models and images to give us some "insight into the mystery" (Eph 3:4) of Christ and his church.

Models can be liberating, even revolutionary. A new model can be dangerous, as Galileo and others like him found out.

Revolutions, in fact, often spring from the discovery and exploration of new models. This has been true in science, economics and other fields. And this has been happening in the church in recent decades as the power of seeing the church as the *community* of God's *people* has been challenging and undermining entrenched models of the church as a religious institution dedicated to a kind of technical spiritual work that does not disturb the political, social and economic status quo.

Thomas S. Kuhn has argued that scientific revolutions spring from a change in fundamental models of understanding—what he calls a "paradigm shift." The root models or paradigms by which a scientific community understands itself and its work undergo a change which, in turn, produces new insights. "Led by a new paradigm," says Kuhn, "scientists adopt new instruments and look in new places. Even more important, during revolutions scientists see new and different things when looking with familiar instruments in places they have looked before."[4]

This is happening in the church. Today's ferment signals, in part, a paradigm shift and the accompanying struggle of new models to displace old ones in the corporate consciousness (or perhaps the collective unconscious) of the church. The Holy Spirit, it seems, is at work in this ferment, and that is potentially liberating.

This book, then, is an exploration of the church's life and renewal —its liberation—using various models and images. The arrangement of the book is not formally logical, nor is the book a systematic examination of models, such as those found elsewhere.[5] Rather, the arrangement is more like an informal conversation, or perhaps like a musical composition woven around a few major themes with several secondary or minor themes intertwined and reappearing intermittently. The basic theme is the liberation of the church viewed ecologically and explored through the use of several models and images. The basic thesis is that a fuller understanding and appropriation of fitting models will help free the church to be the community of the King and the agent of the Kingdom as God intends.

The book proceeds as follows: The first chapter examines the nature of the church's calling as liberating agent of the Kingdom. It also surveys where the church has been and where it appears to be headed, noting some related tendencies in contemporary society. The primary focus here, as throughout the book, is on the local church (but with reference to the larger context) and on churches mainly in the North American evangelical tradition (but with application to the church more generally). The next two chapters then outline and explore a new way of looking at the church, an ecological model which underlies the discussion through the rest of the book.

The major portion of the book examines several key issues affecting the liberation of the church—among them the role of leadership, the meaning of community, the function of Scripture, the ministry of women, the question of lifestyle, the place of theology, and the concerns of justice and the poor. These are treated not as separate topics but ecologically, as aspects of the total life and liberation of the church. Models either proposed or presupposed in dealing with these issues are, primarily, the church as sacrament, community, servant and witness, and, less explicitly, as universal priesthood and as counterculture. I make no claim to comprehensiveness in this use of models; other images might well be used. But I see these models as particularly relevant and pointed in the present situation of the church and as especially compatible with the liberation and ecology themes introduced in section one.

Theses on Renewal   Reflecting on my experience and study of the church over the past several years, I have come to some conclusions which provide, for me at least, a basic perspective—a "place to stand" in viewing the church's life. These may be considered as theses on the renewal of the church. While most of these are not formally elaborated in the course of the book, they are assumed and often provide the foundation, or substratum, of specific discussions. Perhaps listing these in advance will help clarify where the argument is headed, and why. The reader who disagrees with these thesis statements probably won't find much in the book *to* agree with. I hope those who do agree with these propositions will check whether the theses really lead to or support the various positions and proposals put forth in the book. Perhaps readers who don't initially agree with these theses will have second thoughts by the end of the book.

The ten theses are as follows:

1. The fundamental crisis of the church today is a crisis of the Word of God. The church must recover the full dynamic of the Word, not just as Scripture, but as God-in-communication, especially through the written Word of Scripture and supremely through the Incarnate Word, Jesus Christ. This is another way of saying the church must recover a consciousness of who God is.

2. Behaviors and structures in the church reflect fundamental concepts in the church's self-understanding which often remain unarticulated.

3. The church is essentially the community of God's people, not primarily an organization, institution, program or building. This is a distinction of fundamental importance because it is linked to the basic models of the church which Christians employ.

4. The experience of salvation is incomplete and not fully biblical without genuine experience of the church as the community of God's people and agent of the Kingdom.

5. The most dynamic and prophetic thing the church can do is first of all to be a worshiping and serving community.

6. Every believer is a minister, servant and priest of God. Every believer is called to ministry, and all God's people must be equipped to minister.

7. Every believer receives grace for ministry. Therefore spiritual gifts must be identified and employed to God's glory.

8. Leadership grows out of discipleship. Where careful discipling is lacking, leadership cannot be biblical and a crisis of spiritual leadership results. Worldly qualifications for leadership replace biblical ones.

9. The church's concern for and identification with the poor are sure signs of its faithfulness to the Kingdom and are often signs of fundamental renewal.

10. In North America today a vital, biblically faithful church will be a countercultural community living in tension with the non-Christian elements of society and marked by a lifestyle that is distinctively Christlike and Kingdom oriented.

one

A NEW MODEL
FOR CHURCH AND KINGDOM

1
JUSTICE, LIBERATION
AND THE KINGDOM

Many people talk of liberation these days. But liberation of whom, from what, and by what means?

Liberating the church for the Kingdom comes through the Spirit and the Word. But this liberation requires some understanding of the ways the church is in bondage and the dangers it faces. At this point we may learn some things from Latin American liberation theology.

Liberation theologians have been speaking forcefully about the church's task to work for the liberation of the poor and oppressed. They stress the need to free Third World peoples from North American and Western European political and economic domination. They are right in this, but most North American Christians, mystified, miss the point entirely. It is hard to see a system from the inside out. North American Christians hearing the cries of the Third World are often like the suburban Detroiter who said after the 1967 Detroit riots, "Well, I hope those people made their point—whatever it was!"

Most North American evangelical Christians are good, solid, honest, hard-working, generally law-abiding citizens. They are mostly middle-class, white suburbanites who not surprisingly see Christianity through middle-class, white suburban eyes. The problem is that their sociocultural setting seems to determine their concept of the Christian faith, rather than their faith serving as a starting point for a critique of their culture. Thus many of the best, most sincere, most committed and most honest North American Christians today are simply blind to the Third World (or, more accurately, the Two-Thirds World) beyond their borders—and also to the growing Third World within North America's decaying cities.

Liberation theologians, therefore, have a point. The liberationist critique needs to be heard in North America precisely to help free the church for the Kingdom. As William McElvaney reminds us, "Unless the Christian church is to become no more than a Society for the Preservation of the Privileged and Prosperous, we cannot ignore liberation theologies." He adds pointedly,

The first word I hear in liberation theologies is the reality and the immensity of human suffering. If that does not matter to us, we need not give credence to liberation theologies. If the suffering of others does matter to us, we cannot ignore a theology that calls us to listen, to care, and to respond.[1]

Admittedly, liberation theology has its problems. The major problem is not its focus on the poor and oppressed, for that is largely biblical. It is not the concern with political and economic structures, for these are more important in the biblical economy than most of us have realized. The problem isn't even liberation theology's frequent use of a Marxist critique. While problematic, this is no worse, in principle, than North American Protestantism's cozy alliance with capitalism.[2]

The basic problem concerns the church. As I see it, most liberation theologies sacrifice the church as the distinct community of God's people, owing its allegiance to Christ alone, to the exclusive cause of political and economic liberation. For the church to be a liberating force in the world (even in the political and economic realms), it must itself be liberated for the Kingdom in a way that is biblically authentic. Hence my concern for liberating *the church*. Most liberation theology, it seems to me, misunderstands the fundamental ecology of the church. Yet only a church biblically liberated for the Kingdom will know how to be a faithful church both in North America and in Third World countries. And only such a church, incidentally, will be free enough from both Marxism and capitalism to mount a penetrating critique of both.

Liberating the church does not mean retreating to a stained-glass ghetto or turning away from society to wait patiently and passively for the Kingdom. Rather it means recentering the church's life on

God for the sake of Kingdom work now. W. A. Visser 't Hooft once wrote,

The liberation of the Church does not mean that it turns its back upon the world, but that it becomes again wholly dependent upon its Lord, does not listen to the voice of strangers and is in the midst of the world the spokesman of the Word of God which is not fettered (II Tim 2.9). Thus every renewal of the Church is in one sense a movement of withdrawal from the world and from entangling alliances in the political, social, cultural or philosophical realms. But that withdrawal is never an aim in itself. It is a withdrawal with the purpose of returning to the attack.[3]

The true liberation of the church requires a clear understanding of the church's purpose and how it serves the Kingdom of God.

The Church and the Kingdom One of the goals of God's Kingdom is "the glorious freedom of the children of God" (Rom 8:21). The church is the community of the Spirit, and "where the Spirit of the Lord is, there is freedom" (2 Cor 3:17). God's people are to "stand firm" in the freedom Christ won for them, avoiding the twin dangers of legalism (Gal 5:1) and self-indulgence. The principle is clear: "You, my brothers, were called to be free. But do not use your freedom to indulge the sinful nature; rather, serve one another in love" (Gal 5:13).

The gospel sets people free. It transforms sinners into God's own people so that they may serve God in the freedom of the Spirit (1 Pet 2:9-10). Yet how quickly, how easily this freedom is compromised! Often we may feel the same frustration and astonishment the apostle Paul felt when he saw how quickly the Galatian Christians fell into legalism (Gal 1:6-7). Rarely do God's people live up to their privileges as the children of God.

God makes us a free people by his Spirit. Sooner or later, this freedom is throttled. Like the children of Israel in the desert, we yearn for the predictable, safe bondage of institutional captivity. If we are to live the freedom Christ won for us, we must understand what that freedom is and what it means practically to *live* the freedom of the gospel in the present order.

The foundation of our freedom is Jesus Christ. As the book of Romans makes clear so magnificently, Jesus' atoning sacrifice on the cross saves us from sin and reconciles us to God. "This righteousness from God comes through faith in Jesus Christ to all who believe. There is no difference, for all have sinned and fall short of the glory of God, and are justified freely by his grace through the redemption that came by Christ Jesus" (Rom 3:22-24). "God demonstrates his own love for us in this: While we were still sinners, Christ died for us" (Rom 5:8). We cannot earn our freedom; we become God's people simply by accepting, through faith, the free gift. "For it is by grace you have been saved, through faith—and this not from yourselves, it is the gift of God—not by works, so that no one can boast" (Eph 2:8-9).

All this is foundational. It is accepted without question by most earnest Christians. But what kind of church do we build on this foundation? Is it the church of the Spirit? Is it the community of those who have been set free by the Spirit of God to serve the Kingdom? Because of the way the Christian faith has been overindividualized, privatized and institutionalized in the Western world, the church has often failed to live up to its privileges. It has failed to be the community of the Spirit in ways that would make it the agent of the Kingdom as God intends.

What is the purpose of the church? Some would say evangelism. They point to Mark 16:15, "Go into all the world and preach the good news to all creation." Or to Matthew 28:19-20, "Therefore go and make disciples of all nations, baptizing them in the name of the Father and of the Son and of the Holy Spirit, and teaching them to obey everything I have commanded you."

Certainly these are important texts. But do they give us the *purpose* of the church? Nothing in the context indicates that these verses are intended as a definition of the church's purpose. They state a crucial *commission* which has been given to the church. But there is no biblical basis for taking these, rather than some other texts, as the definition of the church's purpose.

Further, these texts are not, in any case, simple commands to evangelize. Mark 16:15 is a command to "preach the good news to all creation." The good news is the gospel of the Kingdom (Mk 1:15; Lk 4:43). If we take Jesus as our example, to preach the gospel is to proclaim the Kingdom. While this certainly begins with the task of winning people to personal faith in Jesus Christ, this is only the beginning, not the end, of preaching the good news of the Kingdom.

People are to be won to faith in Christ so that they may become sons and daughters of the Kingdom.

Matthew 28:19-20 likewise involves more than just evangelism, narrowly defined. The key command here is to make disciples, and this includes "teaching them to obey everything" Jesus commanded. The context is Jesus' statement that all authority (*exousia*) has been given to him (v. 18). Disciple making here means teaching believers to follow Jesus and live the life of the Kingdom that he taught and lived before them. The purpose of evangelism, then, is to create a believing, obeying people who acknowledge Jesus' supreme authority and thus are free for the Kingdom.

This does not cut the nerve of evangelism in any way. Evangelism is vitally important because the Kingdom is so important. Evangelism is winning people to Jesus and his Kingdom. Problems crop up only when evangelism is made an end in itself, or when it is understood and practiced in a way that makes the church an end in itself rather than the servant of the Kingdom. Too often the way the church practices evangelism is like a nation in wartime drafting its young men into the army—and then sending them all back home to do as they please.

It is misleading, therefore, to say that evangelism is the purpose of the church. It's like saying that enlistment is the purpose of an army. It is more accurate to say that evangelism is the first priority of the church's witness in the world (first in importance, though not always first in time).[4]

On the other end of the spectrum, some would say social justice or political reform is the purpose of the church. They cite Old Testament prophecies about God's concern with justice for the poor and oppressed or New Testament texts like Matthew 25:31-46.

While such themes should certainly be given equal weight with the church's evangelistic mandate, to take them as the definition of the church's purpose is misleading. Scripture itself does not lift these themes up as the purpose of the church. Social justice must also be put in the context of the Kingdom of God, or of God's overall redemptive plan.

Jesus himself tells us what the central focus of the church should be: the Kingdom of God, the righteousness and justice of the Kingdom (Mt 6:33). The church is to pray constantly, and in expectant faith, that God's Kingdom may come, meaning that his will should be done *on earth* as it is in heaven (Mt 6:10). The purpose of the church is the Kingdom of God.

The close linking of righteousness and justice in Scripture requires taking Matthew 6:33 to mean, "Seek to manifest the just rule of God," or "Seek the justice of God's kingdom," rather than indicating a concern with righteousness as something distinct from justice. Given the church's tendency to understand "righteousness" (in this passage and others) too narrowly, and divorced from the Old Testament theme of social justice, we are probably closer to Jesus' intent in substituting the word "justice" for "righteousness" here, or at least in including both words.[5]

The Gospel of Matthew, as a whole, shows how Jesus envisaged the Kingdom and confirms the link between justice and the Kingdom. Justice and righteousness are explicitly connected with the Kingdom several times (Mt 5:10, 20; 6:33; 13:43, 49; 21:31-32). In several other places the connection is clearly implied (Mt 3:1-10; 7:21; 18:21-35; 25:31-46). In every case, justice or righteousness concerns one's behavior in the present world. The point is clear: The Kingdom is for those who practice justice, and only those who live justly and righteously will enter the Kingdom of God.

Matthew 6:33 thus becomes a key verse. Jesus says to seek first God's Kingdom and his righteousness/justice. Here *God's* righteousness is the issue. The Kingdom is marked by God's justice and righteousness. In all other passages in Matthew where justice and the Kingdom are associated, justice and righteousness are qualities to be demonstrated in the lives of Jesus' disciples. The point is not that Christians can have a righteousness of their own, but that if they truly are disciples of Jesus and seekers of God's Kingdom, their lives will be marked by the justice and righteousness which Jesus called for and lived. Those who seek God's Kingdom and justice, who hunger and thirst for righteousness (5:6), will be satisfied. They are able to live justly in the world, and they receive the Kingdom (Lk 12:31-32).

The words "righteousness" *(diakaiosunē)* and "righteous" *(dikaios)* are used a total of twenty times in Matthew. Only in 6:33 is the reference clearly to God's righteousness (although 5:6 may be thought of as God's righteousness—or, alternatively, as seeking for a righteous life). All other references are to people as righteous, or to people practicing righteousness.

Whereas "righteous" and "righteousness" always translate *dikaios* and *dikaiosunē* in Matthew, the situation is different with "justice." "Justice" occurs only three times in Matthew (in the NIV), always translating *krisis* (and two of these are quotations from Isaiah 42). *Krisis* occurs a total of twelve times in Matthew, but in all but these three cases the meaning is "judgment" (usually "day of judgment").

We face here the problem of adequately translating the Hebrew word for and concept of justice into the Greek. The Old Testament background is fundamental here. Since righteousness and justice are so closely associated in the Old Testament, we will misunderstand the New Testament view of righteousness if we overlook their connection. In other words, when Jesus talks about righteousness, he is also talking about justice, for the two are part of one and the same truth. The righteous in Matthew are those who are just. Thus Joseph acted righteously or justly toward Mary in not wanting to disgrace her (1:19); Jesus' disciples are to do "acts of righteousness" or justice (6:1); and the righteous at the judgment are those who have shown justice to the needy (25:37).

All this means that the Kingdom of God is fundamentally concerned with righteousness and justice.

What, then, is the Kingdom of heaven (or God) in Matthew? Clearly the Kingdom was the theme of Jesus' teaching (4:17, 23). The Kingdom is mentioned some fifty times, generally in direct quotations from Jesus. What did Jesus mean by the Kingdom? From his own teachings we may conclude the following:

1. The Kingdom is for the poor in spirit (5:3), the humbly child-like (18:3-4; 19:14); for repentant sinners (21:31), those who forgive others (18:23-35), producing the fruit of the Kingdom (21:43). It is for all peoples who believe and obey Jesus (8:11), but it is hard for the rich to enter (19:23-24).

2. The Kingdom is tied to faith in and obedience to Jesus Christ, to teaching and practicing his commands (5:19; 7:21), and to following his example of servanthood (20:20-28).

3. The Kingdom is good news (4:23; 9:35) of surpassing value (13:44-45) and is worth renouncing marriage for if necessary (19:12).

4. The Kingdom is a mystery (13:11); it is the reversal of purely human expectations (20:1-16).

5. The Kingdom is the demonstrated power and authority of God over disease (4:23; 9:35; 10:6) and demonic powers (4:24; 10:6; 12:28).

6. The Kingdom is the way of righteousness and justice (18:23-35; 5:10; 6:33; 21:31-32). The people of the Kingdom are those who demonstrate and practice true righteousness and justice in their lives (5:20; 25:31-46).

7. The Kingdom is really present now, but not yet fully revealed. It is near (3:2; 4:17; 10:7) and is revealed by the powerful work of the Spirit (12:28). It is forcefully advancing (11:12) and growing in the present world, but alongside evil and in often hidden, imperceptible ways (13:24-30; 13:31-33; 13:47-50). It will permeate all of society (13:33). It is both on earth and in heaven (16:19) and combines things both old and new (13:52).

8. The Kingdom is to be sought, prayed for, proclaimed and expected by the church in the present order (3:2; 4:17; 6:10; 6:33; 9:35; 10:7). It will be preached to the whole world (24:14).

9. The Kingdom is assured of final victory over evil (13:30; 13:41; 13:47-50). Its final climax includes the judgment of the evil and the triumph of eternal life for the righteous (13:43; 13:47-50; 8:12; 18:23-34; 25:46). It will mean judgment for those who are unprepared for its coming (25:1-13).

Combining the material in Matthew with the broader sweep of Scripture, we may say that the Kingdom of God means recognizing, glorifying and serving God as the one sovereign, just and holy God —the God revealed in Scripture and supremely in Jesus Christ. The Kingdom means living gladly and obediently under God's rule. For the church, it means living as the Kingdom community, putting into practice its righteousness and justice. It means serving as witness, herald and agent of the Kingdom in the world. This most certainly involves both evangelism and social justice, as well as other Kingdom concerns.

Scripture makes this same point in several ways. Paul, for instance, says that God has a plan for the fullness of time "to bring all things in heaven and on earth together under one head, even Christ" (Eph 1:10).[6] God's "plan" spoken of here is his *oikonomia*, his "economy."[7] Paul is pointing to the economy of God, in effect suggesting an ecological way of looking at God's world and his redemptive work. We will examine this divine economy in greater detail in the next two chapters.

To speak of God's overall redemptive plan is to speak of the Kingdom of God. These are two ways of saying the same thing. The economy of God is the Kingdom of God. God's plan is that all creation acknowledge and serve him as Sovereign King. God's Kingdom is the fulfillment of his plan, the working out of the divine economy through Jesus Christ. So the purpose of the church is to serve God's plan and Kingdom.

We may also say that the purpose of the church is to glorify God. Paul declares in Ephesians 3:21, "To [God] be glory in the church and in Christ Jesus throughout all generations, for ever and ever!" The goal is "that in all things God may be praised through Jesus Christ" (1 Pet 4:11). The church is God's chosen people so that it "may declare the praises of him who called [it] out of darkness into his wonderful light" (1 Pet 2:9). The most basic concern of the church is that it may live "to the praise of [God's] glorious grace" (Eph 1:6, 12, 14).

Does saying the church's primary purpose is to glorify God mean saying something different than that the purpose of the church is the Kingdom of God? Not at all. At the most basic level, Matthew 6:33, Ephesians 1:10 and Ephesians 3:21 all make the same point. The fundamental issue is the church as God's own people in the world. To put the matter in composite form, the purpose of the church is to glorify God by submitting to his sovereign lordship in faith, love and obedient action, thus carrying out God's plan or economy.

God has freed us for the Kingdom. This is the point. Once not a people at all, we are now the very people of God (1 Pet 2:10), the people and community of the Kingdom. God's Kingdom defines our focus, our ultimate loyalty. It integrates our social and cultural existence, providing our center of gravity. This perspective serves as the plumb line of the church's authenticity, its faithfulness or unfaithfulness. The church that does not seek first God's glory and Kingdom *and order its life accordingly* is unfaithful, compromised, undermined, subverted.

The church's heritage, right and privilege is to be free for the Kingdom. But often it is not. When it exists only for itself as a religious institution or is seduced into serving as agent or legitimizer of any political or economic system (whether capitalist or socialist, totalitarian or democratic), it is no longer free for the Kingdom. When it loses the ability to hold together in redemptive tension the physical and the spiritual, or the present and the future, or the individual and the social, it is to that degree not free for the Kingdom. It is true that "the Gospel pertains to the liberation of the poor as well as to the salvation of the soul."[8] But when either focus is lost, the church is not really free for the Kingdom.

Frederick Herzog points out in *Justice Church* that the problem with North American Christianity is not merely its massive cultural accommodation but its split-level view of the church. It has become blind to its own accommodation and subversion. By distinguishing between an ideal and a real church, Christians permit themselves to be at home with the church's actual unfaithfulness (after all, the true, ideal church, wherever and whatever that is, certainly must be holy and perfect) while missing the reality and significance of their own involvement in history and culture.[9]

Observing that "Christians are involved in history, but never notice it," Herzog rightly insists that "in our day we need to be keenly aware of the shift from theologizing about an ideal church to analyzing the actual church."[10] Liberation theology is driving this fundamental biblical insight home. God's plan is a plan for real human history in all its social, personal, political, economic, scientific, and spiritual beauty and ugliness—or else Paul's repeated emphasis on "all things" and all authorities, principalities and powers is meaningless. The tricky but crucial task for would-be biblical Christians is to ground the meaning of God's Kingdom where Scripture does, not where any of today's competing ideologies or theologies ground it.

To be free for the Kingdom, the church must see the world from the perspective of "all things"—the total history (past, present and future) of God's Kingdom plan. This means seeing the world from the perspective of the justice and righteousness of the Kingdom, and not merely from the perspective of Western culture. As Herzog comments, "Our vision in the churches is not yet focused on our global village existence. The Gospel is still interpreted in terms of the *splendid isolation* of that 'tiny island of Christianity' called the United States. But can the Gospel still be understood at all in terms of such splendid isolation?"[11] Certainly only in a partial and distorted way. How many North American Christians, for instance, are daily conscious that the vast majority of our believing brothers and sisters (to say nothing of the rest of humanity) are nonwhite, poor, and politically and economically repressed, and that the burden of suffering always falls most cruelly on women and children? In light of this can we really claim to be free for the Kingdom? Are we really the Kingdom community of justice and righteousness?

But Jesus has freed us for the Kingdom. Through his life, death, resurrection and current reign he has conquered *all* the principalities and powers, visible (social, political, economic and physical) and invisible (Satan and his legions, and all spiritual forces, including those dimensions of earthly power structures which represent the invisible parts of the social, political and economic iceberg).

God has freed us for his Kingdom and for Kingdom work. To live out that freedom we must broaden and deepen our allegiance to God alone, repent of our idolatries, and learn to live the life of the Kingdom community. And we must understand the economy of God in the context of the present actual history of the church and the world.

Tomorrow's Church   Where is the church headed? What is the context in which the liberation of the church must be worked out? Noting several trends in society and in the life of the church will help clarify just what liberating the church means today. The following currents seem especially significant.[12]

1. *A shift in the church's center of gravity to the Third World.* Third World church growth has outstripped North American growth for some time. Many mission-minded denominations now find they have significantly more members overseas than at home.

This numerical shift—coupled with the general decline of the United States, the greater vigor of newer Third World churches, the re-emergence of the Chinese church and related developments —is producing a major shift in the church's center of gravity from Europe and North America to the Third World.[13] Numerical growth will be followed by a burst of Third World Christian institutions and a broadening economic base under the influence of the gospel. Already the dramatic growth of Third World mission societies has been well documented.[14]

This shift will touch North American church life at several points. Among other things, it will probably mean greater diversity as patterns, styles, assumptions, methodologies and theologies from Third World churches infiltrate the American scene.

2. *The increasing pressure of environmental and economic concerns.* The most prominent such concern now is energy, which is already shaping church life and architecture.

The inescapable limits of natural resources and the environment in general seem certain to bring a broader range of ecological concerns to the fore in the near future. As the vulnerability of earth's environment becomes clearer, major economic and lifestyle shifts will affect America's culture and way of life. The economy will suffer wrenching changes, and ecology and conservation will become pressing issues.

These developments may undermine much of evangelicalism's economic prosperity, bring a renewed dimension to and emphasis on discipleship, and give impetus to the house church movement.

3. *The continuing impact of technological materialism.* Many evangelicals and charismatics speak of "secular humanism" as the great foe of the church today. In an increasingly materialistic society governed by technology, however, we must also speak of "technological materialism." This is the view that all value and meaning are limited to this life and that the solution to all problems lies in applying increasingly sophisticated technology. Americans seem to possess an unshakable "can do" faith that just around the corner is another technological breakthrough that will solve all our problems.

Technological materialism will influence the church at several levels. The ethics of using more and more sophisticated and manipulative techniques in evangelism, Christian broadcasting and various local church programs may become an increasingly acute issue. Technological materialism will continue to undermine secular and religious forms of community, keeping the issue of community before the church. The possibility of taxing church property and growing governmental harassment of religious institutions may significantly affect church life as well—possibly for good as much as for evil.

4. *The increasing impact of urbanization, internationalization and mass migration.* Earthquakes, famines, wars and rumors of wars, political repression, and economic collapse have dislodged millions of people on several continents. Urbanization continues. Many of the great cities are growing increasingly diverse and internationalized as the refugee problem reaches flood proportions. One need only think of Cubans and Haitians in Miami or Hispanics and Orientals in Chicago to sense the dimensions of this trend. In Chicago, for instance, Hispanics now constitute about twenty per cent of the population, and Greeks, Koreans, Filipinos, Assyrians and East Indians each number fifty thousand or more.[15]

In the United States, these developments, coupled with the trends previously discussed, will likely bring much greater heterogeneity in church membership as well as in methods and styles. As never before, Protestant evangelicals will have to deal with the issue of diversity.

5. *The resurgence of Roman Catholicism.* Right now the Roman Catholic scene is too diverse and volatile to permit firm projections. The shakeup produced by Vatican II and the subsequent substantial Catholic membership losses, however, may have paved the way for a rebirth of Roman Catholic vigor. In their recent book *The Search for America's Faith,* George Gallup and David Poling speak of "a new flowering of the faith and a new confidence about being a Catholic Christian in America" and project "a golden era of growth and power ahead" for U. S. Catholics. They note that Catholics have moved from twenty-five to twenty-eight per cent of the nation's population in the past decade (largely through Hispanic immigration), and that Catholic church attendance has now begun to rise.[16] In urban areas the continuing decline of public education may well spark a rejuvenation of the extensive Catholic parochial school system.

The combined impact of the charismatic renewal, the base-church movement, and a vigorous, activist pope who is theologically conservative but socially progressive may further make Roman Catholicism a vital force in the United States. If so, this may significantly affect Protestant church life and growth, in part because Catholicism's seemingly greater ability to handle diversity may give it an evangelistic edge in the future. This could be especially critical in major urban areas.

6. *The drift toward a new fascism.* Perhaps most ominous in the current scene is the drift toward a new fascism in the world, especially in the United States. This development is not a political movement as such; it is more basic and subtle. Political and economic power are increasingly concentrated in the hands of an interlocking network of governmental, corporate and military structures.

Bertram Gross has documented this development in great detail in his book *Friendly Fascism: The New Face of Power in America.* From long years of experience in government, Gross warns that the same forces which bred fascism in Japan, Germany and Italy in the thirties are at work today in America. These forces center, above all, in the growing partnership of big business and big government.

An American fascism would, of course, be different from earlier varieties. It would be grounded in the comfortable manipulations of the technological society. American fascism, Gross writes, "would be super-modern and multi-ethnic—as American as Madison Avenue, executive luncheons, credit cards, and apple pie. It would be fascism with a smile. As a warning against its cosmetic facade, subtle manipulation, and velvet gloves, I call it friendly fascism."[17]

The new fascism, as Gross defines it, is a growing supranational force resting on intricate, interlocking complexes and the power of giant transnational corporations. Today the military-industrial complex, Gross writes,

has many partners: the nuclear-power complex, the technology-science complex, the city-planning-development-land-speculation complex, the agribusiness complex, the communications complex, and the enormous tangle of public bureaucracies and universities whose overt and secret services provide the foregoing with financial sustenance and a nurturing environment. Equally important, the emerging Big Business-Big Government partnership has a global reach. It is rooted in colossal transnational corporations and complexes that help knit together a "Free World" on which the sun never sets.[18]

Not only do the sales of huge transnationals outstrip the gross national products of many countries, but such corporations are linked with even larger complexes. For example, Gross notes, "the multinational automobile-highway-petroleum complex (within which General Motors plays a vital role) controls far more money, scientists, and technicians than provided for in the entire budget of *any* capitalist country's national government, including the United States itself."[19]

What all this reveals, Gross argues, is *"the outline of a powerful logic of events.* This logic points toward tighter integration of every First World Establishment. In the United States it points toward more concentrated, unscrupulous, repressive, and militaristic control by a Big Business-Big Government partnership that—to preserve the privileges of the ultra-rich, the corporate overseers, and the brass in the military and civilian order—squelches the rights and liberties of other people both at home and abroad. That is friendly fascism."[20]

And it also explains much of the political and economic news we encounter daily through newspapers and television.

If this is, in fact, where contemporary industrial society is headed, it underscores the need for vigilance and Kingdom awareness on the part of the church. It raises with new urgency the question of the church's allegiance and integrity in much the same ways these questions were raised for the church under Nazism. Does the North American church have the strength to be a Confessing Church in the current scene?

These varied currents touch the life and potential liberation of the church in fundamental ways. They may well hasten the need to sort out different models of the church over the next several years.

In many evangelical churches today one senses a subsurface struggle between two fundamentally different models. One model is essentially institutional and organizational, at home with programs, committees, modern management techniques and elaborate physical facilities, and fascinated with sophisticated technology and mass communications. Partly because of its institutional investment in the economic status quo, this vision of the church tends to be politically and economically conservative.

The contrasting church model is essentially organic, communitary and person-centered, and it often manifests a deep distrust of technology, mass communications and institutional structures. While these two contrasting models of the church lead to fundamentally different patterns of local church life, many churches are a mixture of the two models both conceptually and structurally.[21]

The major tensions and cleavages in North American churches over the next quarter-century may well be more along these lines than along strictly doctrinal or church polity lines (though clearly some major doctrinal struggles are on the horizon). These strains may produce tensions and splits within denominations and local churches, some strange new alliances and networkings, and two distinctly different forms of local church life. There will probably also be some innovative attempts to combine the two contrasting models in various kinds of hybrid structures—some of which may be quite dynamic.

The coming years will almost certainly also witness the continuing growth of house churches and intentional communities. The spread of new Christian communities, though not highly visible since the decline of the Jesus Movement in the early seventies, goes on apace and appears to be of major significance. At least three things are happening in this area: (1) various kinds of new Christian house churches and intentional communities continue to be formed; (2) many of these communities are linking up in wide-ranging, sometimes international, networks; and (3) there is increasing contact and fellowship among several of these networks. For example, the Shalom Covenant network, including Reba Place Fellowship near Chicago, has recently expanded from five to eight communities. One of the new members is Austin Community Fellowship, a group midwifed by Chicago's innovative Circle Church. Further, representatives of this and several other community networks—charismatic and noncharismatic, Roman Catholic and Protestant—are in increasing contact with each other.

Fellowships of this type correspond to the second of the two models mentioned above. Their style emphasizes community, mutual liability, personal relationships, family life, discipleship and the use of spiritual gifts. Many such groups are consciously countercultural, particularly at the point of materialism and technology, but often also on the issue of leadership styles, militarism, politics and economic questions. Many of these communities, in fact, actually constitute an alternative economic system.

Several of the trends and currents we looked at earlier may give additional impetus to house church and intentional community forms of Christianity—for example, the breakdown of community in society, increasing internationalization and heterogeneity, and environmental, ecological factors. If so, the church of the next generation may resemble the church of the first-century Roman Empire or of present-day China more than the American Protestantism of the fifties and sixties. Many indicators point in this direction. Clearly there is a thirst for closer community today and a growing recognition that the church must move in the direction of more intimate and responsible community life. Jürgen Moltmann has recently written, "I believe that the future of the Protestant church lies in this direction, toward which I see more and more people going."[22]

Many of these issues touch on lifestyle questions, and we may expect to see a growing concern with questions of Christian lifestyle as well. What it really means to be a Christian in an increasingly amoral, technological, materialistic and militaristic world will become a foundational question for the church. This may in turn affect patterns of education and discipleship in local churches, leading to greater use of small groups, house fellowships or other forms of face-to-face community.

This whole discussion brings us back to the point where we began: the need for biblically faithful and yet culturally relevant models for understanding the life and liberation of the church and its role as servant of God's Kingdom. The next two chapters outline a comprehensive model which helps to meet this need.

2
THE ECONOMY OF GOD

Should we build roads or save trees? Burn coal or clean the air? Search for oil or safeguard the ocean?

Economy and ecology, the twin truths of our time, constantly push such dilemmas before us. We are trapped between economic necessity and ecological limits. Many critical issues, especially in North America, boil down to either a choice or a compromise between economic development and ecological responsibility.

In the Bible, economic and ecological issues are spiritual issues, and vice versa. Since economy and ecology are matters of value, order and survival, they concern God's plan and purpose for his creation. *In today's world, we can no longer speak of the life and liberation of the church apart from questions of economics and ecology.* These very issues, however, may help us find a new biblical understanding of God's Kingdom. We can learn what it means to say the Kingdom of God is the economy of God.

An economic-ecological perspective is a uniquely helpful way to view the life, liberation and mission of the church in a techno-materialist age. U.S. Senator Mark Hatfield has written,

Several economic assumptions have . . . been regarded as gospel since the time of the Reformation and Enlightenments. First, nature is generous, able to yield the necessary new wealth and resources continually. Second, the individual's pursuit of self-interest leads to the social good. Third, the goal of economic order is constant expansion. . . . Fundamentally, we are still living with the same world-and-life view we inherited from the beginning of the modern age.

Hatfield points out that while these assumptions have been "made to look trustworthy" by America's dramatic economic growth, still that growth has produced neither economic justice nor personal fulfillment. "The gaps have increased and the poor have been left on the bottom." Hatfield adds,

We are, in fact, now reaching the fringes of the modern vision which has been guiding our culture. We are now confronting the finite limits of our economic and technological possibilities. We can begin to see how the guiding assumptions and values of the past are inadequate. This is creating a vacuum philosophically, politically, and spiritually. Therefore, the key question for our future is: What forces and what vision will fill this vacuum? [1]

Hatfield's comments are on target. The ecology-economy crunch we face today points to a coming fundamental shift in economic and social reality worldwide, and ultimately to an altered self-understanding of humanity and its environment. Jeremy Rifkin contends,

We are embarked on a course of sweeping global change. America, as the most aggressively materialist culture on earth, will feel that change more than any other nation. Our liberal disposition is ingrained in the concept of unlimited material advance. Now we are confronted with the economic reality of a finite planet which simply cannot sustain our expansionary value system. . . . Ultimately, the end of the expansionary economic period will usher in an entirely new philosophical ethos that will be as radically different from liberalism as the Reformation and Enlightenment were from the Middle Ages. [2]

Awakening to Ecology   We are coming to an ecological awareness that is unprecedented in human history. The atomic bomb and the theory of relativity dramatized the interplay of matter and energy and the tremendous power packed in the atom. The growing problems of air and water pollution show the delicate balance of our ecosystem and its ultimate vulnerability. The energy crunch is making us aware that earth's bounty is finite and that the key resources fueling our economic growth are rapidly running out. The dawning awareness of the economic and ecological implications of the law of entropy is raising the most basic questions about technology and progress. We have begun to think in terms of a small planet, of Mother Earth or Spaceship Earth, of a global village. Computer technology, cancer research, food studies and other areas of investigation impress on us the intricate balance of systems and forces which make up our habitable globe. We are beginning to understand, for instance, that petro-agriculture is spoiling the land for the future, that acid rain from pollutants is threatening our environment, and that the coming cancer epidemic, in which one of every three Americans will contract the disease, is due mainly to environmental factors.

We are just beginning to think ecologically. We inhabit an intricate, vulnerable biosphere consisting of a few inches of topsoil and a few hundred feet of oxygen. Although our ecological awareness is growing, it may be too late. We may not have enough time for making the required economic and lifestyle shifts to permit human life to continue past the middle of the next century. Our present economic system is buying disaster for our children and grandchildren, even if somehow we avoid nuclear war in our time.

The worldwide ecological crisis is much worse than many have thought, and more fundamental than most politicians yet believe. The most critical problems revolve around the rapid depletion of the earth's resources by the industrialized nations, the growing gap between rich and poor, malnutrition and starvation on an unprecedented scale, and the gradual decline of productive arable land because of chemical pollution (including fertilizers and herbicides), overintensive farming, growing deserts and urban sprawl. While population continues to climb, the world's long-range ability to grow food is declining. In addition, more than thirty nations face severe water shortages by the year 2000.[3] And the situation grows worse as rich nations gobble up the resources of poorer countries in order to fuel an ecologically irresponsible technological materialism and safeguard extravagant lifestyles, raising the specter of nuclear war over oil wells and mineral rights.[4]

While this situation clearly raises ethical questions for the church, my point here is more basic. The human family and the world we live in constitute one ecological system. The very word *ecology*, based on *oikos*, the Greek word for house, tells us that the world is our habitation and that everything within it is tied to everything else. *Ecology* describes the essential interdependence of all aspects of life on this planet; *economy* (from the Greek *oikonomia*) describes the ordering or managing of these interrelationships. The more closely we look at economic and ecological concerns, the more we see that the two concerns merge.

Ecosystem, Egosystem or Technosystem? Ecology makes us aware of systems. The ecologist studies particular ecosystems within certain environments. As ecological awareness grows, we come to see the whole earth as our ecosphere. It is our earthly environment, made up of seemingly endless varieties of ecosystems, all interacting with each other.

Ecology and *system* are closely related ideas. A system may be defined as "an organic or organized whole" or "a set or arrangement of things so related as to form a whole." One definition of ecology is "the study of organisms in their mutual relationships with their environment." Thus ecology is the study of natural systems, or of those systems operating within the natural environment. In the broadest understanding of ecology, every person, plant, animal, and in fact every speck of matter and pulse of energy are part of our ecosystem and interact with many other subsystems in the environment.

We are all part of the earth's ecosystem. But more than any other part of the environment, man and woman are capable of creating many auxiliary systems. Or, more accurately, since these systems are merely the increasingly sophisticated ordering of the finite stuff of the environment, humankind increasingly extends, expands and complicates its own ecosystem. This extending, complicating function has increased dramatically in recent years through scientific discoveries and computerized technology.

We live in systems, we create and adapt systems, and our lives are carried out within the constraints of systems. These are simply the ecological facts of life. But we must examine the *kinds* of systems we create and ask whether or not our manmade systems harmonize with or work against the constraints of the natural world. For the human animal, more than any other creature, has the capacity to change or reorder the environment.

We face a choice today: *eco*system, *ego*system or *techno*system? An egosystem is narcissism and individualism, everything revolving around the Almighty I. It is self on the throne, with each person attempting to order everything for self-satisfaction without regard for anyone or anything else in the environment. Raised to a racial or national level, this means every group looking out for itself, seeking its own way and through war, oppression, discrimination, exploitation or other means, seeking to impose its will and defend itself.

To a large degree this has, of course, been the history of humankind. Spiritually, it points to the Fall and the power of sin. Sin has always had disastrous effects in the natural world. But now the effects of living with disregard for others and for the environment are catching up with us. If we continue to view and live life as an ego-system, we are headed for environmental collapse. This is true simply within the natural, physical world, let alone in the world of the spirit.

Facing the threat of ecological ruin, society tends to move in the direction of a technosystem. Technology will provide the way out. Technology shows us how to make, run and control systems. Systems analysis is the thing. Another technological breakthrough is always just around the laboratory corner, ready to save us from the effects of our own environmental wastefulness and lunacy.

At least two problems, however, come with a technosystem. First, technology does not operate in a magic vacuum; it operates within a finite ecosystem and therefore is limited in what it can do. Technology is simply a way of using sophisticated tools for shaping and ordering the matter and energy of our planet. But these resources are limited. Technology is not a power in itself; it is merely a way of using energy sources in a more concentrated way. Technology has given us the illusion of limitless progress because it has released enormous amounts of energy for human use. But in using up more and more energy, we are in fact borrowing from future generations. Thus dependence on technology is a kind of ecological deficit spending ensuring an eventual, and unpleasant, day of reckoning.

We are nearing the limits of the technological fix. We are not there yet, because new "breakthroughs" may spark a few more bursts of quick energy. But as we reach the limits of the possible in a finite world, technology becomes increasingly dangerous, pushing us to the brink of extinction. The hope of new energy through nuclear fusion and genetic engineering illustrates the risks we face. Genetic engineering may modify earth's delicate gene system in lethal ways, and nuclear energy threatens either to poison the environment with radioactive wastes or lead to war. Further, such technologies raise fundamental questions of regulation and control. As Warren Johnson points out, "Some technologies are inherently totalitarian, and nuclear energy is one of them."[5] And genetic engineering may well be another.

A fundamental problem with both nuclear energy and genetic engineering is the level of technology they require. Such high technology ventures are almost by definition inaccessible to poor nations. They require massive capital investment and highly specialized expertise rarely found outside the rich industrialized countries. They are capital-intensive just when the world's expanding population and shrinking resources require a shift back to simpler, labor-intensive technology. The dream that these technologies hold the key to solving worldwide poverty will never be more than a dream because their proliferation around the globe would mean turning poor nations into even more dependent colonies of the rich, at least if history is any guide. Limited, inadequate amounts of food and energy would be made available to the poor in exchange for economic dependence and the continued rape of Third World natural resources. Thus these and similar "high-tech" schemes are fundamentally antidemocratic, anti-ecological and therefore irredeemably unjust in today's world.

This leads to the second problem with a technosystem which is even more basic. *A technosystem is fundamentally anti-ecological.* We are faced with a choice. Will we view the world essentially as a machine or as a garden? Will we see the earth as a factory or as a home? Will we opt for technology or ecology? This is not an either-or choice but a question of dominant models. Controlled by a proper regard for ecology, technology can be simple, appropriate and human—as advocated, for example, by E. F. Schumacher and others. If ecology is kept as the controlling reality, technology can have a human face. But if the controlling reality is technosystem, mechanistic technology takes over and life suffers from being squeezed into the "clockwork orange" habitat for which it was never meant. Then the world becomes essentially what Jacques Ellul describes in *The Technological Society* and *The Meaning of the City:* mankind's substitute Eden—its symbol of rebellion and sign of autonomy. But this is suicidal, for we are *not* autonomous, not from each other, not from God, and certainly not from our earthly habitat.

The dangers of a technosystem do not mean, however, that all technology should be condemned. Neither a biblical nor an ecological perspective need be anti-technological. Technology may be used in human and humane ways, especially when it is used on a small or intermediate scale. Even large-scale and highly sophisticated technology (for instance, in communications) may be appropriate, provided its dangers are recognized and accounted for. We must at all costs, however, recognize that technology is not amoral, that it tends to create its own morality of means, and that it has an inherent tendency toward totalitarianism and depersonalization.

Technology may be controlled in an ecosphere where the primary paradigms and principles are organic, person-centered and spiritually vital—and perhaps only there. In such an environment technology can be a useful adjunct to a life and culture of ecological sensitivity. Where life is lived in harmony with God's plan, human-scale technology may witness to the creative capacity of the image of God in man and woman. God himself may be thought of as the divine technologist, the craftsman or architect *(technitēs)* and builder of the city to which we look forward (Heb 11:10). God, however, uses technology only in a subsidiary way that never manipulates or dehumanizes. God's technology is always human-friendly.

We should not, therefore, issue a blanket condemnation of technology, but rather within a Christian perspective see its role as somewhat parallel to the function of reason. Technology is, in fact, rationalization taken to its ultimate extent. God has given us reason to use and not abuse, as an aid to faith and understanding. Where reason is placed above faith or Scripture, it betrays God's purposes and betrays faith. And the same is true of technology.

The question, then, is one of dominant themes and controlling models. As the environmental crisis deepens, our situation boils down to a fundamental choice—either cooperating with the world as God created it or trying to fashion a "better" world, which is in fact worse because it rests inevitably on injustice, oppression and depersonalization. As man and woman become like their gods, so they become like their models. A machine model (a technosystem) produces human robots; an organic model (an ecosystem) produces healthy persons.

These are issues of church life and renewal. In fact, we face here the same choice of models confronting the church itself. For survival and fulfillment, humankind must cooperate with God's plan. This is true for life in the world just as it is true for life in the church. In both cases we face limits built into the nature of God's universe. We can cooperate with God's plan, or we can take the route of autonomous rebellion. In the church, we can choose an organic model or an institutional model. In the natural environment we can choose an ecosystem or a technosystem. In both cases the choice is, quite literally, the choice between life and death.

Christians live in two worlds. They inhabit two households: the church and the natural environment. Yet, viewed both ecologically and biblically, these two realities are linked. Here we begin to see how important it is that the church think ecologically.

How to Think Ecologically. As ecological awareness grows, Christians will increasingly think in ecological terms and will begin to apply the model of ecology to the church's life and thought. Already this is happening, with some initial attempts at an ecological approach to theology.[6] But how can the church respond legitimately to ecological awareness and make use of ecological categories?

There are three possible ways for the church to view ecology: as a *problem* for the church's attention, as a *paradigm* for its self-understanding, or as a *perspective* for the church's encounter with Scripture.

1. The first approach represents the church's initial encounter with ecological realities. Ecology and the environment are seen as one more social question which the church must address. The perspective is that of the church versus ecology. But this is an inadequate approach, for by definition ecology is an all-encompassing perspective and raises questions about the church's own life and reality.

2. Viewed as a paradigm for the church's self-understanding, ecology itself becomes the controlling reality. Here the perspective is that the church must be conformed to the ecological model. The problem with this approach is the problem the church always faces in using a human system or philosophy. Most ecological thinking thus far is so undeveloped, and as a science is still so dominated by evolutionary presuppositions, that the effort to use ecology as the fundamental paradigm for the church's self-understanding runs

the strong risk of doing violence to Scripture.[7]

3. The more valid approach, therefore, is to see ecology as a perspective for the church's encounter with Scripture. Ecology does provide a model. But that model must be controlled, tested and clarified by the biblical revelation. The question, then, is to what degree an ecological perspective is compatible with Scripture, or to what extent the Bible actually views the church and the world ecologically. Taking this approach, we may find some surprising results.

Ecology and Scripture   Do Scripture and ecology agree? I suggest that the Bible presents the world to us in a way that is remarkably consistent with ecological realities. Several parallels between the biblical and ecological perspectives deserve attention and show that ecology points to a key theme woven throughout Scripture.

1. *Both ecology and the Bible view the world in a long-range time frame.* Human beings are accustomed to measuring time in terms of a life span, at most. Ours is a short-range view. Most human planning reaches only a few years or decades into the future. But to understand ecological reality, we must speak of hundreds or thousands of years. Ecological problems, for example, may be many generations in building and can seldom be solved in a few years' time.[8]

The biblical perspective is similarly long-range. The Bible itself was written over a period of some fifteen hundred years. It traces history back to our first parents, back to creation itself. It makes the historical connections straight through from Adam and Eve to Jesus Christ and on to the final culmination of the Kingdom of God. Each human life is seen as important, but as fitting into God's long-range purposes in history.

2. *Both ecology and the Bible see the natural world as one interconnected whole.* This, of course, is the point of the ecological perspective. But it is also true of Scripture. Here the doctrine of creation is central. Everything is interrelated because everything comes from the hand of God and finds meaning in God's purposes. God creates matter, and the human form is fashioned from the dust of the earth. Each form of life reproduces "after its kind" and is related to the rest of creation. Even the heavenly bodies come from the hand of God. From this perspective the Bible is profoundly ecological.

Ecology speaks of the web of life—of diversity and mutuality, of dynamics and change. So does the Bible. Life's interdependent web is pictured historically in many of the narrative sections of Scripture and poetically in Job and many of the psalms. A large number of the psalms are really creation hymns, glorying not in an abstract God but in the wisdom, power and care God displays in the intricate ordering of the natural environment.

3. *Both ecology and the Bible focus on the significance of land.* Man and woman do not live independently of the land. They are linked to the land and exploit or ruin it only at their peril.

Walter Brueggemann has shown the fundamental significance of land for biblical faith in his book *The Land.* The Bible is not, Brueggemann argues, the story of God and his people only, but of God, his people and the land. Land, both as "actual earthly turf" and as symbol of rootedness or "historical belonging," Brueggemann believes, is "a central, if not *the central theme* of biblical faith."[9] Keeping the biblical focus on land before us "will protect us from excessive spiritualization, so that we recognize that the yearning for land is always a serious historical enterprise concerned with historical power and belonging."[10]

Though some of Brueggemann's analysis may be open to criticism or qualification, the stress on the central place of land in God's economy is borne out by Scripture. We may recall here the many biblical promises concerning land, beginning especially with God's covenant with Abraham (Gen 12:7; 17:8). This emphasis on the land is particularly interesting and significant from an ecological standpoint. In both Scripture and ecology, the ideal is man and woman living at home on the land in an environment of balance, harmony and mutual dependence. It is neither biblically nor ecologically sound to view humankind as living independently from the land, and it is fundamentally unecological, both spiritually and physically, to attempt autonomous life divorced or alienated from the land.[11]

4. *Both ecology and the Bible present us with an awareness of limits.*[12] This is one of the hardest facts to face, but also one of the most stubborn ecological realities. Above all, our ecosphere is limited in its matter and energy. Even solar power is limited, both absolutely and in the degree to which it can be captured and used on earth. Resources which appeared limitless to an expanding frontier population now are seen to be finite as population bulges into the billions.

But Scripture already provides us with an awareness of limits. At creation God separated the light from the darkness (Gen 1:4) and established the limits of earth and sea (Gen 1:9). Creation itself may be viewed as a process of separating and setting limits. The psalmist says God "set the boundaries of the earth" and "made both summer and winter" (Ps 74:17; see also Deut 32:8; Prov 8:27-29). Man and woman are limited because of their physical existence, even though created in the image of God. And God marks off moral limits for man and woman, initially (Gen 2:15-16), after the Fall (Gen 3:16-19), and on down through the course of salvation history and the formation of a special people of God. God provides structures and boundaries for the well-being of his creation. So the apostle Paul says, "From one man [God] made every nation of men, that they should inhabit the whole earth; and he determined the times set for them and the exact places where they should live" (Acts 17:26).[13]

God is forever saying to man and woman, in effect: Here are the limits. Abide by them, according to my purposes, and you will live. Disregard them and you will die. As we view things ecologically, we see that this is true not just in some arbitrary sense, and not just spiritually, but physically as well because of the nature of the world God has given us.

5. *Both ecology and the Bible see the natural order as subject to decay.* Plants and animals die, hills erode, and some species become extinct. Ecologically, we face here not just the transitoriness of nature but the fact of entropy, the second law of thermodynamics. Entropy is a measure of disorder in a system. According to the law of entropy, the disorder in our universe is increasing as more and more resources are transformed from usable to unusable form.

Entropy may turn out to be the premiere natural constraint of the new age of ecology, as basic as gravity. Its significance lies in the fact that earth's matter and energy are limited and that no process is one hundred per cent efficient. Whenever work of any kind is performed, matter is changed from one form to another. While some of the energy derived is used to do the work, some is irretrievably lost as heat or waste products. For example, when gasoline is burned in an automobile, power is released to drive the machine, but most of the energy in the gasoline is lost as heat. Physicists tell us that even the most efficient machine produces some waste, and the energy lost as waste can never be fully recovered. Thus available energy is always decreasing; waste (as various forms of pollution) is always increasing; and overall the universe is moving from order to disorder as more and more matter and energy are turned into waste products. This process is becoming critical in our age because of the awesome power of technology to speed up the entropy process.

Jeremy Rifkin has popularized the entropy model in his book *Entropy: A New World View.* [14] Rifkin argues that since the law of entropy is grounded in the very nature of our physical existence, it will soon replace the dominant machine-progress view of history which has held sway for the past several hundred years. While some critics think Rifkin has seriously overstated the case for entropy and has applied it more broadly than can legitimately be done, a number of scientists and environmentalists have been voicing the same concern for over a decade. At the very least, entropy seriously affects energy questions on earth. Whether it provides the basis for a world view will continue to be debated. [15]

Regardless of the entropy debate, ecology does show us that the natural world is subject to decay. And this is consistent with the biblical revelation. We read that "the creation was subjected to frustration, not by its own choice, but by the will of the one who subjected it, in hope that the creation itself will be liberated from its bondage to decay and brought into the glorious freedom of the children of God" (Rom 8:20-21). The natural world is not in a perfectly balanced, self-sustaining state. Human sin and rebellion have had their negative impact on the natural order. While we may not know the precise ways sin has affected our world, nature is in some fundamental sense disordered because of the Fall. [16] Like human nature itself, the physical world suffers not only from human sin but from some more basic derangement, some "bondage to decay." This is reflected in part in the curse pronounced after the Fall (Gen 3:17-19) and may be in part the result of the catastrophic event of the flood (Gen 6:13; 8:21; 9:3). The natural environment was significantly different after the flood, as can be seen in Genesis 9 and in the sharp drop in longevity after Noah's time.

It would appear, then, that in the judgments of the Fall and flood the created order was subjected to decay. The original harmony and balance were broken. Marvelous as it still is, ours is a spoiled world. Like man and woman, the earth still shows forth the glory of its maker but in a defaced, partially ruined way.

6. *Both ecology and the Bible show that all behavior has consequences.* Ecologically speaking, we can never say that anything we do simply doesn't matter. The effect of one person's life may be minimal, but it does have environmental impact—physically, socially, economically and spiritually. Every breath breathed, every dollar spent and every relationship created modifies the environment. We are tempted to think one person's impact is so small as to be irrelevant, but that is a profoundly anti-ecological attitude. Our new environmental awareness is showing us that when added to the experience of hundreds or millions of others, every person's behavior is ecologically significant *in all its dimensions.*

Ecology also tells us to watch out for long-range consequences. Our behavior touches not only the present world but all future generations. Whether we are speaking about biology (for instance, the creation of families), economics (for instance, the accumulation of wealth) or technology (for instance, the production of radioactive wastes), our behavior as humans makes ripples that radiate ahead into future generations. Thus even from a purely ecological perspective we can say that ethical questions are an inevitable part of life on earth.

In all these respects, the biblical perspective closely parallels that of ecology. The Bible contends that all behavior has meaning and consequences because of who God is and because of the nature of the physical-spiritual universe in which God has placed us. We are faced again with the perspective, "Do this, and you will live; do that, and you will die." We have tended to think of such consequences as arbitrary fiats of God. God has set the rules and, for his own sovereign and inscrutable reasons, if we break the rules we get zapped. But the ecological perspective points to a deeper truth: We suffer the consequences of our actions because of the nature of the physical, spiritual, moral universe God has created—which reflects, of course, the very character of God himself.

The rule is, "The soul who sins is the one who will die" (Ezek 18:4). But this is not an arbitrary rule; it is the nature of the case, part of the spiritual ecology of God's world. In giving the law to his people Israel, God said, "I, the LORD your God, am a jealous God, punishing the children for the sin of the fathers to the third and fourth generation of those who hate me, but showing love to thousands who love me and keep my commandments" (Ex 20:5-6). Viewed ecologically, this is a very interesting passage. When God's people sin, they feel the effects down through several generations. But when they love and obey God, the blessings also radiate into the future. This is not to deny, of course, that God's judgments may be specific and individual, but it is to underscore that the world and God's plan are profoundly ecological. In the biblical perspective, as in the ecological, all behavior has consequences. Those consequences are often long-range, and ethical questions are inescapable. It is probably in this perspective that the effects of the Fall on the physical environment are to be understood.

In all these ways, then, the ecological and biblical perspectives are similar. From the viewpoint of Christian faith, this is not surprising. If the biblical revelation is reliable, then the closer ecological science comes to the real nature of things, the closer it will approach the biblical picture.

Fundamentally, the universe is ordered not logically, psychologically, nor sociologically, but ecologically. The ecological perspective affirms and encompasses all other dimensions. Both the Bible and ecology show man and woman living interdependently with the natural environment. Ideally the relationship between humanity and our environment is a *symbiosis*—a mutually supportive, interdependent living *with*—rather than a parasitism. But in our disordered world, man and woman have become parasites on the environment. Both ecological and spiritual health require understanding the necessary interdependence of humankind and the natural environment, and of taking both ecology and Scripture seriously.

Scripture, however, claims a fundamental priority over ecology because it reveals what ecology cannot fully understand or explain: the realm of the spirit, the dimension of spiritual reality. According to the Bible, we do not really understand the ecology of the world until we recognize its source, the Lord God, and see that the space-time physical world is interpenetrated and held together by a spiritual world and by spiritual energy which comes from God himself.[17]

From this standpoint, we really are not thinking ecologically—even from a scientific point of view—if we do not include the dimension of the spirit.

The Bible gives us a fundamentally accurate, spiritually balanced and scientifically trustworthy understanding of the essential ecology of human existence. And modern ecological awareness can provide a key for understanding what is happening in the world today and relating this to the divine economy "for the fullness of time to unite all things" in Jesus Christ. As we examine Scripture, we see that the Bible pictures both the church and the Kingdom in fundamentally ecological ways. The Bible presents the church through what might be called ecological word pictures. The significance of this will be explored in the next chapter. Further, the biblical conception of God's rule or Kingdom is an ecological conception. The fruit of God's unhindered rule is *shalom*—a life of harmony, health and peace. Thus biblical *shalom* is very close to the concept of ecological balance so far as its implications for nature are concerned—though of course *shalom* is much more than this because it includes righteousness and justice and the full restoration of the image of God in human life and community.[18]

Discovering God's Economy   As we have already noted, God's plan is his *oikonomia,* his economy for the fullness of time. The economy of God is the manifestation of the Kingdom of God. It is the reconciling and uniting of all things, visible and invisible, under the authority of Jesus Christ.

Is it mere chance that we find the word *economy* in the New Testament? Or is God's Kingdom plan in fact economic and ecological in the modern sense?

We have already seen that the biblical revelation is profoundly ecological. But the biblical economy is profoundly economic as well. Economics and ecology trace back to the same basic issues. And Scripture addresses precisely these issues when it speaks of God's purposes and plans.

Economy, House and Kingdom. The word *economy* means the proper or efficient arrangement of parts in a system. We have come to understand economics as "the science of how people produce goods and services, how they distribute them among themselves, and how they use them." As does ecology, economy focuses on the interrelationships and interdependence of parts in a whole. Like ecology, the idea of economy is based on the metaphor of a household. It is rooted in the idea of a Greek house or household *(oikos)* made up of a large family, including servants or slaves. The "economy" *(oikonomia)* was the efficient and proper ordering of the affairs of the *oikos*.

House or household is a key image, then, when we speak of economy and ecology. Household management requires the ordering and arranging of many resources—food and clothing, space and time, money, people, and social relationships. Each person in the household influences all the others, and each person must be cared for. Both modern economics and the biblical economy are concerned with these matters. Properly understood, the biblical revelation encompasses all reality, including economic issues; and, properly understood, economics is not just a matter of goods and services but also of values and relationships. It is important here to note both these facts: God's economy and Kingdom deeply and inevitably involve economic issues, and economics always (and especially today) raises ethical and spiritual issues.

Before dealing with the biblical perspective, let us see just how significant economic issues and questions have become today.

The economic dislocations of the past decade and the advent of "Reaganomics" in the United States have brought economic questions to center stage as at no time perhaps since the Great Depression. But public concern with economics is only symptomatic of a more basic and longer-range debate over the economic options available to us as we move into an age of scarcity.

We are now in a period, argues J. Philip Wogaman, of "a great debate" over economic realities:

Humankind is engaged now in a great debate of worldwide and historic magnitude on the question of how economic life should be organized. Aspects of the debate are peculiar to each country, but it will ultimately be decided in world, not national terms. The broad outlines of the great economic debate call forth a new global consciousness. It is not likely to be resolved quickly.[19]

Wogaman contends that this historic debate will affect life on earth for many years to come and is inevitably a debate in part over values and ethics. "What is at stake in economic questions," he notes, "is the well-being and community relationships of the whole human family, each of whose members is a person of incalculable worth."[20]

One of the problems of economics as currently practiced is that it deals too narrowly with material, quantifiable and monetary matters. In the process it creates, like technology, its own values and morality in which the highest good is efficiency and profitability. As E. F. Schumacher observes, "The religion of economics has its own code of ethics, and the First Commandment is to behave 'economically.' " And "if economic thinking pervades the whole of society, even simple non-economic values like beauty, health, or cleanliness can survive only if they prove to be 'economic.' "[21]

Such an economic perspective is too narrow, both because it tends to ignore ecological realities and constraints and because it shuts out the realm of the spirit.[22] The inevitable result is suicide—ecologically, spiritually, and thus also economically and physically, for these dimensions cannot be divorced. To think exclusively or even primarily in economic terms is like feeding and clothing a baby but ignoring its emotional and social needs. The result is a cripple, something much less than human.

The point, however, is not just that economics provides too narrow a perspective, but rather that when limited to the material and the quantifiable, economics betrays the very concept of economy itself. By definition economy is concerned with *all* the factors which affect people and their environment. Economics, ecology and spiritual reality are not three isolated spheres. They are three ways of viewing the one sphere which is our human environment, our *oikos* or house. Economically, we need a new understanding of the importance of the spiritual dimension, just as spiritually we need to understand the significance of economic issues. The ecological perspective is a pressing reminder of the interpenetration of the economic and spiritual spheres. Figure 1 illustrates how the biblical ecological view contrasts with popular "Christian" views.

In part the pressure of environmental constraints pushes the debate over economic options to the fore. As the scarcity of resources becomes clearer and "the struggle to prop up a way of life that is no longer practical becomes too great, a new economic orientation will emerge."[23]

The church has a key role to play here—both as participant in the

Figure 1. Comparative Views of Reality

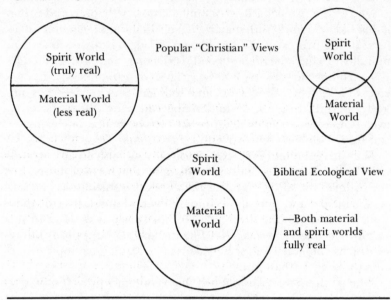

great economic debate and as sign and agent for the economy and Kingdom of God. In fact, a key part of the church's Kingdom work today should be exploring, advocating and modeling economic arrangements which are both ecologically and biblically sound.[24] In this chapter I have indicated some of the elements such economic arrangements would have to incorporate. Theologically, this means seeing God's economy through the biblical images of God's house and Kingdom.

The House of God. Hebrews 3:1-6 exhorts us to fix our thoughts on Jesus, our apostle and high priest, who "was faithful to the one who appointed him, just as Moses was faithful in all God's house." Moses, we read, "was faithful as a servant in all God's house," but "Christ is faithful as a son over God's house." Further, we are told that we, the church, are God's house *(oikos).* Here is a web of biblical ideas which recur in various ways throughout Scripture and which provide a timely perspective for understanding God's plan in the world.

Hebrews begins with a ringing affirmation of who Jesus is: "the

radiance of God's glory and the exact representation of his being,"
the one through whom the world was made and is sustained (Heb
1:2-3). Now we see this same Jesus "crowned with glory and honor
because he suffered death" (2:9). Note that the author links this fact
with Psalm 8:

What is man that you are mindful of him,
the son of man that you care for him?
You made him a little lower than the angels;
you crowned him with glory and honor
and put everything under his feet. (Heb 2:6-8)

This is how man and woman were created—very much like God,
and with dominion over God's world and a charge to care for it. God
initially left nothing in the created order that was not subject to humankind, the writer says. But as we look around us today, we do not
see this. We do not see a fully ordered, balanced, peaceful world.
In many ways we see just the opposite. But what else do we see? "We
see Jesus, who [like us] was made a little lower than the angels, now
crowned with glory and honor."

Note the perspective here. Man and woman were created by God
in his very image to have fellowship with him and to care for a beautiful, balanced, dynamic world. They failed. But Jesus has come,
very God and very human, to restore the ecological balance of God's
order. Through his once-for-all death and resurrection a new, restored order is now at work within the fallen world. And we, the
church, are a part of God's restoring work, for Jesus "is not ashamed
to call" us his brothers and sisters (Heb 2:11). Therefore, as Moses
was faithful, and as Jesus was faithful, we are to be faithful servants
in God's house.

At first glance, "house of God" may look like a rather static idea—
that is, until we remember who God is. God is the great initiator and
his "house" is wherever he chooses to act and make himself known.
"I will put my presence there"—this is what transforms a wilderness
tent into a divine sanctuary, a stone temple into God's dwelling, a
scattered group of people into Christ's body, or the physical cosmos
into God's house.

The New Testament word for "house," *oikos,* means "house,"
"household," or "family." In the Bible it corresponds to the Hebrew
word *beth.* Both words commonly have the meaning of "family," for

"Greek and Hebrew have no word for 'family'; they use the terms *oikos* or *beth* respectively."[25] The significance of the house motif in Scripture becomes clear when we note several biblical words and ideas which are rooted in the word *oikos*. Stewardship, steward, building up or edification, economy or overall plan, the whole habitable globe, God's family or household—all these concepts are grounded in the Greek word *oikos*.

Biblically, God's economy *(oikonomia)* is to put all things in proper order within his *oikos*. This is the image involved in saying God has an *oikonomia* for the fullness of time to unite or reconcile all things in Jesus Christ (Eph 1:10). It is important, then, that we see just what this "house" means and includes.

The Bible employs the idea of God's house in several senses. These boil down to two fundamental ideas: The church is God's household or family, and the whole created order is, metaphorically, God's house.

First, *the church is the house, household and family of God.* The common designation for "temple" in the Old Testament is, literally, "God's house" *(beth-El)*. The Old Testament speaks much about the tabernacle and temple of God. These were the places where God, symbolically but really, established his presence among his chosen people. But these realities were shadows of things to come. God's will is to dwell in people, not in bricks and mortar, not in crystal and steel. His intention, and the goal of salvation history, is to lead, dwell with and work through a special people, his servants and stewards. This is what the church is—the family and household of God.

Where does God dwell today? Not in temples made with hands but in human temples. Not in places but in people. In human hearts certainly, but also, and especially, in a community of people who confess Jesus Christ as Lord and determine to be faithful to him in their life together.

Nearly all the biblical images of the church are figures from life. The church is a living organism. It is a community taking its spiritual life and power from the living presence of the Spirit of Jesus. Combining the images of the body of Christ and the family or household of God, we get a clear picture of what the church really is in God's plan. This understanding comes through with striking force in Ephesians 2:19-22 where, after describing the church as Christ's body, Paul goes on to say, "You are no longer foreigners and aliens, but fellow citizens with God's people and members of God's household [*oikeioi*], built [*epoikodomēthentes*] on the foundation of the apostles and prophets, with Christ Jesus himself as the chief cornerstone. In him the whole building [*oikodomē*] is joined together and rises to become a holy temple in the Lord. And in him you too are being built together [*sunoikodomeisthe*] to become a dwelling [*katoikētērion*] in which God lives by his Spirit." No fewer than five words in this passage are based on the word *oikos,* "family" or "household." This complex of ideas reinforces the biblical picture of the church as the community of God's people and the agent of God's *oikonomia* and Kingdom.

God has a well-ordered plan for how the church is to live and function. Part of God's economy concerns the way the local congregation is to function—what we might call the ecology of the local church.

Second, *the whole created order is God's house.* The church is not the only place God works; rather it is a sign pointing to what God is doing in his larger "house," the created universe. The whole cosmos is, metaphorically, God's *oikos* for which God has an *oikonomia,* a plan for the proper ordering of everything in the world.

God does not dwell in a house made with hands; not even the whole universe can contain him.[26] Yet God inhabits his world.[27] As Israel's psalmists often sang, every part of the created order testifies to God's power and goodness and is the sphere of his presence and mighty acts.

In the Old Testament, first the tabernacle and then the temple at Jerusalem became the focal point of God's presence and dwelling. From this point two lines of development can be traced. The one sees God's people, rather than a physical structure, as God's house and temple. This provides the basis for the New Testament understanding of the church as the household, family and community of God. The other line of development is equally significant, however, for understanding God's plan. Here the idea of God's house or dwelling is expanded to become a metaphor for the whole created order. The cosmos is the house of God, inhabited and sanctified by his presence.

This development is seen especially in the book of Psalms. Often references to God's house or dwelling clearly mean the Jerusalem temple, or Jerusalem itself (for instance, Ps 5:7; 42:4; 55:14; 116:19). But in some cases the idea is expanded so that the whole earth is pictured as God's house. This is most clear, perhaps, in Psalm 36:5-9:

> Your love, O LORD, reaches to the heavens,
> your faithfulness to the skies.
> Your righteousness is like the mighty mountains,
> your justice like the great deep.
> O LORD, you preserve both man and beast.
> How priceless is your unfailing love!
> Both high and low among men
> find refuge in the shadow of your wings.
> They feast on the abundance of your house;
> you give them drink from your river of delights.
> For with you is the fountain of life;
> in your light we see light.

Here the earth is God's house and the object of his care. God is present in his world. A related idea is that God himself is the dwelling place for his people (Ps 90:1; 91:9). In the Old Testament, this does not have an otherworldly sense. Rather the thought is that God is present on earth with his people. God provides a habitation for his people in himself and in the world he has made. The perspective is ecological.

From this perspective, several passages in the Psalms which appear at first to refer to the physical temple may well have a broader sense. "I love the house where you live, O LORD, the place where your glory dwells" (Ps 26:8) can be seen as referring to the whole created world, especially when we compare it with such passages as Psalm 19:1-6 and Psalm 24:1-2. "We are filled with the good things of your house" (Ps 65:4) praises God not just for "spiritual" blessings but for the abundance of the earth. Several other passages may similarly have a broader reference (for example, Ps 27:4-6; 52:8; 61:4; 84:1-4; 92:12-13; 134:1; 135:2).

Many of the psalms come from the time of David and Solomon, when the idea of "house" carried also the idea of lineage or royal line. In this connection notice how the ideas of "house" and "kingdom" are linked in several Old Testament passages which clearly point ahead to the coming of Christ and the Kingdom pictured in the New Testament.[28]

This Old Testament background enriches the New Testament picture of God's saving work as the manifestation of his Kingdom and the proper ordering of all things in God's house under the headship of Jesus Christ. God's salvation centers in the life, death, resurrection and reign of Jesus, and the New Testament shows how God is working out his economy and Kingdom through Jesus Christ.

The way the New Testament speaks of Christ underscores the double sense of house (both the church and the cosmos) which we have been describing. In Colossians 1, for instance, Jesus is described as both "the firstborn over all creation" and "the firstborn from among the dead" (Col 1:15, 18). In Hebrews, Jesus is both the sustainer and "heir of all things" and the apostle and high priest of the church (Heb 1:2-3; 3:1). Jesus Christ, Lord of the church, is also Lord of the universe. This is the jolting significance of the original cry of the first Christians, "Jesus is Lord!"

This perspective is further reinforced by the way the New Testament speaks of Jesus Christ as "head." Jesus is head not only of the church but of "all things." "God placed all things under [Jesus'] feet and appointed him to be head over everything for the church, which is his body, the fullness of him who fills everything in every way" (Eph 1:22-23). Thus God's plan, as the New International Version correctly translates Ephesians 1:10, is "to bring all things in heaven and on earth together under one head, even Christ." The verb here (anakephalaiosasthai) derives from the noun kephalē, "head," the word used for Jesus as head of the church. The verb means "to head up" or "to bring under the headship of." Jesus Christ is now head of the church, and God's plan through the church is to fully reveal Christ's headship over the whole created order.

These passages all point in the same direction. The whole created order is God's house, his habitation, though now disordered by sin and human unfaithfulness. But God is creating a new humanity, a new family or household, which is the present manifestation of the future reconciliation of all things. And far from operating in a separate sphere greatly removed from the world, the church is God's household right smack in the middle of the disordered cosmos, existing there both to show what God intends and will do and to be the body of Christ—the presence and agency of Jesus in the world today. For the Lord, the Father of the Christian household, is also the "Father of all" (Eph 4:6), "the Father from whom all fatherhood in heaven and on earth derives its name" (Eph 3:14).

The Significance of God's Economy. In summary, God's economy is his plan to bring justice, harmony and health—his perfect *shalom*— to his creation. This he accomplishes through Jesus Christ and the church. The church is God's *oikos* in a special sense, charged with showing forth and helping to bring about God's peace in the larger *oikos,* the created order. The church does this in part through understanding its own real ecology in all its dimensions, and through cooperating with God's design in its life and witness.

Economy or *oikonomia* is a particularly apt word today for picturing God's design. The word *oikonomia* occurs nine times in the New Testament and is variously translated "management," "administration," "stewardship" or "plan."[29] In its larger sense, according to Oscar Cullmann, it is the word "whereby the divine plan of salvation is viewed in its entirety."[30] Cullmann suggests that God's economy is equivalent to salvation history.[31] The term has, in fact, a long and noble history in Christian thought from the patristic period on, as well as an important history in Greek thought outside New Testament and patristic use. When set in the thought world of the first century, Paul's use of *oikonomia* proves more significant than its few New Testament occurrences might at first suggest.

John Reumann notes that "*oikonomia* and its related terms *(oikonomos, oikonomein, dioikēsis,* etc.) were 'in the air' with a variety of meanings in the first-century A.D. world. There had been a steady development of usages from the root meaning of 'management in a household *(oikos)*' to management of a city-state *(polis)* to management of the world *(kosmos)*. Especially important is the fact that by late Hellenistic times *oikonomia* was regularly applied to God's ordering and administration of the universe."[32]

In using this term, then, Paul was plugging into a common and very lively Greek notion of "the economy of God," giving it a Christian understanding. Reumann notes that apparently "Hellenistic-Judaism increasingly took over this *oikonomia*-vocabulary in order to speak of God's rule in the world" and "Christian writers soon took over this language too."[33]

G. L. Prestige has traced the extensive use of *oikonomia* and related terms in the Greek church fathers and shows that "divine economy was conceived as extending to things great and small indifferently—from the ordering of natural law on the widest scale to the particular disposition of unimportant details in daily life." He notes in summary,

the Greek Fathers recognized, in principle and in detail, the providential activity of God in nature, human history, and the sphere of grace. It need only be added that the supreme instance of divine economy, whether in the sense of dispensation, condescension, or special providence, was exhibited in the Incarnation, for which the word "oekonomia," without any verbal qualifications, is the regular patristic term from the third century onwards.[34]

Thus in the New Testament and the early Greek fathers, God's plan of salvation was understood in this fundamentally economic-ecological way. Since *economy* became virtually synonymous with Incarnation from the third century on, much of the earlier power of the economy motif was eventually lost. The significance for today, however, is that this economic-ecological way of understanding God's saving plan is both biblically based and precisely relevant to the realities of today's global village.[35]

God is the divine economist, the creative Lord who from the foundation of the world has established a plan for the fullness of time. And this plan centers in Jesus Christ and the work of the Holy Spirit in and through the church.

The significance and breadth of God's economy can be gauged by correlating it with three other New Testament words which are also based on the metaphor of "house." Each Christian is an *oikonomos,* a steward or good manager in God's house. To us is given the task of *oikodomē*, of edifying or building up God's house. And God's plan extends to the whole *oikoumenē*, the entire habitable world. Thus steward, edification and ecumenical are all *oikos* words which suggest the dimensions of God's redemptive plan.

Stewards and Earthkeepers. In light of the contemporary ecological crisis and the divine economy presented in Scripture, we are called to be stewards in God's house and keepers of the earth. We are called to work together with Christ in building and managing his house—both the church and the world—in a way that is biblically faithful and ecologically responsible. We are given a stewardship *(oikonomia).*

We are to be good managers of the resources which God has placed in our hands—resources which are fully adequate to accomplish God's will and plan through the church.

Stewardship, like so many rich biblical concepts, has been robbed of much of its biblical punch by being restricted to questions of the tithe and the use of time. The biblical idea of stewardship is much broader and richer—first, because it ties in with God's overall economy, and second because it involves the stewardship both of the created order and of God's grace.

Men and women have obviously been very poor stewards of the created order. Unfortunately, we Christians haven't done much better than the human race generally. Much of the destruction and disruption of the natural world has been carried out with the blessing of the church. Christians need to recover a comprehensive biblical understanding of the stewardship God has given us of the created world. This concerns both our lives in the world (how we treat the physical environment; the quantities and kinds of food we consume; our use of land and energy; the kinds of homes and church buildings we erect) and our lives in the Christian community (how well we understand the spiritual ecology of the church and work harmoniously with God's principles to build a community of the Spirit which is in fact a sign of the Kingdom of God). If we are to live ecologically responsible lives as Christians, we must cooperate with God's ecology for the church.

In order that we may be good stewards of the created order, God has given us his grace. Peter says we should be "good stewards of God's varied grace" (1 Pet 4:10 RSV). We have been charged with stewardship of the most precious of all resources—the grace of God.

We have been saved by grace through faith, and God has given us gifts of grace by his Spirit. These are our most precious and valuable resources, and we are charged to be good stewards of them. God gives his own life to us. The body receives its life from the head, Jesus Christ. We are to grow into his fullness and likeness. We are to have the mind of Christ. Only as this happens will we have the spiritual strength to build the church as God intends and to witness effectively to and among the principalities and powers of the present age.

The church, however, also has a wider stewardship in God's

world. The mission of the church is to glorify God by showing forth his nature and works, the reconciliation and redemption God brings through the death, resurrection and reign of Jesus Christ. "God . . . reconciled us to himself through Christ and gave us the ministry of reconciliation: that God was reconciling the world to himself in Christ, not counting men's sins against them. And he has committed to us the message of reconciliation. We are therefore Christ's ambassadors, as though God were making his appeal through us" (2 Cor 5:18-20). God's plan is that *"now,* through the church, the manifold wisdom of God should be made known to the rulers and authorities in the heavenly realms, according to his eternal purpose which he accomplished in Christ Jesus our Lord" (Eph 3:10-11).

In other words, the life and work of the Christian community are intimately bound up with God's cosmic-historical plan for the redemption of his world. It most certainly matters *what* the Christian community does and how authentically it demonstrates the mind of Christ and the values of the Kingdom in its daily life. We are saved by grace, not by our works, but "we are God's workmanship, created in Christ Jesus to do good works"—specifically those good works "which God prepared in advance for us to do" (Eph 2:10).

Kingdom Economics. As I have already argued, a practical concern with economic issues must be high on the agenda of the church's Kingdom responsibility today. Liberating the church means freedom from current economic ideologies and idols so that the church can bring the biblical perspective to bear on all economic questions.

While this is not the place to discuss economic questions thoroughly, I want to emphasize some elements which should be part of any economic system that is consistent with the biblical economy. Translating the economy of God into contemporary economic reality means incorporating the following perspectives:

1. *God is the owner of everything,* including all resources and the means of production. He owns both land and capital. All these are held in trust, for God's glory and the common good, by the human family. This fact places serious limitations on private ownership of resources and on the private accumulation of wealth.

Whether it is ultimately more functional and more just for most resources to be held in trust by "private" individuals and corporations or by the state is, of course, a point of dispute between capitalists and socialists. Most economies are in fact a mixture of private and public ownership. A biblical economic perspective, however, will insist that divine ownership is the fundamental reality, and that this consciousness must permeate all economic thinking and practice. Economic and political arrangements must be structured so that in fact all resources are held in trust for the common good and the glory of God, consistent with God's economy.

2. *Economics must recognize that man and woman are fallen, though imaged after God.* It therefore must take account of human greed, perversity and selfishness, as well as human creativity, freedom and idealism.

Much economic thinking, especially toward the socialist end of the spectrum, seems to assume a naively optimistic view of human nature. It is easy to think that evil and injustice are rooted in the system only, that if only a more just system were instituted, human goodness and creativity would blossom, sprouting a perfect society. The biblical perspective, however, is that because of sin human beings are perverse and self-seeking. This is true in any economic system. Economic arrangements which are most consistent with Scripture, however, will recognize human perversity, place limits on its effects and also provide space so that all that is good, beautiful and productive in man and woman may blossom to its fullest.

3. *Economics must reject both doctrinaire capitalism and socialism,* seeking new economic options which incorporate the valid elements of both these systems. Traditional capitalism and socialism both assume unlimited economic growth and thus tend to be anti-ecological. For these and other reasons, they must be severely questioned today.

Perhaps out of this questioning may come some new, creative economic options which draw on the strengths of both capitalism and socialism while taking ecological limits seriously. One of the strengths of capitalism, for instance, is the freedom and opportunities it provides for the entrepreneur. This often spurs innovation and new economic vitality, as well as new products and services. But where the profit motive and private ownership are uncritically assumed, this freedom is often abused, producing private wealth at the expense of the public good. Are there ways to preserve entrepreneurial freedom while harnessing it more directly to social benefit and the preservation, rather than the despoiling, of the environment? Some new models are emerging, and others certainly must be possible.[36] Tremendous opportunity exists today for Christian and other public-minded entrepreneurs to develop new businesses which provide for broader profit sharing or joint ownership and which provide useful services or products *which work in fundamental harmony with God's economy.* One can imagine new ventures that create jobs for the unemployed, use more cooperative forms of ownership and management and provide ecologically sound services in recycling, energy conservation, alternate energy, food and transportation systems. Such ventures would use "small-tech" rather than "high-tech" approaches.

There are no inherent reasons why many new options along these lines would not be workable. What is needed is the new paradigm of a broadly ecological understanding coupled with the daring to innovate.

4. *Economics must recognize the finiteness and vulnerability of our ecosystem and the seriousness of environmental issues,* seeking to preserve and protect earth's biosphere.

The limitations which the environment places on economic activity are very real. This should be seen as a friendly fact, however, not a hostile one. Economic arrangements which are consistent with the Kingdom will delight in the adventure of working with, not against, the environment. As environmental constraints become more obvious and pressing, those economic systems and enterprises which understand and cooperate with the ecological realities will be a jump ahead of those which ignore or only grudgingly accept the limits of our ecosystem.[37]

5. *Economics must recognize and focus on the genius of human community* as a key factor in economic policy and organization. This means, among other things, working to support and encourage human-scale economic arrangements which tend to build neighborhoods, local communities and families.

Many cultures, including some primitive tribal groups, have an ethos of community and shared responsibility which is markedly different from the unquestioned individualism of industrialized Western cultures. The recent experience of Japan shows that a greater sense of community or group cohesiveness and responsibility is just as economically viable as is the more individualistic approach. These realities suggest that economic theory and practice in the future must learn that the inherent genius of human community has tremendous economic potential. Some of the more successful uses of co-ops in the United States and elsewhere in recent decades may be pointers in this direction.

6. Given the vulnerability of the biosphere, the limits of resources, and the nature of human community, *economics must focus on small- and intermediate-scale organization and technology* rather than large-scale capital- and energy-intensive technology and economic arrangements.[38] In the world today, most economic organization tends either to combine high technology with capital-intensive production or else to join labor-intensive production with very primitive technology. One result is that industrial investment by large corporations in Third World nations may actually produce greater unemployment among the poor. You need a few skilled workers, not masses of untrained laborers, to operate a modern factory.

But again, are not other options possible? Much more can be done in combining sophisticated but small-scale technology with labor-intensive production so that everyone has a productive job without demeaning or backbreaking labor. The most ecologically sound economics of the future will likely move in this direction. The exciting thing about this from a Christian standpoint is that this style of economics can work with, rather than against, God's Kingdom purposes.

7. Realizing that every person has moral and ecological significance, *economics must give special attention to the poor and oppressed,* working toward economic and social justice. It must be based on the recognition that the welfare of the whole human community depends on the well-being of every person, and indeed every creature, in the ecosystem.

Kingdom economics will demonstrate that, when the real ecology of our world is understood, caring for the poor and oppressed is actually economic wisdom as well. Properly understood, this means not simply providing a safety net at the bottom of society but rather involving all people, including the poor, in the economic system. The year of Jubilee and the other economic provisions in Scripture, provide ample demonstration that caring for the poor makes sense economically, as well as morally and spiritually.

Much more could be said in this area, especially from the perspective of the Kingdom of God. Each of these seven points could be developed at length. The point here, however, is principally to trace a perspective; to stress that God's Kingdom plan is in part a matter of economics and that the Kingdom of God does point in some specific economic directions. Business executives are always concerned about economic indicators and the bottom line. The Kingdom of God gives us some economic indicators and a bottom line of a different species.

The economic and ecological realities of our time point us back to fundamental issues of value and human community. In this perspective the significance of seeing the Kingdom of God as God's economy and ecology emerges with special force. Viewed ecologically, God's plan in Scripture becomes clearer and its significance for today is sharpened. Liberating the church in our day means freeing the church for the economy and ecology of God.

3
THE ECOLOGY
OF THE CHURCH

Today much of the church moves with a massive misunderstanding of its own nature and mission. Especially in North America, the church shows little perception of the economy of God and therefore of the ecology of the church in God's plan. Many believers still operate with a static, institutional understanding, seeing the church as buildings, meetings, programs, professional clergy and special techniques of communication, evangelism and church growth. Worse, in the United States this whole mentality is often wed to a political and economic perspective which clashes directly with God's economy. Most Christians in our land are so tied to a perspective of unlimited economic growth, continued exploitation of resources, militarism, extravagant gadget-fed lifestyles and patriotic narcissism that they instinctively repel a more biblical view of the church and God's plan before they really understand it.

We need a massive awakening to the church's cultural accommodations and a fundamental rethinking of the church itself. By and large, North American Christians are so enamored with the American dream that they have become immune to several fundamental biblical themes. We have picked and chosen—spiritualizing here, literalizing there—in the process conforming the gospel to a comfortable, materialistic lifestyle. Where Scripture speaks of preaching the gospel to the poor, maintaining justice, caring for the widow and orphan, or preaching liberty to the captives, we have said, "Oh, that must be understood spiritually. Everyone is spiritually poor without Christ." But where the Scriptures speak of getting blessings from God or receiving "the desires of our heart," we have said, "Oh, that is literal and material. God helps those who help themselves. God wants us to be prosperous. We are children of the King." To many, this is gospel. But in reality this inversion of material and spiritual values is hypocrisy and heresy. It is a biblically unfaithful splitting up of the wholeness of God's house.

This is why the church needs a fundamental paradigm shift in its self-understanding. We must have a more faithful overall model for understanding the church in God's economy. Talk with another Christian for only five minutes, and you can tell what model of the church he or she is operating with. Where the model is the institutional-technical-hierarchical model of contemporary pop Christianity, a whole set of assumptions follows which make it difficult to really grasp the New Testament picture of the church. But where the model is that of the body of Christ, the household of God and the community of God's people, the door is opened to understand the economy and ecology of God and to see the church as a charismatic organism which, united to and dependent on Christ, is at the center of God's plan for the reconciliation of all things.

In this chapter I want to explore what it means practically to view the life of the church ecologically and then to propose an ecological model for the internal life of the church.

We have seen that God's house, his *oikos*, has a dual sense: the *oikoumenē*, or whole habitable world, and the church as the prototypical community of the Kingdom of God. We have seen that God has an economy for his entire creation and that because of this dual sense of "house" we have been given a stewardship in the church and in the physical environment to care for and build God's household. For this task God has given us the resources of his grace. We need then to understand *the real ecology of the church* and what it means to be servants, stewards and earthkeepers for God. We need to grasp both the *internal ecology* of the church (how it functions as a spiritual-social organism) and its *extended ecology* (how it interacts with and affects the whole ecosphere of God's world).

We must learn to think ecologically at all levels in the church. Ecological thinking reminds us that everything is related to everything else, and it emphasizes the need to trace and comprehend these interrelationships. This may seem like an impossible task, and it is, if we think comprehensively. If we have an ecological mindset, however, we can trace those interdependencies which bear most directly on our own lives and stewardship.

A few examples will illustrate the point. Within the church, Christians need to see how their lives really do touch the lives of other believers. In the neighborhood, Christians should ask how their lifestyles affect the environment. This ecology includes the kind of housing and transportation used, relationships with neighbors, and many other strands in the physical, social and spiritual environment. In their work, Christians should ask how the products and services they design, manufacture or distribute touch the overall environment—including, especially, their impact on the world's poor. For those who have investments, a critical question is where funds are invested and how those investments are used. Generally, invested capital operates either for or against the environment and the poor, for it is impossible for investments to be environmentally (and therefore morally) neutral. Ecological stewardship means concern as much with the impact of investments themselves as with how investment earnings are spent. And if this is true of individual investments, it is true even more of the investments of church-related institutions.

The Real Ecology of the Church   Once we understand the intertwining of social, physical, economic and spiritual dimensions of reality, we must pursue the real ecology of the church and guard against unbiblical and unecological divisions between the spiritual and material realms. When we limit our perceptions to spiritual matters only, we see not the church's real ecology but only some parts of it.

What, then, is the real ecology of the church? Here we face two immediate problems: identifying all the factors which constitute this ecology, and distinguishing between what the church's ecology ought to be and what it is in fact. Much of this book is addressed to the normative ecology of the church—what it ought to be and can be if we cooperate with the given spiritual and material constraints. We have also looked to some degree at how the church actually functions.

The real ecology of the church encompasses an extremely large number of variables. The church, in fact, may be the most complex ecosystem in existence since it includes the total human environment and experience—physical, social and spiritual. Although these three categories are not totally satisfactory or mutually exclusive, we may use them to probe further into the church's actual ecology.

Physical Ecology. The church's physical ecology consists of the physical bodies of believers and all the material aspects of their lives. It includes the food and clothing Christians use, the products they use or help produce, and the physical energy they consume. It includes their houses and church buildings. Transportation, land use and the treatment of other life on earth are also part of the actual ecology of the church. *We cannot speak of the real ecology of the church without taking into account the combined impact Christians have in all these areas.* The key question, then, becomes whether the church's use of money, buildings, food supplies, energy and other physical resources is in harmony with God's economy or works against it. If Christians claim to be worshiping and serving God in the spiritual realm while furthering injustice through extravagant consumption of the earth's resources, then they are giving mixed signals. They are in fact working against God's economy in fundamental ways. From an ecological perspective there are no such things as *adiaphora,* "things indifferent."

Social Ecology. The social ecology of the church concerns the church as a social organism, a community. It includes the social impact of each believer, but it especially concerns the social reality and impact of Christian families and homes, Christian congregations, and the influence of Christians in their neighborhoods and in the larger human community.

The social ecology of the church thus includes the total social impact of the church and of individual Christians, as well as how the church is shaped by society. Part of this impact involves the moral and ethical values which Christians hold. These values are shown and transmitted by Christians' actual behavior. This is one reason the economic and social behavior of Christians is so important. Whether or not Christians are really cooperating with the economy of God will be revealed in the way they behave in the economic realm.

The real ecology of the church, then, includes every aspect of the social behavior of Christians. It includes the social and economic impact of the jobs Christians hold, and not just Christians' dependability at work or how they spend their off-the-job hours. And it includes the social impact of how Christians treat the physical world —for instance, whether they care for the earth and work for equitable distribution of food and clothing or are concerned only with their own accumulation and comfort.

Spiritual Ecology. The spiritual ecology of the church is even more complex than its physical and social ecology and is less available to our understanding and analysis. But Christians insist, on the basis of both Scripture and personal experience, that the spiritual dimension is the most fundamental in the church's ecology, the reality which gives ultimate meaning to all the rest.

The spiritual ecology of the church incorporates the moral and spiritual values by which Christians live, but it includes much more. It incorporates the reality of the spirit world—the actual presence of the Spirit of God in the world and the reality of angels, demons and whatever other unseen principalities and powers the universe contains. It is profoundly unecological to overlook this dimension. The church's spiritual ecology includes its battle with the kingdom of darkness, "the ruler of the kingdom of the air, the spirit who is now at work in those who are disobedient" (Eph 2:2).

The spiritual impact of the church is tied especially to the influence Christians have on one another, the impact of righteous living on society and the power of prayer. Since prayer is the primary channel of communication between believers and God, it is a key means through which God's energy is released into the world. Here faith and hope are crucial, for through these, Christians are enabled to work constructively for the manifestation of the Kingdom of God in the present order.

The key dynamic in the church's spiritual ecology is faith working by love (Gal 5:6). Much of this book focuses on the spiritual ecology of the church, for this is the key to everything else.

The Church's Environmental Impact. Only when we take into account the physical, social and spiritual ecology of the church can we begin to gauge her true environmental impact.

We may consider the life of a local congregation in a particular community. What is its impact? Some of the congregation's impact could actually be measured through sociological, economic or ecological analysis. One could determine, for instance, the combined effect of the energy consumed by Christians or gauge their impact on the community's social fabric. It is true, of course, that much of the church's impact could not be measured or quantified. But since the social, physical and economic life of a group of people reflects their spiritual values, some judgment could be made about the total environmental impact of a congregation and its fundamental fidelity or infidelity to the economy of God.

The next question is: What would be the result of intentional changes in the church's life? What would be the ecological impact if a congregation decided to align its life more closely with God's economy and Kingdom? This is where the lifestyle changes advocated by a growing number of thoughtful Christians come into focus.

Many Christians ask what difference it makes to live a simpler, more Kingdom-oriented lifestyle. When we view this question ecologically, we see that it makes all the difference in the world. For the ecological perspective reminds us that every life is linked to every other, that all our behavior has consequences socially, physically and spiritually, and that our behavior has long-range effects that may continue for generations. In other words, from an ecological standpoint living for Kingdom priorities has far-reaching and highly significant results. Such responsible living in fact helps to manifest the Kingdom of God and contributes significantly to the reconciliation of all things in Jesus Christ.

It is not necessary to follow this out in further detail right now. We will look more closely at the question of lifestyle in chapter eleven. An example, however, may be useful.

Consider the church's relationship to nature. The church should be a model of reconciliation between people and nature, thus pointing ahead to the Kingdom. The church could start, for instance, with ecological responsibility for the land it owns corporately—the millions of acres tied up in church and college campuses and in the church's sacred-cow pastures, church camps, which not uncommonly run into the hundreds of acres. Just as industrial holdings are managed with no other motive than profit, so church properties are often managed with no other motive than narrowly religious programming. Such property should be used as a model of ecological responsibility. This would mean, at the least, preserving as much as possible of the land in its natural state; protecting resident wildlife; developing as environmentally balanced an ecosystem as feasible; and using such areas as educational tools to heighten a sense of environmental awareness and ecological stewardship. A similar perspective and concern could be applied also to the land held "privately" by Christians in the form of homes, farms, and vacation or investment property.[1]

An Ecological Model for Church Life The church is a sociospiritual organism. Its life may be viewed ecologically as a dynamic interplay of several parts. Like any other organism, its health depends on the proper balance and functioning of the parts. Understanding the ecology of the church means discerning the elements of church life and how they relate to each other.

Paul presents one ecological view of the church in 1 Corinthians 12, using the analogy of the human body. Each believer is a member of the body, and the health of the whole depends on the proper functioning and interplay of all the members. Paul uses a fundamentally ecological model when he says, "The body is a unit, though it is made up of many parts; and though all its parts are many, they form one body. So it is with Christ" (1 Cor 12:12).

Paul speaks similarly but from a slightly different angle in Ephesians 4:1-16. This is also a picture of church ecology, but the stress is not so much on individual members and gifts as on the dynamic of growing up into Christ and living from the fullness of Christ's grace. The emphasis is on the dependence of the body on the head, Jesus Christ. But the picture here too is highly ecological: "Speaking the truth in love, we will in all things grow up into him who is the Head, that is, Christ. From him the whole body, joined and held together by every supporting ligament, grows and builds itself up in love, as each part does its work" (Eph 4:15-16).

These passages underscore the fact that the church is a living, charismatic organism dependent on the grace of God. Examining Ephesians and other New Testament passages, we may construct an ecological model which traces the basic elements of the church's life and shows how these relate to each other.

The following model is a synthesis of the New Testament teachings on the ecology of the church. I emphasize that this is a model. That is, it is not a complete description of the church's life, nor is it the only valid way to view the local church. It is a fairly comprehensive model, however, and it is consistent with Scripture and particularly apt for church life in today's world.

The Purpose of the Church. The model begins with the church's purpose. It is easier to understand the church's ecology when we know why the church exists.

I stress this starting point because it determines everything else. Just as a saw does not serve well as a hammer, so the church is powerless when it functions contrary to God's intentions. The church has tremendous force when its purpose and functions match God's design. Too often, however, we expect the wrong things from the church—in part because we are not clear regarding its purpose.

We have seen that the church is to be sign, symbol and forerunner of the Kingdom of God. The church exists for the Kingdom. More basically, as we noted in chapter one, the purpose of the church is to glorify God.

An ecological model for the church, then, orients church life toward God's glory. If we conceive the Christian community as a circle, the model begins to take form as in figure 2.

Figure 2.

Functions of the Church. The church glorifies God in many ways. In order to avoid the pitfall of justifying anything and everything the church does simply by saying it is "done for the glory of God," however, we need to identify the most basic functions of the church. What are the essential components of the church's life?

In portraying the church as God's household or *oikos,* it is helpful to view the church as a fellowship of worship, community and witness. Given the proper biblical and practical rhythm of worship, community and witness, the church maintains a spiritual ecological balance. This provides the dynamism and health which allow it to be used dramatically in God's larger plan of redemption.

We find the New Testament church living a life of worship, community and witness. These functions are indicated to some extent by the New Testament words *leitourgia* ("service" or "worship," from which comes the English word *liturgy*), *koinōnia* ("fellowship" or "sharing"), and *martyria* ("witness" or "testimony," from which comes the word *martyr*).[2] The church is a community or fellowship of shared life, a *koinōnia.* The church witnesses to what God has done in Jesus Christ and in its own experience, even when its *martyria* leads to martyrdom. Above all, the church performs the service of worship (*leitourgia*) to God, not just through acts of worship but by living a life of praise to God.

Drawing these three elements together, and giving a certain priority to worship as the church in the act of praising God, the model then becomes that of figure 3. Here the church is seen as glorifying God through its worship, its life together in community and its witness in the world. Recalling that this is an ecological model, we must stress not only that these functions are oriented toward the glory of God but also that each one interacts with and influences the others. This dynamism of interrelationships is highlighted by the arrows in the figure.

These functions stood out clearly in the early days of the Christian church. In Acts 2:42 we read that the first Christians "devoted themselves to the apostles' teaching and to the fellowship, to the breaking of bread and to prayer." Further, we read that they shared their goods and homes with each other so that no one had need and all had a house fellowship in which to worship God and be strengthened for witness in the world.

Figure 3.

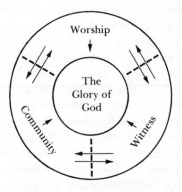

1. *Worship.* The early Christians "devoted themselves ... to the breaking of bread and to prayer." This describes the church at worship. Bread breaking probably indicates the early Christian *agape* meal in which believers celebrated the Lord's Supper in their house fellowships. Meeting together in their homes as well as in large-group worship, first-century Christians kept their church life vital through frequent praise and prayer.

In Acts 4:22-31 we get a picture of the church at worship. Peter and John had been arrested and then released by the Sanhedrin. The believers came together to praise God and to pray for boldness. And God answered: "After they prayed, the place where they were meeting was shaken. And they were all filled with the Holy Spirit and spoke the word of God boldly" (Acts 4:31).

Paul tells the Ephesians: "Speak to one another with psalms, hymns and spiritual songs. Sing and make music in your heart to the Lord, always giving thanks to God the Father for everything, in the name of our Lord Jesus Christ" (Eph 5:19-20). We are to "teach and admonish one another with all wisdom," singing "psalms, hymns and spiritual songs with gratitude ... to God" (Col 3:16).

Worship—praising God and hearing him speak through the Word—is the heart of being God's people. Often in the Old Testament we read of the special festivals of the children of Israel. These, as well as the whole sacrificial system, focused on worshiping God.

Down through history, in every land and language, worship has been the central activity of the church, its very life blood. This is appropriate, for worship is, above all, the church praising God. In worship the church celebrates who God is and all he has done for his people, and renews its covenant to live for his glory. Worship comes first among all the things the church does, for its special concern is the glory of Almighty God.

Worship means more, however, than worship services. We are to live a life of worship. Everything we do is to glorify God. But this life of worship comes to special focus and intensity in the regular weekly worship celebration of God's people.

Each week is a journey through time. The journey brings us face to face with the values, pressures and seductions of an idolatrous age. Getting through the week means turning a deaf ear to countless advertisements for clothes, cars, magazines, video recorders and other items, even while we listen for the cries of human need. Unless we plan otherwise, the week will be programmed for us by job or school commitments, errands, TV schedules, our acquaintances and many other demands. The world closes in on us.

This is why Paul says in Romans 12, "Don't let the world around you squeeze you into its own mold" (Phillips). Rather we are to offer ourselves as living sacrifices to God. This is genuine worship (Rom 12:1-2).

Worship is the opening in an enclosed world. The world tries to make us like itself. It draws a circle around us, blocking out the higher, brighter world of the Spirit. We are not to deny the present world nor to flee from it. Rather we are to learn how to live like Jesus within society. We are to be lights in the world (Mt 5:14-16; Phil 2:15).

Here is the key. In worship the curtains of time and space are thrown back, and we see anew the realm of the Spirit. Worshiping God in spirit and truth gives us a window on eternity. It changes our lives as we see again that we really do live in two worlds. We begin to see from God's perspective: "I entered the sanctuary of God; then I understood" (Ps 73:17).

Certainly each Christian worships God privately in his or her own times of prayer and devotion. But worship is especially the business of the church gathered. Alone in prayer, we tend to focus on our own needs, problems and hurts. There is nothing wrong with this, provided private prayer is balanced by corporate praise. God made us to glorify him *together*. We are to be a worshiping, praising community. There is something about being together, blending our hearts and voices together in praise, that lifts us away from our own concerns and focuses our eyes on Almighty God. And then something strange happens: In looking at God himself, we find our own lives turned around, healed and prepared for service in the world.

This is what worship can and should do for us. But the ways *we* benefit from worship are, in fact, secondary. The great concern is God himself. We worship God, not to feel better nor even to be more "spiritual," but because he commands and invites us to worship him. In our praise to God, we worship the King.

2. *Community.* One of the things the first Christians devoted themselves to was "the fellowship" (Acts 2:42). The word *koinōnia* here denotes communion, community or fellowship—a group of people bound closely together by what they share. As sharers in God's grace, the believers devoted themselves to being and becoming the *community* of God's people. One basic function of the church as seen in Acts and throughout the New Testament is building Christian community or fellowship. The believers "broke bread in their homes and ate together with glad and sincere hearts, praising God and enjoying the favor of all the people" (Acts 2:46-47). This was one of the basic ways they glorified God.

God has made us a community and wants us to grow continually as a fellowship of believers, being "built up [*oikodomēn*] until we all reach unity in the faith and in the knowledge of the Son of God and become mature, attaining to the whole measure of the fullness of Christ" (Eph 4:12-13).

This is edification in the New Testament sense of *oikodomein,* building up the household or community of faith. As W. A. Visser 't Hooft has noted, "In the New Testament edification is not used in the subjective sense of intensification and nurture of personal piety. It means the action of the Holy Spirit by which he creates the people of God and gives shape to its life."[3] Biblically, edification is community building with the person and character of Jesus as the goal.

In the biblical ecology of the church, community is as important as worship. Just as a household is not really a family if it doesn't meet and spend time together, so believers don't really experience the church without Christian community. Just as the human body cannot live without its vital organs, so the church cannot thrive without life in community.

Biblically, community means shared life based on our new being in Jesus Christ. To be born again is to be born into God's family and community. While forms and styles of community may vary widely, any group of believers which fails to experience intimate life together has failed to experience the real meaning of Christ's body. To be the Christian community means to take seriously that believers are members of each other, and therefore to take responsibility for the welfare of Christian brothers and sisters in their social, material and spiritual needs.

3. *Witness.* In the life of the church, worship and community spark the church's witness.

This was so in Acts. The praise and fellowship described in Acts 2:42-47 brought an interesting result: "The Lord added to their number daily those who were being saved" (Acts 2:47). Later when the Jerusalem church was persecuted and many believers fled to other areas, "those who had been scattered preached the word wherever they went" (Acts 8:4). Jesus told his followers before his ascension, "You will be my witnesses in Jerusalem, and in all Judea and Samaria, and to the ends of the earth" (Acts 1:8). The book of Acts is the history of the church's witness throughout the Roman world in response to Jesus' words.

A church weak in worship has little will for witness, nor does it have much to witness about. Similarly, a church with no vital community life has little witness because believers are not growing to maturity and learning to function as healthy disciples. Where community is weak, witness is often further compromised by an exaggerated individualism. Witness may degenerate into inviting people to God without involving them in Christian community.

In a healthy congregation, witness springs not only from Jesus' specific commission (Mt 28:19-20; Acts 1:8) but also from the impulse of Pentecost and the dynamic of Christian community life. These are the primary springs of the church's will to witness in the world. A living Christian community has both the inclination and the power to witness. It witnesses both from concern for human need and for the sake of the coming Kingdom of God. In God's economy, the church's witness has Kingdom significance.

Viewed ecologically, witness is not the primary purpose of the church but the inevitable and necessary fruit of a worshiping, nurturing community. Thus it is a high priority of the church's life in the world.

Exploring the Model   The basic elements of worship, community and witness may be expanded to clarify their function in the ecology of the church. Just as these parts combine to shape the life of the church, so each in turn depends on the proper functioning of its component parts.

Worship, community and witness may be analyzed in several ways. One way, which seems to possess a certain internal logic and balance, is to view worship as the interplay of instruction, repentance and celebration; community as consisting of discipline, sanctification and the gifts of the Spirit; and witness as a combination of evangelism, service and prophecy. Thus the church's ecology may be more fully pictured by figure 4.[4]

Let us look briefly at the way each of these aspects functions in the church's life. I will not discuss these elements in depth here, since the point is primarily to show the importance of each to the total ecology of the church and how each interacts with the other elements. In the course of the book, however, I will take up most of these elements further as they relate to other issues.

Celebration is the church in the act of praising God. In worship the church celebrates God's person and works through music, liturgy, spontaneous praise and other means.

The Christian life is a life of celebration. The word *celebrate,* like the word *worship,* suggests honoring someone else. In worship we celebrate God's worth. But because of who God is and what he has done, celebration means joy as well. Christians are a joyous, singing people because they know the secret of who God is. Their joy comes from the freedom God gives from the bondage and hopelessness of sin.

Giving praise to God for who he is touches the deepest fibers of our being. Praise reaches down even below the conscious levels of our personalities because deep within us God has made us for himself. As we praise God, the deepest wells of soul and spirit are stirred.

Figure 4.

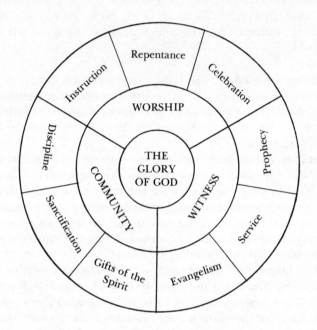

This is why worship not only glorifies God but also frees, cleanses and strengthens us.

The church at worship celebrates a God of action, not abstraction. Worship is celebrating God's acts in history and especially in Jesus Christ. This includes celebrating God's work in our lives and our life together in the Christian community. Coming together as sisters and brothers in Christ, we share the mystery and secret not only of sins forgiven but also of fellowship given. So we "rejoice with those who rejoice; mourn with those who mourn" (Rom 12:15).

Special joy comes to believers in celebrating the coming new age. *Worship liberates the church for the Kingdom.* We praise God not only for what he has done but for what he will do. Already in faith we anticipate and celebrate the day when we will sing, "The kingdom of the world has become the kingdom of our Lord and of his Christ"

(Rev 11:15). In worship we celebrate God's economy and Kingdom
—now and for the future. The church celebrates the future present,
knowing that "the kingdom of God is not a matter of eating and
drinking, but of righteousness, peace and joy in the Holy Spirit"
(Rom 14:17).

In the church's worship life the Lord's Supper especially is part
celebration. The Eucharist recalls God's work in Christ and signals
forth both the reality of the church and the promise of the Kingdom.
The church is in fact a sacramental community. Some of the rich
meaning of understanding the church sacramentally will be explored in chapter four.

Instruction as part of worship involves the church in hearing God's
voice through the Word read, taught or otherwise spoken. In worship, the movements of celebration and instruction are the movements of the Spirit and the Word.

The church is the community of the Word as much as it is the
community of the Spirit. It is the environment where we learn from
God. Not only do we speak to God in worship; even more important-
ly, we listen to him speaking to us. We worship in the Spirit as we
receive the Word. This is a basic part of worship. God has revealed
himself through his Word. We can be his faithful people only as we
hear, understand and obey it.

The community of God's people lives by the Word applied to our
hearts by the Spirit. Paul gives us a picture of God's Word in the life
of the church when he says, "Let the word of Christ dwell in you
richly as you teach and admonish one another with all wisdom, and
as you sing psalms, hymns and spiritual songs with gratitude in your
hearts to God" (Col 3:16). Thus Paul reminds us that sharing the
word in worship is something believers do with one another; it is not
something for one person alone to do. This passage suggests also
that instruction often merges into celebration.

Public worship should be built around the Word of God. Often
worship begins with a verse of a psalm or other Scripture calling
us to worship, uniting our focus on God himself. This reminds us
of our primary vocation to glorify him.

We often hear God's Word also in Scripture lessons from the Old
and New Testaments. The regular use of Scripture reading in worship teaches us the ways of God with his people—all that he has done

in the past and all he intends for the present and the future.

Scripture can be used profitably and creatively in a variety of ways in worship. Readings can be tied to the main events of the Christian year. For many centuries the church has patterned its yearly worship around the events of Jesus' life. The Christian year begins not with New Year's Day but with Advent, the announcement of Christ's coming four weeks before Christmas. Then follow the seasons of Christmas, Epiphany (the public appearing and ministry of Jesus), Lent (centering on Jesus' suffering and death), Easter and Pentecost. Pentecost, celebrating the coming of the Holy Spirit and the life of the church, begins the longest season of the year (about six months), bringing us around again to Advent. This is a good period to recall also how God has worked down through history and right up to the present, using Scriptures that recount God's mighty acts. Following the Christian year keeps our attention on God's acts through Christ rather than allowing us to slip into a rhythm dominated by secular holidays and commercial seasons.[5]

Besides the normal reading, reciting or singing of the Word, the Scriptures can be presented in drama, responsive or antiphonal reading, dance and other ways. Just as the psalms tell us to use poetry and music in worship, so they also speak of liturgical dance.

Many of the psalms are especially adaptable for dramatic or responsive readings. Psalm 107, for instance, recites the story of God's faithfulness to his people. A refrain occurs four times: "Let them give thanks to the LORD for his unfailing love and his wonderful deeds for men." Dividing the psalm into sections according to these refrains, a group of readers (or the whole congregation, divided into sections) can read the entire psalm, stressing the rising chorus to God for his unfailing faithfulness.

Particularly important in worship is the public proclamation of the Word through teaching and preaching (1 Tim 4:13; 5:17). God has chosen through the "foolishness" of preaching "to save those who believe" (1 Cor 1:21). Preaching means both public proclamation of the Word to unbelievers and teaching the Word to believers as part of regular worship. While God enables all believers to read and understand the Word on their own, he gives special gifts to some believers for the ministry of preaching and teaching (1 Cor 12:28; Eph 4:11; Acts 6:2). The church should both seek to identify and encourage members who have these gifts, and pay special attention to the words of those so gifted, even while it continues to "test everything," holding on to the good (1 Thess 5:21) through private study and small-group gatherings.

Repentance is perhaps seldom seen as part of worship, but it really fits into the rhythm of Word and response. To celebrate God when our lives contradict the gospel and we remain unrepentant is false worship. Yet this is true of much of the church in North America.

God broke into the sacred worship of unrepentant Israel to say, "I hate, I despise your religious feasts; I cannot bear your assemblies. . . . Away with the noise of your songs! I will not listen to the music of your harps. But let justice roll on like a river, righteousness like a never-failing stream!" (Amos 5:21, 23-24). Worship is closely linked with God's Kingdom and justice in the ecology of the church, and therefore with repentance.

At several points in its history, Israel truly heard God's Word, repented and was renewed. It was then enabled truly to celebrate the Lord's goodness. When Isaiah saw the Lord "high and exalted," he repented of his own uncleanness and was thus prepared to serve God effectively (Is 6:1-10). The proclamation of the Kingdom in the New Testament begins with a call to repentance (Mt 3:2). And James says to the church, "Wash your hands, you sinners, and purify your hearts, you double-minded. Grieve, mourn and wail. Change your laughter to mourning and your joy to gloom. Humble yourselves before the Lord, and he will lift you up" (Jas 4:8-9). God's word to the church is often "Repent!" (Rev 2:1—3:22). When the church is unfaithful to God, worship without repentance is blasphemy.

One of the rhythms of worship, then, is the rhythm of instruction, repentance and celebration. In these acts we celebrate not only God's acts in the past, but also his mercy in renewing us, forgiving us and accepting us as his people.

Practically, this means we must provide for repentance as well as praise in our worship. Often repentance is part of the church's liturgy, as in the General Confession in the Book of Common Prayer or the ritual of Holy Communion. This is most appropriate and reminds the church of the need for repentance. But repentance needs to be made specific, both in the personal lives of believers and in the corporate life of the Christian community.

As the economy of God and the priorities of his Kingdom become clearer to the church in North America, repentance will increasingly be seen as a key to Kingdom faithfulness. Repentance from self-centeredness, gluttony and oppression, and from trusting the false gods of wealth, nationalism and military power can open the doors to renewal and to a new identification with the poor and suffering around the globe. In this sense, repentance can be a key to liberating the church. In North America it is not so much the nation that needs to repent as it is the church, which claims to be serving God and his Kingdom.

Discipline, Sanctification and Spiritual Gifts. The church's life together in community requires as much attention as does worship. Vital worship depends largely on how much care is given to nurturing the church's shared life. We may think of this aspect of church ecology as including discipline, sanctification and spiritual gifts.

Discipline means discipleship, building a community of people who are truly Jesus' disciples. The church is not a social club or a chance catch of people; it is a community of believers called and united together by the grace of God. The church is a covenant people. In fidelity to God as revealed in Scripture and in Jesus Christ, Christians accept responsibility for each other and agree to exercise discipline as needed in order to keep faith with God's covenant. In this way the church takes seriously the many scriptural injunctions to warn, rebuke, exhort, encourage, build and disciple one another in love.

Jesus said in Matthew 18:20, "Where two or three come together in my name, there am I with them." This verse, however, comes at the end of a section where Jesus speaks of sins and conflicts and the need to confront one another. So Jesus is talking about more than merely *being with* him. He is speaking about what it means to be a community of disciples. To be "together with Jesus" for a short while is no problem. But when we start living our lives together as Christian brothers and sisters, helping each other to be faithful to our calling as Christians, problems arise. Sins crop up. We offend each other. And so confrontation, discipline and reconciliation become necessary. This, too, is part of what it means to "be with Jesus." Part of the ecology of the church is learning how to live and function together as a community of discipline.

We don't naturally follow the Jesus way. We tend to stray, to do our own thing instead of God's thing. We need someone to guide us, to encourage us, to praise us when we do well and to correct us when we do wrong. We need discipline—both the internal discipline which flows from centering our lives in Christ and walking in the Spirit, and the external discipline which comes from being accountable to and for one another.

God has saved us and made us responsible for each other. This is why Paul says, "Each of you should look not only to your own interests, but also to the interests of others" (Phil 2:4). Believers must be ready to take some agreed responsibility for their own lives and for the lives of their sisters and brothers in the faith.

For this reason, small-group structures are essential in the church. The New Testament depicts a level of Christian life which is distinct from the world and which simply fails to happen without some form of small-group structure. Hebrews 3:13 says we should "encourage one another *daily*, . . . so that none . . . may be hardened by sin's deceitfulness." This requires frequent intimate gatherings, for without such constant mutual support we will likely be deceived by sin. Hebrews 10:25 is a related passage: "Let us not give up meeting together, as some are in the habit of doing, but let us encourage one another." These passages seem to suggest frequent gatherings for encouraging one another apart from the worship celebration of the church. They point to times of meeting in smaller groups for nurture and discipline, as well as other frequent contacts among believers.

A number of Scriptures speak of the need to encourage, exhort and even rebuke one another in the church—for example, James 5:16, 1 Thessalonians 5:11, Colossians 3:16, Romans 12:15 and the passage from Matthew 18 already mentioned. These passages picture a level of Christian commitment and behavior which requires some form of small covenant-cell to sustain. These qualities are simply lost to the church when it does not meet with sufficient frequency, intimacy and commitment to permit them to develop.[6]

Sanctification is closely related to discipline and to the edification (*oikodomē*) of the church that we discussed earlier. Sanctification is the Spirit's work of restoring the image of God in believers and in the believing community. It is having the mind of Christ and displaying the fruit of the Spirit. It is the manifestation of Christ's character in his body.

Jesus gave himself for the church "to make her holy, cleansing her by the washing with water through the word, and to present her to himself as a radiant church, without stain or wrinkle or any other blemish, but holy and blameless" (Eph 5:26-27). This is part of what it means for the church to "become mature, attaining to the whole measure of the fullness of Christ" (Eph 4:13).

The focus here is on the work of the Holy Spirit in believers and in the Christian community. Jesus wants to make us like himself. Part of the purpose of life together is the sanctification of believers. God wants a holy people—a people distinct from the world in order to be engaged with the world. And this holiness is not to be molded after some abstract or otherworldly notion of saintliness, but according to the character of Jesus Christ.

Personal piety has a place in God's household. The disciplines of devotion and growth in grace are legitimate concerns for those who are determined to put God first in their lives. Yet the church always runs the danger that this focus may turn into spiritual narcissism or subjectivism. Other aspects in the total ecology of the church, if kept in balance, can effectively counter this tendency. As Richard Foster suggests in *Celebration of Discipline,* the inward life and disciplines must be balanced by the outward and corporate life and disciplines.[7] Bible study, devotional reading, prayer and fasting, and other means toward a holy life are important disciplines in themselves. They become potent in Christian experience when they are part of the larger balanced ecology of the Christian community.

Christians should be those who are concerned, as John Wesley often said, with "all inward and outward holiness." Thus our personal habits, stewardship of our bodies and commitment to the values of honesty, integrity and purity are as important for the health of the church as are our more outward witness in the world. Both are part of the sanctified life.

Sanctification is, above all, the ministry of the Holy Spirit. We are saved "through the sanctifying work of the Spirit and through belief in the truth" (2 Thess 2:13). God continues his sanctifying work in us and in his body as we allow his Spirit to cleanse, fill and liberate us. "Where the Spirit of the Lord is, there is freedom. And we, who with unveiled faces all reflect the Lord's glory, are being transformed into his likeness with ever-increasing glory, which comes from the Lord, who is the Spirit" (2 Cor 3:17-18).

This takes place when the church functions according to God's ecology and economy. It does not happen otherwise, or at least not to the extent God intends. For sanctification is part of the larger picture of the church's life.

The priority of sanctification is another reason why the church needs close-knit small groups or covenant cells to undergird its life. Such groups are just as important as the other aids toward spirituality and edification which the church provides.

Spiritual gifts are a particularly important part of the community life of the church. The gifts of the Spirit become vital and practical when they are awakened, identified and exercised in the context of shared Christian life. In God's ecology, the fruit of the Spirit and the gifts of the Spirit go together, and to stress one over the other is to distort God's plan for the church, crippling the body.

Spiritual gifts are not "things" which God gives. Rather they are manifestations of his grace in the church. Spiritual gifts are God's grace working through the personalities of believers, preparing and enabling them for their particular ministries, in order that the church may be edified, that the Kingdom of God may be established and that God may be glorified in all. The key biblical passage here is Ephesians 4:11-12.

Spiritual gifts are one of the foundation stones of the ministry of God's people. Gifts are awakened, identified and channeled as believers are intimately tied in to the community life of the church. Further, as the range of gifts is awakened and begins to function, these gifts quicken other aspects of the church's life and mission. Thus gifts are one of the most important keys in the ecology of the church. The functioning of gifts provides much of the dynamism of the church's witness and worship, as well as building community. If we trust God and his working in the body, we will find that the Spirit raises up people with the necessary gifts to make the full ecology of the church function. And this, then, becomes a key to the church's witness in the world.

In sum, we may say that discipline, sanctification and spiritual gifts constitute the ecology of the church's community life. The purpose of their functioning together is to build the household of God so that it can indeed live "to the praise of his glorious grace" (Eph 1:6).

Evangelism, Service and Prophecy. The key elements in the church's witness may be seen as evangelism, service and prophecy. With these we get a fairly complete picture of the total ecology of the church.

Historically, the church has found it difficult to hold evangelism, service and prophetic witness together. But where the church's evangelistic witness has been buttressed by loving service in the spirit of Jesus and an authentic prophetic thrust, the church has been at its best and has made its greatest impact for the Kingdom.

Evangelism—sharing the good news of Jesus and the Kingdom— is always important in a biblically faithful church. In a healthy church usually evangelism simply happens, and very little need be said about it. This is probably why the New Testament gives us examples of the church's evangelistic witness but says little about the need to evangelize. Today, however, we must stress evangelism in the church's ecology because church history and accumulated church tradition show the tendency either to exaggerate or neglect the missionary thrust of the gospel.

From an ecological perspective, the point is that evangelism strongly affects the other areas of the church's life. A church which is not evangelizing runs the risk of becoming ingrown and self-centered. With time, it may well become legalistic through the weight of tradition, the lack of new blood and the loss of the vitality which new converts bring. Evangelistic fruitfulness enlivens both the church's worship and its community life. The church was made to grow and reproduce itself; where this does not happen its vitality suffers. Adding new converts to a church fellowship is like the birth of a baby into a family.

Service means the church's servant role in the world, following the example of Christ. Like evangelism, service is part of the overflow of the life of the Spirit in the church. It is rooted in the church's community life because Christian service means both serving one another in the household of faith and reaching out in service to the world. Service is grounded also in worship, for in worship we are reminded of what God has done for us and we hear his Word calling us to follow Jesus to the poor, the suffering and the oppressed.

Prophecy is part of the church's witness to the world. Prophecy here means not primarily the charismatic gift of prophecy as it may be exercised in Christian worship, but rather the church's corporate prophetic witness in the world. This, of course, may include the exercise of the gifts of particular believers. The church's evangelism and service, in fact, are part of the church's prophetic witness when they grow out of healthy church life and genuinely point ahead to the Kingdom.

The church is prophetic both by what it is and what it does. As I have suggested in *The Community of the King,* the church is prophetic when it creates and sustains a reconciled and reconciling community of believers, recognizes and identifies the true enemy, renounces the world's definition and practice of power, and works for justice in society.[8] Most of all, the church is prophetic when by its worship, community and witness it points toward and manifests the new age of the Kingdom.

In today's world, the church is God's prophetic word in the world when it stands with and for the poor. Jesus made it plain that this is where he intends us to stand (Mt 25:31-46). When we serve the poor, we are not taking Christ to them; we are merely going where he already is and making him known (Mt 25:40). Thus the church's evangelism and service themselves become prophetic. Standing with the poor is both a pointer to the new age and a condemnation of the powers of the present age (whether political, economic, physical or spiritual) that are content with providing protection for the rich and advice for the poor. This is another way of saying the church must be a visible sign of the Kingdom.

From the ecological viewpoint, then, evangelism, service and prophecy combine and interact to constitute the church's witness in the world. And this witness is nourished and authenticated (or else starved and betrayed) by the quality of the church's worship and community life.

Using the Model   Such an ecological model for church life can be strategically useful. In addition to being a tool for understanding church life, it is helpful in diagnosing the condition of a church and in handling the question of church structure.

Problems in a church frequently trace to an imbalance in the ecology of worship, community and witness. Viewing the church as a living organism, we may say that the church often exhibits some sickness, some pathology, which needs correcting so that the fellowship can have a balanced and healthy life. The need, therefore, is to diagnose the problem and correct it.

When the church is weak in *worship,* its life becomes humanistic and subjective and the impulse for evangelism is often lost. When *community* life is anemic, believers remain spiritual babes, failing to grow up in Christ. Worship may become cold and formal, and witness weak or overly individualistic. If the church's *witness* is the problem, the fellowship may become ingrown and self-centered. The church may drift into legalism in order to guard its life, and it will have little growth or impact. Investigating these various areas can be very revealing to a church which is seeking to be free for the Kingdom but senses something is wrong.

From this perspective, renewal is a matter of bringing the church to the level of normal health which God intends. Actually the goal is not *renewal* so much as it is *vitality.* Put another way, renewal should be understood as building a vital fellowship which works together with God's Kingdom purposes.

This model can be used similarly to explore the question of church structure. If worship, community and witness are basic for church health, then the question arises whether the church has the necessary functioning structures in these areas. Some of the components of church life require more structure and attention than others. But if the various elements presented in the model are all important, then we must ask whether the church is structured for life in these areas. Structure won't bring life, but its absence can bring death. A family can live without a house, but it will be healthier if it has shelter. Structure is the skeleton which gives shape to life.

In raising the question of structure, we must remember that the church is primarily a charismatic organism rather than an institution or organization. Therefore structures created for the church's life must fit a charismatic-organic model. They ought not to be a mishmash of programs and organizations that clash with the essential nature of the church itself.

These are the dimensions and some of the dynamics of the ecology of the church as a liberating community of the Kingdom. In the remaining chapters we will explore these elements in greater depth, drawing on a range of different but ecologically compatible models. While the remaining chapters are not organized formally around the elements of the model, all the elements are treated in some way. On the other hand, given the present situation of the church, some issues and aspects of church life need to be treated more extensively than others.

The next four chapters explore four models of the church, treating them ecologically: the church as sacrament, community, servant and witness. In a general sense, the first of these relates most directly to worship, the second to community, and the third and fourth to witness. The ecological perspective reminds us, however, that these conceptions are all interrelated and interwoven in the day-to-day life of the church.

two

LIBERATING MODELS
OF THE CHURCH

4

THE CHURCH
AS SACRAMENT

Something strange is happening in the church, especially where renewal reigns. On the one hand, community and servanthood are being rediscovered. With this is coming a new emphasis on the Kingdom of God, the social-political-economic-spiritual reality not of this world but of God which challenges the present world system.

But another reality, another consciousness, is also penetrating much of the more renewal-oriented evangelical church. This is the reality of sacrament. Renewal communities often find that the Lord's Supper becomes an essential focal point of their worship. Why? In part because of the mystery of symbol and sign. How can we stand it that the Kingdom has not come and the church is so often unfaithful? We can stand it only through faith in what God has promised. And that faith is powerfully fed, symbolized and proclaimed in the sacramental reality of the Lord's Supper.

Just as the Lord's Supper points beyond itself, so the very concept of sacrament outgrows the Eucharist to provide a clue and model for understanding the church and the Kingdom. At first glance sacramental and community-centered models may appear in tension or even in conflict. But this is not so. It only looks that way because of the institutional sacramental overtones we have inherited from medieval Christendom. In fact, at the deepest and perhaps even subconscious level, the reality of the Kingdom community draws us to the reality of sacrament.

These four themes, then, properly belong together: community, servanthood, sacrament and the Kingdom of God. The church is God's servant community on earth for the sake of the Kingdom. And the reality of sacrament helps us understand and feel just what this means.

The Idea of Sacrament   Saint Augustine said that God "has welded together the community of his new people through the bond of the sacraments."[1] But what is a sacrament? The word *sacrament* is not found in the Bible. In fact, no New Testament word carries the idea of sacrament in the sense used by most Protestants (baptism and the Lord's Supper) or by Roman Catholics (baptism, the Lord's Supper, confirmation, ordination, marriage, penance, extreme unction). Much of the church's sacramental thinking is inherited from the medieval church. But the root idea goes back to the church's earliest days.

Essentially, a sacrament is a "visible form of invisible grace" (Augustine). More formally, a sacrament may be thought of as "an outward and visible sign of an inward and spiritual grace given unto us; ordained by Christ himself, as a means whereby we receive the same, and a pledge to assure us thereof."[2] Properly understood, a sacrament is a sign and yet more than a sign. It both witnesses to the operation of God's grace and, in some way not fully definable, is a channel or means of that grace.

Augustine (354-430) identified many different things as sacraments, including the Lord's Prayer, the church's feasts or celebrations, and the sign of the cross, as well as baptism and the Lord's Supper. Hugh of St. Victor (d. 1142) enumerated as many as thirty sacraments. It was Peter Lombard (ca 1100-1160), especially, who emphasized the sevenfold list of sacraments which was accepted by Thomas Aquinas (ca 1225-74) and confirmed by the Council of Trent in 1545-63. The sacramental idea started as something flexible and dynamic and became increasingly technical and mechanical, culminating with Trent and the Counter Reformation. In this century, Roman Catholic theologians have begun rethinking the whole sacramental idea, culminating in the Second Vatican Council's more organic, dynamic understanding of sacrament.

From the beginning, the church faced the problem of how to understand itself. The New Testament gave clues which they developed in various directions, depending on the social context in which the church found itself. Changing sacramental ideas corresponded to the changing circumstances in which the church lived.

Sacramental ideas and language can be useful for the church's self-understanding. But is the concept of sacrament itself biblically valid? The medieval sacramental system was a distortion of biblical truth in fundamental ways. Is this true of the very idea of sacrament itself? Is the very concept of sacrament tainted? This question requires a look at New Testament teachings.

Four New Testament words and ideas lead us to a proper understanding of sacrament: *sign, covenant, mystery* and *thanksgiving.*

Sign and Covenant. Some of Jesus' miracles were signs that God had come in the flesh, fulfilling his promise (Jn 2:11; 20:30). Jesus spoke of Noah as a sign (Mt 12:39; Lk 11:29). The rainbow was the sign of God's universal covenant with humankind after the flood (Gen 9:12).

The New Testament does not use the word *sign* with reference to baptism or the Lord's Supper, but the idea of sign is present. "For whenever you eat this bread and drink this cup, you proclaim the Lord's death until he comes" (1 Cor 11:26). Both baptism and the Lord's Supper are signs of the new covenant (Col 2:11-12; Rom 6:3-4; 1 Cor 11:25). The new covenant concerns the heart and the Spirit, not laws, commandments and animal sacrifices. New covenant signs must have new covenant meaning. They are not Old Testament signs.

We must guard against falling back into an Old Testament understanding of these signs, even though Old Testament understanding enriches their meaning greatly. An improper return to Old Testament categories is precisely what happened in the Middle Ages. The Old Testament understanding of the tabernacle, priesthood and sacrifice was taken over wholesale, compromising the newness and uniqueness of Jesus Christ. But we must insist, rather, that Jesus Christ fulfills the Old Testament system. He is Sacrifice and High Priest. He is the great Sign and Sacrament of our salvation. He fulfills the Old Testament signs. So no signs or sacraments in the church can have an Old Testament meaning, nor should they be permitted to overshadow or displace Jesus Christ as our Sign and

Savior, or his presence with us daily by the Holy Spirit. How often human nature prefers a touchable sign to God's invisible living Spirit!

Mystery. This brings us to the New Testament word *mystery* and to the origin of the word *sacrament.*

Paul speaks of "the mystery of Christ" (Eph 3:4), or "the mystery of the gospel" (Eph 6:19) or of the faith (1 Tim 3:9). A key passage is Ephesians 5:32, where Paul speaks about marriage: "This is a profound mystery—but I am talking about Christ and the church." Mystery in these passages refers to God's economy of redemption and reconciliation through Jesus Christ. It clearly has no special reference to the sacraments of baptism or the Lord's Supper.

Significantly, the Greek word "mystery" *(mystērion)* became "sacrament" *(sacramentum)* when the Bible was translated into Latin. Pagan ideas of mystery and sacrament from the Greek and Roman world gradually colored the church's understanding of Christian worship, and especially the Lord's Supper.

Greeks and Romans knew about "mysteries." They knew about, and some practiced, the mystery religions where sacred meals were eaten and sexual immorality was sometimes indulged. This is why early Christians were occasionally suspected of having sexual orgies in their closed worship services and why Tertullian had to say, "All things are common among us except our wives."[3]

With time, and especially after the Emperor Constantine was converted in 323, these pagan understandings filtered into the church and twisted its concepts of baptism and the Lord's Supper. The idea that these observances were mysterious, almost magical rites giving mystical powers began to displace the New Testament understanding of the new covenant of the Spirit. This led to the medieval view of the mass as a repetition of the sacrifice of Christ in which bread and wine literally become Jesus' flesh and blood. It led finally to the whole medieval system of seven interlocking sacraments all keyed to the mysterious power of the priest.

The medieval sacramental-hierarchical system, which reached its climax at the Council of Trent partly in reaction to the Reformation, was highly complex, rational and consistent. It was both mystical and rational, for the mystical element of faith was captured and routinized by means of religious technique. The sacraments came to constitute the ecology of the church. In the New Testament, *mystery* has to do with God's Kingdom plan of salvation through Jesus Christ—the whole economy of God. Economy *(oikonomia)* and mystery *(mystērion)* are closely related, and both point to the Kingdom of God and the church as the Kingdom community. Paul says his commission was "to bring to light the economy of the mystery" of the gospel (Eph 3:9, literal translation). God has made known to us "the mystery of his will" which involves "an economy of the fullness of the times, to head up all things in Christ" (Eph 1:9-10, literal translation).[4] This is the biblical economy, based in the church as community. But in the medieval synthesis mystery became sacrament, and the sacramental system came to be the economy of the church. Quite literally, the New Testament economy was transmuted into the sacramental economy—a system based on hierarchy, institution, cathedral, law and technique rather than on community, mutuality, charisms, discipleship and free grace. It was precisely this system which most of the Reformers protested so strongly.

Thanksgiving. Another word that entered the church's vocabulary was *Eucharist.* The New Testament speaks of "giving thanks" *(eucharistia).* Since thanksgiving was associated with worship and the Lord's Supper became the principal act of worship, the word *Eucharist* became synonymous with the Lord's Supper. In much of the Christian church today the Lord's Supper is commonly called the Eucharist.

The Sacramental Community   Since sacrament is not a New Testament word and medieval sacramentalism led to a serious distortion of the gospel, it could be argued that the whole concept of sacrament should be dropped in our quest for a truly liberated church. But for a number of reasons it seems wise to retain the notion of sacrament, applying it, however, in more biblically faithful ways. Sacramental language may indeed spark greater clarity about the church and its mission.

The New Testament use of *sign* and *mystery* (both the terms and the ideas) lead to an understanding of the church for which *sacramental* seems an apt term. If *sacrament* does not mean precisely the same thing as *mystery,* it does help us deal with the meaning of the mystery of the church as a sign of the Kingdom in the present age.

As a term and concept, *sacrament* is like *Trinity*. It is a legitimate extension and extrapolation from biblical truth, even if not explicitly taught in Scripture. Sacrament (understood and controlled by Scripture) is an appropriate vehicle for understanding not only baptism and the Lord's Supper but the Christian community itself. But can we say that the church is *itself* a sacrament? Can we legitimately speak of the community of God's people sacramentally?

This is precisely what a number of contemporary Roman Catholic theologians have been doing in an attempt to gain a newer and more faithful understanding of the church.[5] Rather than focusing on the sacramental system itself, this approach sees the church as "the primordial sacrament" in which the traditional sacraments are grounded. In the words of Karl Rahner, "As the primordial sacrament, the Church is the constant presence in the world of the saving mystery of Christ and his grace." "Since the Church exists in this sense (as the sacrament), there are sacraments in the New Testament sense."[6] This conception found expression in Vatican II. The Dogmatic Constitution on the Church *(Lumen Gentium)* says in its first paragraph, "By her relationship with Christ, the Church is a kind of sacrament or sign of intimate union with God, and of the unity of all mankind."[7] Later the document describes the church as "the universal sacrament of salvation" through which Christ is still active in the world, but which exists now on earth as "the pilgrim Church."[8]

The sacramental conception provides a way of understanding the church in relation both to the world and to the Kingdom which is, it seems to me, more biblically faithful that the visible-invisible distinction and more potent for liberating the church. As Eric Jay comments, "Here is the seed for a fruitful doctrine of the Church." He continues,

A sacrament is a gift of God: something earthly is set aside for holy use, a sign and representative of what all things earthly are meant to be, and an instrument of sanctification of all that is earthly. In the idea of the Church as the sacrament of the world, then, we have the concept of a society instituted by God which is itself in microcosm what the world must be, and which exists to enable it to be that which itself is, the body of Christ.[9]

The appropriateness of seeing the church as sacrament can be shown by examining the classical Anglican definition quoted above: "an outward and visible sign of an inward and spiritual grace given unto us; ordained by Christ himself, as a means whereby we receive the same, and a pledge to assure us thereof." Does this apply not only to the sacraments of the church in the individual experience of believers, but also to the very community of God's people itself? Let us consider:

An Outward and Visible Sign. Clearly the church is "outward and visible," not just "inward and spiritual," although this fact has often been slighted. The church is an actual, visible social reality in the world. Its true and proper visibility, however, is not in buildings or structures but in its gathering in worship and in witness and service to the world. "In face of the *world*—which may or may not understand it—the Church is the living and visible congregation which listens to the divine Word and responds to it, and which proposes it to the world, but by it, inevitably scandalizes the world," as Karl Barth says.[10]

While the church takes its life from its "inner and spiritual" relationship to God through Christ, its life and relationship to God are also outward and visible, just as Christ's were. And in this outward, visible life in the world, the church is a sign of the Kingdom. Jesus said, "Anyone who has seen me has seen the Father" (Jn 14:9); "I am in my Father, and you are in me, and I am in you" (Jn 14:20). "As the Father has sent me, I am sending you" (Jn 20:21). Many biblical passages and images of the church show that the church is not only the community of the redeemed but also a sign of God's presence, activity and coming reign. And the church is a sign of these things precisely because it is the community of the redeemed.

Of an Inward and Spiritual Grace. A sacrament signs forth, specifically, the gracious activity of God, his grace that works inwardly and spiritually. This is true of the church itself. It is saved and lives by grace. The church can never be fully explained sociologically, psychologically, politically or economically. It requires an invisible, inward operation of God's grace to accomplish the new birth and to transform individual men and women into the body of Christ. The church, when biblically faithful, is an unmistakable sign and witness of God's grace.

Given unto Us. It is both the sacramental sign and God's grace which are given to us. The Lord's Supper is a sacrament because it was given to the church by Christ. It wasn't instituted by human action alone. If this is true of baptism and the Eucharist, it is even more true of the church itself. The church was and is called together and formed by Jesus Christ. In a healthy church believers have the sense of God's gracious gift. We did not earn or achieve this life together; God gave it.

Ordained by Christ Himself. Traditionally, an authentic sacrament must trace back in some way to the specific action of Jesus Christ. This is clearly and dramatically so with the church itself. Not only did Jesus say "I will build my church" (Mt 16:18); his very life, death and resurrection constituted his ordaining the church. The church is ordained specifically to be Jesus' body, his worshiping and witnessing community in the world.

As a Means Whereby We Receive the Same. A sacrament, as we have noted, is more than a sign; it is a means of grace. A sacrament is a channel and agent of God's grace as God works through it and as persons respond in faith and obedience. On this point, also, the definition of sacrament fits the church. The church is a channel of God's grace, both internally and to the world. As noted earlier, this is part of the meaning of the priesthood of believers. We receive God's grace not by the Spirit without the church, but by the Spirit through the church.

A Pledge to Assure Us Thereof. A sacrament always points beyond itself to the future. It is a pledge in the sense of a foretaste, first-fruit or initial realization. It is not the full reality but a real sign of what God has promised. And the church, animated by the Spirit, is just this. Life in Christian community is a promise to all believers that the Kingdom will come in fullness, that every knee shall bow and every tongue confess Jesus as Lord (Phil 2:10-11), that "the earth will be full of the knowledge of the LORD as the waters cover the sea" (Is 11:9).

A sacrament is both a means of grace and a pledge of grace. It is a promise that God will in fact accomplish what he has graciously promised. In this sense also the church is a sacrament. It has been formed by grace and is a sign that God's Kingdom will come by grace —in God's way, not in the ways of the world.

In sum, the church may truly and properly be seen as a sacrament, as a sign and microcosm of the Kingdom of God. It is crucial, however, that such a sacramental understanding be applied consistently with the New Testament understanding of the church. The church as sacrament is one model among many, not an exclusive definition of the church, and needs to be balanced by other models. It has both advantages and disadvantages which need to be considered.[11]

There are, perhaps, two primary dangers in a sacramental understanding of the church. Such an approach will surely go awry if wedded to an institutional-organizational rather than charismatic-organic view of the church. What might be called the institutional-sacramental view leads straight back to medieval Christendom, while an organic-sacramental view can lead to greater freedom and fidelity for the church and points ahead more authentically to the Kingdom. The sacramental approach, then, must be joined to and controlled by more explicitly biblical models.

A related danger is that the sacramental model may be seen as holding the institutional and charismatic dimensions together in a way that makes more allowance for institutionalism than is warranted by Scripture. The sacramental model is useful in part because it does help us deal with the institutional side of the church without rejecting institutionalization altogether. But the church must always be critical of its institutional side precisely because of the inherent dangers of institutional self-serving, self-righteousness and self-justification. Properly understood, the sacramental model is not a clever theological justification for the church's institutionalism, but a way of showing how the church points beyond itself to God and his future. And precisely this understanding should help the church criticize and correct its institutional tendencies.

In what sense, then, is the church a sacrament? Not in the sense that its institutional form necessarily says anything redemptive in the world, but in the sense that as the community of God's people it is a sign, symbol and servant of the Kingdom of God on earth. The church is, in this sense, truly a means of grace.

Sacrament and Sacraments The conception of the church as sacrament does not displace the sacraments of the church; rather, it enhances them. Given the understanding of the church as sacrament, we can view the sacraments of baptism and the Lord's Supper in ways that contribute to liberating the church. Several issues call for comment at this point.

1. The church's sacraments are not magical or mystical rites or spiritual techniques which in themselves transmit spiritual power. They are signs which derive their power from Jesus Christ and his work and from God's grace working in the believer and in the Christian community so that the signs may be received by faith. Without faith—in God, not in the rites—the sacraments are nothing.

2. That we must continue to speak of the "mystery of Christ" reminds us, on the other hand, that God's economy of salvation is beyond human comprehension. It remains a mystery, even though we know its key secret: reconciliation (Eph 3:4-6). In Christian worship there is always more than meets the eye. So even though the sacraments are not mystical rites, they do become channels of God's grace in ways we don't fully understand. This has something to do with God's image in us and with our need for symbols, signs and ritual. There is room for proper respect for those sacraments given us specifically by Christ and in which he is really present—even though we don't turn them into magical rites or spiritual techniques.

3. Baptism and the Lord's Supper remind us of God's covenant, his promises. God is faithful. He will do what he says. He fulfills his plan in history. In the sacraments we express our faith that God has acted for us in the past, is present now and will in the future fulfill his plan and manifest his rule. In baptism we find that God does indeed give us new birth and adopt us into his family through faith in Christ; and in the Eucharist we find that, partaking in faith and unity, we are indeed built up as the body of Christ.

4. The sacraments are acts of Christian community. They help form and feed the flock of God. They build *koinōnia*. Every culture has its symbols and signs and cannot exist without them. As God's counterculture in a sinful world, the church is held together, in part, by sacramental signs—even while it knows that "faith working by love" is the fundamental sign of God's presence, and even while it also sees signs in the world of God's working and of the coming Kingdom of God.

5. Since baptism and the Lord's Supper are part of the church's witness, worship and community life, how they are observed is important. As acts of community, they should build the church's sense of communion, fellowship and discipleship. We should avoid ob-

servances which overindividualize the sacraments or make them highly formal. The Lord's Supper should be observed with reverence and order, but not with excessive ritual, formality or mysteriousness. The focus should be on Jesus Christ and his body, the church. The Eucharist should build body life—openness, communication, confession, oneness, reconciliation, sharing, joyful celebration and dedication to the Kingdom. Although for the sake of order the church may prescribe who should lead in this observance, the Bible does not restrict the administration of the Supper to ordained persons or to men only.

6. The Lord's Supper should be observed frequently. In the early church and through much of Christian history, observance was weekly. Because of historical circumstances and reaction against medieval sacramentalism, many Protestants came to celebrate the Supper infrequently, often four times or less per year. Yet some of the great Reformers, Calvin and Wesley among them, celebrated the Eucharist weekly or even daily.

Renewal in the church has often gone hand in hand with a rediscovery and more frequent observance of the Lord's Supper. Christian fellowships today should celebrate the Eucharist often, with the minimum probably being once a month and the normal pattern being weekly.

Some argue that such frequent observance cheapens or formalizes the Lord's Supper, reducing its significance. Curiously, we don't argue this way in other areas. One could argue that the church should keep preaching to a minimum because preaching is so important, or that since prayer and Bible reading are so important Christians should engage in these activities only infrequently in order not to cheapen them or make them routine. But the fact is that sacraments are *means of grace,* and means are to be used, not neglected. The church is to feed on God's grace through the Lord's Supper, and it should do so often rather than staying away from the very table to which Christ calls it.[12]

7. We must always keep before us the realities to which the sacraments point: Jesus, the church and the Kingdom of God. The church is to be the great sign of Jesus' presence on earth and the promise of his return. The world should be able to look at the church and see Jesus. The love, fellowship, worship and service of the

church should be a sacrament before the world of God's love and reconciliation. Our observance of the sacraments should nourish our understanding and experience of the church as a reconciled and reconciling community.

Sacraments spring from, symbolize and sign forth the reality of the church as Christ's body. The most important sign of God's presence on earth is not the sacraments but the body of Christ itself—not the bread and wine on the table but the body of Christ, our own flesh and blood, in the world for the sake of the Kingdom.

This Is Christ's Body   This is the point of the sacraments: The church is the *body of Christ.*

A key passage here is 1 Corinthians 10:16-17. "Is not the cup of thanksgiving for which we give thanks a participation in the blood of Christ? And is not the bread that we break a participation in the body of Christ? Because there is one loaf, we, who are many, are one body, for we all partake of the one loaf."

The word translated "participation" here is the New Testament word for community, *koinōnia.* In other words, the Scripture says that our participation in the Lord's Supper is a sharing in Christ himself. It is our community in Christ. In the New Testament, baptism and the Lord's Supper *are* our membership in the body of Christ. In the New Testament church *koinōnia* (sharing, community, participation) was the meaning of church membership. Thus these observances given by Christ are the signs and determiners of the meaning of membership. This means two things: (1) church membership is highly important and necessary for every believer, and (2) church membership should be understood primarily as participation and community in the body of Christ, rather than as joining an organization or having one's name on a membership list.

Because of the prominence of organizational-institutional models, Western Christians tend to think of church membership as joining an organization rather than as participating in a community. The sacraments, however, are community acts and make much more sense when understood this way. Biblically, one does not become a Christian and then later join the church. To be born again is to be born into God's family. A Christian is by definition a part of the community of God's people. One can't be joined to the head without being joined to the body. The sacraments, integrated into the worshiping and serving life of the community, are important in order to keep this affirmation from being merely theoretical or invisible. Membership in the body of Christ is neither organizational affiliation nor an invisible mystical communion. It is a visible participation and sharing in the visible community of God's people.

It is especially significant in this connection that the New Testament calls the church the body of Christ. The body of Christ is one, and yet in Scripture the phrase "body of Christ" has a threefold meaning. As Barth says,

There are not two or possibly three bodies of Christ: the historical, in which He died and rose again; the mystical which is His community; and that in which He is really present in the Lord's Supper. For there are not three Christs. There is only one Christ, and therefore there is only one body of Christ.[13]

Yet the New Testament does give a threefold meaning to "body of Christ": Jesus' physical body, the church and the bread of the Lord's Supper. The distinction, however, between these three senses is not always clear, precisely because there are not three but only one body of Christ.

The close identification between the church and Jesus' physical body is seen especially in Ephesians. Paul says, "But now in Christ Jesus you who once were far away have been brought near through the blood of Christ. For he himself is our peace, who has made the two [Jew and Gentile] one and has destroyed the barrier, the dividing wall of hostility, by abolishing in his flesh the law with its commandments and regulations. His purpose was to create in himself one new man out of the two, thus making peace, and in this one body to reconcile both of them to God through the cross, by which he put to death their hostility" (Eph 2:13-16). "This one body" in verse sixteen may mean either Jesus' physical body, crucified, or the church. Better, it may mean both. Through his body we are made his body—historically through Jesus' death and resurrection, and sacramentally through the Lord's Supper.

The Physical Body of Jesus. Here we face the mystery of the Incarnation, the Word made flesh. This is the mystery of God-in-Man, God in human person. We can't explain the Incarnation and we can't explain the life of Jesus. Yet neither can we account for the life of Jesus apart from the miracle of incarnation.

Even so, despite and through this mystery, Jesus is our pattern and model. *Because* Jesus is Lord and Savior, and because of the mystery of his presence in us now through the new birth, he is also our example and pattern (1 Pet 2:21; 1 Jn 2:6).

In Jesus' physical body, then, as God incarnate, we have both *model* and *mystery*. While the Incarnation is a mystery, it provides the essential model for the believer and especially for the church's corporate life and mission in the world.

The Church, Christ's Body. Why is the church called Christ's body? In one sense the idea is a mystical one, but it is more than that. The church is the body of Christ in something close to a literal, physical, space-time sense. It is "the earthly-historical form of existence" of Jesus Christ (Barth). The church is the body of Christ because it is the presence of Jesus Christ in the world by the work and indwelling of the Holy Spirit in the flesh-and-blood bodies of Christ's disciples and especially in the historical social reality of the Christian community.

In this sense, the church as Christ's body is also *mystery* and *model*. To call the church Christ's body is to speak a mystery—the mystery of just how Jesus is joined to the church and the mystery of how the church, in all its imperfections, is a sign of the Kingdom. "This is a profound mystery—but I am talking about Christ and the church" (Eph 5:32).

Yet the mystery is consistent with the model. The church *is* a sign of the coming Kingdom. It is called to model the age to come, to be a microcosm of the Kingdom. Following the model of the Incarnation, the church's mission is to be the firstfruits of the Kingdom, present now, as Jesus was, in humility and service.[14]

Christ's Body in the Lord's Supper. Given this perspective, the church's sharing of Jesus' body and blood in the Eucharist takes on deep significance. The bread we break in the Lord's Supper: Is this not our community in Christ? Is this not our membership in his body? Is this not the meaning of the church? In the Lord's Supper, especially, we are the community of God's people—if we feed on the Word by faith and live consistently with it.

The Lord's Supper is an expression of the family of God and a sharing in Jesus Christ. It is both *model* and *mystery*. It is a mystery because we do not know (and the church has never been able to agree) just how Jesus is really present in the eucharistic bread. The Lord's Supper is a mystery of Jesus' presence and a mystery as a means of grace. It participates in the mystery of symbol and sign. It shares in the mystery of the church as the family of God.

But the Eucharist is also a model and sign. As the presence of God in the earthly elements of bread and wine, it symbolizes Jesus' incarnation. It is a model of God's family, for in the Supper we gather *together* as one, equally dependent on God's grace and all dependent on one another. And it is a model, especially, of the Kingdom of God. It signs and signals the future marriage supper of the Lamb (Rev 19:9). In eating bread and drinking wine together the church celebrates and looks ahead to God's new heaven and new earth when every man, woman and child will be fed and none will lack food either for body or for soul.

The threefold mystery of the body of Christ, then, is a model of the church which lives for the Kingdom. The church participates in the mystery and becomes the model when it seeks first the Kingdom of God and his justice. In the language of sacrament, biblically controlled, mystery and model are held together so that the mystery does not become mysticism, and the model does not become mechanism.

Church, Sacrament and Kingdom   Church, sacrament and Kingdom have often been associated in Christian theology, especially in Eastern Orthodoxy and some strains of Roman Catholicism. But this association needs to be animated by the biblical, evangelical spirit. This has been our attempt here.

As the relationship of God to the world may be understood sacramentally, so the concept of sacrament helps us understand the relationship of the church to the Kingdom. The church is not the Kingdom; neither is it unrelated to the Kingdom. While some sacramental theology has tended to identify the Kingdom too closely with the church, some dispensational theology has divorced the two so thoroughly that the Kingdom has no present significance.

The church, however, may be understood as the present sacrament (mystery and model) of the Kingdom in the world. It both signs, points toward, and by God's grace accomplishes God's rule on earth. As sacrament of the Kingdom, the church points ahead to what it claims by faith and works for by faith and does not yet fully experience or understand. It prays that the Kingdom may come on earth, knowing that God by his Spirit must do for us what we cannot do for ourselves, so that we can do for his Kingdom what otherwise would remain undone. The sacramental reality of the church will come in fullness only with the historical return of Jesus Christ when the Kingdom is finally, fully and definitively established.

Liberating the church means understanding that the church is not the Kingdom nor is it unhinged from it, but it is free, by faith and by God's grace, to be the Kingdom community.

5
THE CHURCH
AS COMMUNITY

Listen carefully, and you will hear the muffled cry and sigh for community today. College students and young adults especially seem attuned to the question and quest of community. Many reasons lie behind this, some obvious and some not so obvious. The response in North American society today to anything having to do with community, however defined, suggests a deep hunger for human intimacy and raises the question of community for the church.[1] Many people, Christians as well as nonbelievers, long for more intimate and meaningful relationships with other persons. They want to find a group whose meaning and mission transcend the daily grind and the routine rat race. Something within them says there must be something more, a level of sharing and common life that goes beyond what they have known.[2]

Crisis of Community in Society All the significant social indicators point to a breakdown of community today—in the home, the school, the neighborhood, the church. This goes hand in hand with the advance of a technological society which focuses on either the individual or the mass as it speeds the disintegration of small, intimate groupings. The illusion of total, unrestricted individual freedom ("Have it your way") in fact leads to totalitarian mass society in which close-knit intermediate communities of meaning—the glue of society—are dissolved.[3] Obeying the enticing commands of propaganda and advertising, people fail to perceive that the freedom offered is the freedom to do what someone else wants (for a price) and what everyone else is doing. So "Have it your way" really means "Do it our way—and feel good about it!"

But technological materialism, with its morality of means, is only part of the problem. It is not the only villain. Many forces are at work to undermine community, both in society and in the church. This can be clarified by playing a little game. How would one go about undermining community, isolating people from each other and from shared life with others?

The first thing, of course, would be to fragment family life. The family is the fundamental unit and microstructure of society, the primary form of human community. Undermining community begins with undermining the family. One would fragment the family by drawing off its members in different directions and into different worlds.

Another way to break down community would be to move people away from the neighborhoods where they grew up. Cut the roots. Instead of allowing people to live near relatives and friends and among familiar landmarks and symbols, move them to new neighborhoods. And then, for further disintegration, separate the places people work from where they live. Partition off people's lives into as many worlds as possible.

If we really wanted to break down community, we would certainly bring television into the home. Television is perhaps the modern world's most effective communication blocker. We think of TV as a means of communication. More accurately, it is a means of blocking communication—if communication means two-way interaction.[4]

Another way to undermine community is to move people gradually farther and farther apart through larger and larger yards, bigger houses or through walls, fences and "apart-ments." Here affluence is a great aid to dissolving community.

The automobile further extends the process. The more houses, stores, schools and places of employment or entertainment are physically separated, the more people travel separately to those places in cars, especially in suburbia. Adding a second or third car furthers the process, cutting down even more on the time family members have to be together.

The final clincher, then, in the process of fragmentation would be to cut down on family size. Two parents and several children make a small community. But with one or no children in the home, and the circumstances traced above, real community life expires altogether.

We must not underestimate the role of the media, and especially of television, in this disintegrating process. The role of the visual media in breaking down community in society today is twofold. First, the visual media undermine community simply because they are passive rather than participatory. They block communication. Second, the visual media push values to the sensate level. Because television and motion pictures in the United States are almost totally the tools of technological materialism, programming constantly moves toward the sensate. The media challenge accepted mores of society and push the barriers just beyond what is accepted as normal in real life. The visual media operate less and less at the level of ideas and concepts, more and more at the emotional and sensual levels. And the less the viewers think, the more they respond at the sensate level. The media could operate more constructively and responsibly, but in today's culture they mainly assist the breakdown of community.

All this is part of the crisis of community in society. And it is both related to and compounded by the crisis of community in the church. The question of the role of the church is significant, for *undermining community in the church destroys the best hope for community in the world,* the best chance for rebuilding community in society. When the church is a genuine community experiencing real *koinōnia,* it is the most potent source of community in the world.

Crisis of Community in the Church   We face a crisis of community, of fellowship, in the church today. Lack of community testifies partly to a lack of understanding concerning the nature of the church, partly to the individualism of Western culture, and partly to the influence of broader social currents. The Western church finds itself in a world where Christian consensus has broken down. We may question, of course, whether the consensus that held Western society together was really Christian. But certainly that society was shaped and influenced in large measure by Christian values, even if only partially and imperfectly. In the United States, Christian values permeated the culture rather thoroughly. At least there was a strong sense of the worth of the individual. One simply did not snuff out another person's life easily. Today, however, respect for life is breaking down. Along with other Christian values, it is fast disappearing. Increase in violent and senseless crime, casual acceptance of abortion and mercy killing, and general indifference toward the fate of others are all part of the picture.[5]

Until recent decades, Christians could assume that when a person became a Christian or came up through a Christian family that his or her basic values were at least compatible with Christian beliefs. Because of this, it wasn't as crucial that the church lacked a real basis in community. A church without a genuine experience of community could at least function as a Christian church with some degree of integrity because society's values reinforced and overlapped those of the church.

No more. Christian consensus is gone. A person growing up in North America today simply does not have either a Christian world view or set of values instilled by the culture. And a person entering the church from such a background begins almost at point zero in Christian life and understanding. This means that the church must increasingly take seriously its true nature as a community and counterculture that reinforces and perpetuates its own values. Otherwise the church simply accommodates itself to the culture. This is what is happening, and this is the crisis the church faces.

In sum, the church is confronted by the breakdown of Christian consensus in society, and this is compounded by the absence of real community in the church. Increasingly we will hear calls for the church to recognize its true situation and danger. It must be a community with the social strength to incarnate values that are antagonistic at key points to the world around us.

Merely adopting such a viewpoint will mean nothing. The church must in fact *be* a community that experiences and reinforces biblical values. No group with values which differ significantly from a society can endure long in that society unless the group is a counter-community. Our values and world view are molded by our community context. A group of Christians cannot exist in society and maintain Christian values unless they are part of a community that reinforces those values. This is simply a matter of the sociology of knowledge.

I believe this is a crucial point. "Certainly it is not impossible for individual Christians to maintain biblical beliefs even if a hostile majority disagrees," Ron Sider notes. "But if the church is to consist of communities of loving defiance in a sinful world, then it must pay more attention to the quality of its fellowship."[6] The relation of Christian community not only to Kingdom living but even to doctrinal integrity will increasingly have to be examined. Orthodoxy is no defense. If Christians cease to act like Christians, sooner or later they will stop believing like Christians. So community is a crucial concern. To be Christian at the level of values that influence our behavior means to be part of a community that reinforces Christian values as they confront non-Christian values.

The New Testament Community The New Testament pictures the church as the community gathered around Jesus. We see this, for example, in Matthew 18:15-20, Acts 2:42, Philippians 2:1-11 and Ephesians 4:1-16.

Matthew 18:20 is perhaps the most compact definition of the church in Scripture: "Where two or three come together in my name, there am I with them."[7] What makes a church? One person is not enough. Even one person alone with Jesus ("just Jesus and me") is not the church. Church is community. Where two or three come together in Jesus' name, there church begins. The church is a community of people gathered around Jesus, committed to him, worshiping him and ready to serve his Kingdom in the world. People gathered around Jesus is the irreducible minimum of the church. Then arise questions of preaching, sacraments, liturgy, ordination, doctrine, church government and many other things which separate Christians into denominational families. Some say you can't have the church without the sacraments; others say you can. But Jesus says that at heart the church is the community of people gathered in his name and in his presence, sharing his life.

In its actual history, as pictured in the New Testament, the early church was truly the community of Jesus. This is not, of course, to deny its roots in Jewish culture. On the contrary, the church was born in first-century Jewish society. Its early character and style were largely Jewish. Although the church quickly (but not pain-lessly) transcended its Jewishness as it crossed racial and national lines, still its strong Jewish roots must be understood.

In fact, the early church drew some of its strength from these Jewish roots. The church was born in a culture with a strong sense of community and with an ethos of peoplehood. Jews in Jesus' day were very much aware they were a people. They knew they were a covenant people; they existed as a nation because God had acted in history. The Old Testament writings record that history, showing how God had acted in faithfulness to his covenant, in both blessing and judgment. The church was born in this Jewish matrix. The new reality believers discovered in Jesus Christ was built on this founda-tion of community and peoplehood that God had been building through the millennia of Old Testament history, and pre-eminently through the two thousand years from Abraham to Jesus Christ.

Even though the church outgrew its Jewish character, it brought over understandings, concepts, practices and even structures from the Jewish community which became basic to the Christian church. For example, the church initially built its worship on the synagogue model. Churches were at first largely Christian synagogues.[8] When we look at the first Christians, we do not see a group of people alien-ated from their cultural context, but rather a community rooted in a specific culture. This particular cultural context provided the base from which the church moved out to become more than merely the Jewish sect that it initially appeared to be.[9]

From the beginning, however, the church was much more than simply a Jewish sect because it was the community of *Jesus'* disciples. Jesus was the key. Here was not just another rabbi or philosopher, but the incarnate Son of God announcing a new order and King-dom. The impressive thing about Jesus' three years with his dis-ciples is not just the miracles and the teaching and the crowds, but *the embryonic community that Jesus himself formed.* This was a new social reality consisting of the Twelve plus a larger community of disciples beyond the apostolic core. Tracing the word *disciple* through the Gospel of Luke reveals a community of several concentric circles of disciples, beginning with the Twelve.

The church pictured in Acts and the Epistles was based on the community Jesus had formed. The disciples after Pentecost simply repeated what Jesus had done with them. Acts 2:42, and in fact the first several chapters in Acts, shows the pattern. Jesus himself provided for the many converts of Pentecost by preparing a community of people—not a disconnected corps of experts, but a prepared community of disciples. How different from today's missionary and evangelistic methods!

Picture the scene. Your small church of a few hundred members suddenly gains three thousand converts in one day. A few days later several thousand more are added. Soon the church has grown to twenty or thirty thousand. And you don't even have a board of directors, an organizational manual, a budget, a doctrinal statement, committees or buildings. Can you survive?

From our perspective, the church on the day of Pentecost was hopelessly handicapped. It should not have survived. But Jesus had prepared for Pentecost. He had prepared his disciples not only to receive the Pentecostal outpouring of the Spirit; he had also prepared them as a community. The church at Pentecost knew the basics and was not distracted, as we often are, into looking elsewhere.

Jesus could have left a book of instructions or set up an organization. He could have created a ready-made system so that when the thousands of converts appeared, the church would have known exactly what to do. But Jesus worked at a more fundamental level. He gathered a community of believers, working intensively with them so that they would understand who he was and why he had come. God, through Jesus Christ, had such confidence in the Twelve that he left it to them and their fellow disciples to figure out questions of organization. They could handle the problems as they came up, guided by the Holy Spirit and following Jesus' teaching and example. In the book of Acts we see believers using their own intelligence but guided by the Holy Spirit in nurturing the growth of the church.

Here is a vital lesson about church life and structure, about wine and wineskins. It is easy to look at Pentecost and see the Spirit but miss the structure. It is easy to be amazed at what was new but blind to what was old. At Pentecost the disciples clearly got a taste of new wine. But Jesus provided also the basis for new wineskins in the community he had formed—wineskins created not out of thin air but from patterns, customs and understandings derived from centuries of God's acts in history. As he delights to do, the Ancient of Days did a new thing. Jesus drew on centuries, even millennia, of God's work in forming his new community—and then baptized the little group with his Spirit at Pentecost.

And so the first disciples did what Jesus had done. As Jesus had met with them in small groups, and as they had met together outdoors and in homes, so did the first Christians.

The early church took shape primarily in the homes of the believers. Its life was nourished in homes in two ways. First, the church was built through normal family life, drawing on the strength of the family in that day. Second, it was fed through *koinōnia* groups, cells of people who met together for prayer, worship and the Eucharist and who passed on Jesus' teaching by word of mouth.

The church's experience of community as it developed and spread through the Roman world was complemented by the sense of being a distinct people. The Epistles reveal a strong countercultural consciousness in the early church, a consciousness that developed and deepened as the church spread across the empire. Initially Jewish Christians saw themselves simply as Jews who accepted the Messiah. But as the church grew and spread, it learned that God's plan was not just for the Jews. It was for the Gentiles, for all peoples, nations and classes. The book of Acts shows the gospel spreading beyond Jewish confines and beginning to develop a people consciousness.

This consciousness dawned gradually; it didn't come all at once. Through the ministry of Peter, Paul, Barnabas, Philip and others (Acts 8—15) the church came to see that it was a new community and people. The Holy Spirit was poured out equally on Jew and Gentile (Acts 10:44-47; 11:15-18; 19:5-6). The believing community was not just a subcommunity among the Jews but a new work of God in history. Christians began to think of themselves as a third race: neither Jew nor Gentile, but something new transcending both.[10] They were the new Israel, the new people of God fulfilling Old Testament promises and expectations, but as a new social reality transcending the separate identities and allegiances of Jew and Gentile, of slave and free, of male and female. The church became not just a subculture within the dominant culture, but a new counterculture in the Greco-Roman world. Christians were "neither Jew nor Greek, slave nor free, male nor female," but "all one in Christ Jesus" (Gal 3:28; note also 1 Cor 12:13; Eph 2:14; Col 3:11). This was not merely spiritual renewal; it was social revolution.

The modern tragedy is that this consciousness has all but evaporated from the church, especially in North America. Given a test of loyalties, many Christians would place their identity as Americans or Canadians, or as members of a particular socioeconomic, employment, racial or ethnic group, above their identity as God's people. A sad symptom of the loss of true community and peoplehood in the church is the way Christians easily accept massive gaps between rich and poor in the church as normal, or at least as not a pressing Christian concern. The early Christians took steps so that "there were no needy persons among them" (Acts 4:34) and shared with those in need, even in other countries (Acts 11:28-30; 24:17; Rom 12:13; 15:26; 1 Cor 16:3), but few Christians today are so moved.

In North America, most of the Christian church is a subculture rather than a counterculture. A subculture is in fundamental agreement with the dominant culture on major issues and values, but has distinct secondary values and characteristics. By contrast, a counterculture is in tension with the dominant culture at the level of fundamental values, even though it may share many secondary characteristics with that culture. The church functions as a subculture, not as a counterculture, when it fails to oppose the dominant culture at those points where the culture pays allegiance to alien gods rather than to the Kingdom of God.

The Church as Countercultural Community But should the church really be a counterculture? Some say no, wanting to preserve the church's vital, transforming link to society. This is a legitimate concern. But faithfulness both to the New Testament picture of the church and to the church's Kingdom mission points to the church as a counterculture. Understood biblically, the model of the church as countercultural community is both dynamic and missiologically faithful.

The term *counterculture* is an inheritance from the sixties, the days of hippies, antiwar protest, the drug scene and the Jesus Revolution. Observers were quick to see that a sizable number of young people were switching to a set of values which constituted not a mere

---

subculture but rather a counterculture. This development was analyzed in such publications as Theodore Roszak's 1969 book, *The Making of a Counter-culture.*[11]

Counterculture is a useful term in probing the calling and experience of the church. In his study of the Sermon on the Mount, *Christian Counter-Culture,* John Stott says, "If the church realistically accepted [Jesus'] standards and values as here set forth, and lived by them, it would be the alternative society he always intended it to be, and would offer to the world an authentic Christian counterculture."[12] Instead of doing this, the church throughout history has too often developed clever ways of explaining why Jesus didn't really mean what he said or why his teachings are not to be applied to the present time. Fortunately, there have been significant exceptions to this pattern of unfaithfulness.

As applied to the church, counterculture is both a positive and a negative concept. Perhaps the negative side is more obvious: As a counterculture the church takes its stand *against* surrounding culture. The Christian community must be in some sense "other than" the world around it, maintaining fundamental points of antithesis.

But counterculture is also positive. A counterculture offers a genuine alternative to the dominant culture. In fundamental ways, the counterculture claims to be not only other than but also better than the world's culture. In offering a clearly delineated, visible alternative, the counterculture pushes society to self-examination, self-criticism and very often self-defense. Hidden or only dimly perceived questions rise to the surface. In this way the counterculture has a significant social impact, good or bad. Conversely, the counterculture is influenced by its contact with the larger culture and often defines itself in reaction to the mainline view. If the dominant culture emphasizes a work ethic, for instance, the counterculture may champion "dropping out" of the job market and the economic system generally. If the dominant culture stresses materialism and sensuality, the counterculture may move toward asceticism and mysticism. If "straight" culture wears suits, ties, white shirts and carefully manicured hair, the counterculture may sport blue jeans, bright colors, beads and beards. Of course, with time the countercultural trends may be taken over, popularized and exploited by the dominant culture, as happened in the United States from about 1970 to 1975.

In what sense should the church be a counterculture? Is the fidelity of the church to the Kingdom a matter of a countercultural existence? Or is this an unwholesomely negative way to picture the church's life?

The answer depends on the biblical image of the church. Does the Bible picture the church counterculturally? Five portions of Scripture help answer the question.

John 15:18-19–In the World, Not of It. "If the world hates you, keep in mind that it hated me first. If you belonged to the world, it would love you as its own. As it is, you do not belong to the world, but I have chosen you out of the world. That is why the world hates you." With this we may compare John 17:14-16, "I have given them your word and the world has hated them, for they are not of the world any more than I am of the world. My prayer is not that you take them out of the world but that you protect them from the evil one. They are not of the world, even as I am not of it."

These passages show that Jesus' disciples must maintain a critical tension: *in* the world but not *of* it. Christians are neither to withdraw from the world nor to become one with it. Jesus said, "My kingdom is not of this world" (Jn 18:36), but he made it plain that it is *in* the world (Lk 17:21). Jesus plants us in a place of tension. We are to maintain that tension against the strong pull to a more comfortable position either out of the world or totally of the world. This is the tension of incarnation, and it requires the church to be in some sense a counterculture.

Romans 12:2–Conformed to Christ, Not the World. "Do not conform any longer to the pattern of this world, but be transformed by the renewing of your mind." With this we may compare Romans 8:29, "For those God foreknew he also predestined to be conformed to the likeness of his Son, that he might be the firstborn among many brothers." The church is to avoid conformity to the world by being conformed to Jesus Christ through the renewing work of the Holy Spirit in the minds and lives of Christians. The statement that Jesus is "the firstborn among many brothers" suggests that the church is a brotherhood, a family, a community.

The church is to be a community of people who are conformed to the pattern of Jesus, not to the pattern of the world's culture. Is this merely another way of saying that we are to be in the world but not of it? Certainly Paul's statement here presupposes what Jesus said in John 15 and 17. But we find an added note: Jesus calls us to be conformed to himself, to be like him. Jesus' disciples are not of the world just as Jesus himself was not of the world (Jn 17:16). We are to be conformed to the image of God. We are "in all things" to "grow up into him who is the Head, that is, Christ" (Eph 4:15). So here conformity to Christ means nonconformity to the world's culture. This also suggests that the church is a countercultural community.

Luke 12:29-32–The Flock of the Kingdom. "Do not set your heart on what you will eat or drink; do not worry about it. For the pagan world runs after all such things, and your Father knows that you need them. But seek his kingdom, and these things will be given to you as well. Do not be afraid, little flock, for your Father has been pleased to give you the kingdom."

Here Jesus pictures his disciples as the flock of the Kingdom, the Kingdom community. What an amazing contrast of weakness and strength—a flock and a kingdom! You are a little flock, Jesus says, but in your very weakness and dependence on me you will inherit the Kingdom of God (compare 2 Cor 12:9).

The church is the community which has traded the values of the present world for the truth of the Kingdom. So the church is a counterculture. It pledges its allegiance to a sovereign different from that of the citizens of this world kingdom, the dominion of darkness. This goes beyond what has been said already, adding two more elements. First, the church's distinctness from the world is not merely a difference; it is a warfare, a world struggle. A battle is raging between the Kingdom of God and the powers of the enemy. Second, in this warfare the church must be faithful to its King and Lord. It must be faithful to the new covenant. As a covenant community, the church has pledged itself to live by the values of the Kingdom of God and to renounce the values of the world's culture. This is the basis for its concern with justice, truth, reconciliation and God's new order.

John 17:18–Sent into the World. Many Scriptures teach that Christians are sent into the world as Christ's witnesses and ambassadors. In his prayer recorded in John 17 Jesus says, "As you sent me into the world, I have sent them into the world." We are sent to be witnesses and to make disciples in all nations. In other words, the church is to be engaged aggressively with the world in winning the allegiance of increasing numbers of people away from the world and to Jesus as Lord and King. Its task is to win people not just to the church but to the full Kingdom and economy of God. This comes about through the regenerating work of the Holy Spirit in human lives. We are called to make disciples, not just converts, and disciples of the Kingdom, not just of the church.

As God's counterculture the church is not merely to be in the world; it is to pursue the mission of God in the world. It is the agent of God's Kingdom in bringing all things under the headship of Jesus Christ (Eph 1:10).

Revelation 21:23-27–Contributing to Culture. In Revelation 21 the holy city is described. We read, "The city does not need the sun or the moon to shine on it, for the glory of God gives it light, and the Lamb is its lamp. The nations will walk by its light, and the kings of the earth will bring their splendor into it. On no day will its gates ever be shut, for there will be no night there. The glory and honor of the nations will be brought into it. Nothing impure will ever enter it, nor will anyone who does what is shameful or deceitful, but only those whose names are written in the Lamb's book of life."

We may not understand all this passage means, but one thing is particularly striking. The holy city—the consummated Kingdom of God—will include "the glory and honor of the nations."[13] This suggests a positive evaluation of cultural diversity and of human cultural works. All that is good in human works—whatever is pure, lovely, true, honorable and harmonious—will be brought into the city of God. Everything false, ugly and distorted will be rejected. God will somehow gather all our cultural works, purify them and use them in his Kingdom.

This means Christians themselves have a positive contribution to make to culture. In being a Christian counterculture, the church can legitimately be engaged in cultural works that add beauty and harmony to the world. This also is Kingdom work. When we speak of the priesthood of all believers and the ministry of all God's people, we must understand that Kingdom ministry is not confined to religious things or church work, but includes all good work in the world which holds potential for glorifying God.

The Kingdom Community   The danger of a countercultural model
is that it may lead inward, away from engagement with the world.
The antidote to this danger is a deep consciousness that the church
exists for the Kingdom. The model of countercultural community
is essentially negative, despite its positive possibilities. It is therefore
an inadequate model by itself. But as part of the total picture of
what it means to be the church in a hostile world, it is an important
perspective. The church can be free for the Kingdom only if it is
sufficiently detached and distinct from the world's culture to maintain obedience for the Kingdom.

The key fact, then, is the church as Kingdom community. In most
cultural settings, a faithful church will be a countercultural church.
The more important point, however, is simply that the church be
faithful to the Kingdom, whatever this means for its position in
society.

Often the church's notion of community is shockingly shallow.
It fails to see how radical it is to build a community for the Kingdom.
It misses the deeply social, economic and political dimensions of
New Testament *koinōnia*. Being the *community* of God's people is a
social and political reality because to be a Christian is to be part of
a social group.

Government controls or regulates people in social groupings.
Thus a purely individualistic faith is politically irrelevant, while the
shared faith of God's people is a sociopolitical declaration, reality and threat. Individual, isolated Christians are seldom persecuted. Christian communities which dare to follow an alternate,
Christian sociopolitical life together constitute a political challenge
to the status quo and are always in danger of persecution or ex-
termination, as many historical examples show.

The church for the Kingdom is inevitably political, social and
economic. *Political,* because it deals with ultimate meaning and allegiance and aims to change the present order. *Social,* because it forms
people into close-knit, intense social groups organized around questions of values and life meaning, not just around secondary tasks.
Economic, because it involves the stewardship of money and resources and some level of mutual economic sharing and liability.

Biblically, there is no *koinōnia* without some form of economic sharing. If the church poses no threat to the enemy in these areas, its allegiance to Jesus Christ must be seriously questioned. We are, after all, involved not merely with a religious organization but with the *people* of God, the *community* of the Spirit and the *Kingdom* of Jesus Christ, our sovereign Lord.

Jim Wallis addresses this issue prophetically in his book *The Call to Conversion*. He suggests that we ask Christians, "What is the most important social reality in your life? What place, what group of people do you feel most dependent upon for your survival?" In asking this question, Wallis says, he finds that most Christians respond by indicating their work place or some other nonchurch organization or institution, "usually something associated with economic livelihood, personal advancement, or social influence." Then Wallis makes his key point:

If in fact most Christians are more rooted in the principalities and powers of this world than they are in the local community of faith, it is no wonder that the church is in trouble. Clearly, the social reality in which we feel most rooted will be the one that will most determine our values, our priorities, and the way we will live. It is not enough to talk of Christian fellowship while our security is based elsewhere. We will continue to conform to the values and institutions of our society as long as our people's security is grounded in them.[14]

This rings true, both spiritually and sociologically. It is important to emphasize Wallis's point. This is not simply the common sermon line that, regardless of our involvements in the world, our deepest commitment *should* be to the church, and we *should* remember to keep that commitment first. That is merely a mental exercise devoid of real historical significance. The point is the one Jesus makes: Where your security is, there your heart is. Jesus didn't divide people's allegiances into political, economic and spiritual compartments, merely asking that we not neglect the spiritual box. He said plainly, "Do not store up riches for yourselves here on earth. . . . For your heart will always be where your riches are. . . . You cannot serve both God and money" (Mt 6:19, 21, 24 TEV). The question is basic loyalties. Do we find our fundamental meaning and security in the Kingdom community or in material and economic resources? It is a choice between the Kingdom of God and the kingdom of this world. Wallis says,

We have to create a base that is internally strong enough to enable us to survive as Christians and to empower us to be actively engaged in the world. The community is the place where the healing of our own lives becomes the foundation for the healing of the nations. The making of community is finally the only thing strong enough to resist the system and to provide an adequate spiritual foundation for better and more human ways to live.

There is no greater moral authority than that given by standing before the world free of its securities. There is no greater threat to the system than that of being free of its rewards and punishments, and therefore free of its control. And there is no greater power than that which comes from being free to offer ourselves for what we know to be true.[15]

Only one kind of community can possibly have such strength and exercise it redemptively, and that is the community of Jesus that lives for the Kingdom of God. This is what it means to discern and live by the economy of God.

Building Community Today   The church has redemptive significance not when community is a theoretical perspective but only when it is an empirical fact, a social and historical reality. It means little to call the church a community if socially speaking it is not. The community model is helpful only if it serves as the basis for building authentic community in the church.

This is where an understanding of local church ecology comes in. Building community means applying basic biblical principles of church life, such as those outlined in chapter three. Building genuine Christian community today involves especially the following aspects.[16]

Commitment and Covenant. Christian community starts at the point of commitment and covenant. There is no genuine Christian community without a covenant. Whether this is a formal or an informal commitment is secondary. The point is, Christian community cannot exist without commitment to Jesus as Lord and to each other as sister and brother. And this must be more than a general mental commitment. It must be specific and explicit, involving our time, energy and resources. Covenant is not just a nebulous commitment to each other; it takes specific shape in history.

Shared Life. This means, first of all, spending time together. The church exists in time and space and must therefore come together in time and space. Real community means shared time, shared meals, shared priorities and some level of economic sharing, some genuine economic mutual dependence. While specific patterns of such sharing may vary, *koinōnia* in the New Testament sense does not exist without this level of shared life. Such life finds its real meaning in the balance of shared worship, nurture and witness.

The Dimension of Transcendence. It is possible to have *human* community based on covenant and shared life without having *Christian* community. But we are talking about building the church, the community of Jesus and his Kingdom. Human community is the Kingdom community only when it is formed around Jesus and lives by the Spirit for the sake of the Kingdom. The church transcends mere human community when the horizontal, human dimension is married to the vertical dimension through Jesus Christ. This dimension of transcendence constitutes the church and builds the church into a true community of the Spirit. It causes the Christian community to look not just inward or outward but also upward to God and ahead to God's future in the promised Kingdom. The presence of Jesus Christ through the Holy Spirit creates true New Testament *koinōnia* in the church.

To be the community of the Spirit the church must live in the atmosphere of worship. The first priority of the church is always worship. If community itself, or the church's witness in the world, takes the place of worship, the dimension of transcendence may be lost, and the church may forfeit both its unique character and its peculiar power.

Service in Community Building Servanthood is an essential mark of authentic Christian community and should characterize the church's internal life and its life in the world. The church is called to be a community in the world at the service of the Kingdom.

The church's most potent role as community is in community building, particularly at the levels of family, church and neighborhood. Although society's macrostructures must be changed or replaced before universal justice can reign, much of the battle for justice today is taking place at the level of the microstructures of family, church and neighborhood. These structures are the building blocks of a just society and the school where justice, mercy and truth are learned. Christians can and must work in other areas, but if the church fails to make its unique contribution in building community at these foundational levels, it will have little significant impact at broader levels.

If the church is seen primarily as an institution, its ministry will be largely institutional and program-oriented. But if the church is viewed as a community, its ministry will be person-oriented, focusing on building structures of human interaction. And in this perspective, the structures of family, church and neighborhood are most basic. All are fairly intimate forms of human community based on face-to-face personal relationships. Together they provide the glue of society. We have seen how these foundational structures are being undermined today. But the church as community has the answer.

1. *Family Building*. The church builds families first by recognizing that the church is the family of God and that the family is the church of God. Family was the original form of human community. Both in Scripture and in history the family preceded the church. Indeed, the Old Testament initially makes no distinction between church and family.

To understand what this means we must think beyond the nuclear family. Mother, father and two kids, virtually divorced from grandparents, cousins and other kin, may be the hallowed ideal of twentieth-century Middle America and of church bulletin covers, but it is not the biblical ideal. Effectively building family life today means rediscovering the extended family. With so many fractured and isolated families and so many people living singly, the church should see itself as an extended family where every believer finds a home, not just figuratively but literally. The church must work to build strong homes, exploring extended family models, so that each home truly is a church and the church truly is a family.

2. *Neighborhood Building*. Beyond family life, a key ministry for the church is building vital, healthy neighborhoods. This is true especially in the city, but it has application elsewhere too. In urban neighborhoods the church has often been guilty of "ecclesiastical redlining"—failing to invest in, or abandoning, neighborhoods which most needed a Christian presence. Neighborhoods decline when the key institutions sustaining their social and economic life-

blood begin to pull out. When a bank refuses to grant mortgages or loans in a particular area or an insurance company refuses to offer policies there, this is called "redlining" (from the practice of either literally or figuratively drawing a red line around areas where service is no longer to be offered). Such practices simply hasten neighborhood deterioration which otherwise could be prevented. For this reason redlining is now illegal in many cities.

The church practices redlining when it abandons or bypasses needy communities. Too often it becomes a party to institutional disinvestment, the pattern of pulling from a neighborhood the very institutions most needed for healthy community. In so doing the church fails to live up to its mission as a builder of community.

When biblically faithful, the church has the two things the world needs most: the love of God and life in community. When its love extends to the building of healthy community, the Kingdom of God is advanced. Then the church meets society's crucial need for functioning communities where people trust one another and everyone is treated fairly and justly.

What happens in a neighborhood when the church takes seriously its commission to serve in Jesus' name in building community? Let us imagine:

Here and there, couples on the brink of divorce discover that God's love can put their homes back together again.

Fearful neighbors get acquainted and begin to work on community problems (crime, the schools, energy conservation, discrimination, rent control, poor city services or whatever the needs are), as Christians help bring people together, reducing fear and building understanding.

Poor families find that someone cares as Christians reach out to them in love, giving material aid when needed and working to improve housing conditions and employment opportunities.

Aimless children with no real home life find that God has a plan for them and a loving, caring family where they are welcome as the church opens its doors to them.

Elderly folks with little meaning in life and perhaps no one to look after them find new security and new opportunities for service, as Christians care for their needs.

These are but a few examples of what can happen when Christians catch a vision for turning neighborhoods into real communities. In these ways the church can literally transform neighborhoods, and the larger society, for Christ.

Liberating the church means freeing Christians to be a community of believers that serves as an agent of the Kingdom of God. As the church *becomes* a community in the New Testament sense, it is able to *create* community and to enhance existing community not only among Christians but in society at large. This is why liberating the church for community is crucial for liberating the world.

When the Kingdom comes, it will come through genuine community in Christ through the power of the Spirit. Where the church today is truly the community of God's people living for God's glory and mission, there the Kingdom is already visibly present as sign, promise and firstfruit.

6
THE CHURCH
AS SERVANT

Both as sacrament and as community, the church is the body of Christ. Since we are *Jesus'* body, the church is called to serve as Jesus served.

Sacrament and service go together. At the Last Supper Jesus washed the disciples' feet. As he served he said, "I have set you an example that you should do as I have done for you" (Jn 13:15). "No servant," Jesus says, "is greater than his master" (Jn 13:16).

So we may speak of the church as servant. Throughout history, and especially among movements of renewal, Jesus-style servanthood has emerged as a redemptive counterpoint to the church's tendencies to institutionalism and triumphalism. Today in major segments of the Christian church servanthood is being reaffirmed as the church's basic style in the world. The motif of servanthood must penetrate much more deeply into the consciousness of the North American church, however, if it is to be free for the Kingdom and redemptively liberating for the world. In far too many churches the unmasked assumption is that the church exists for itself and that people in the surrounding community are "prospects" to be won rather than persons to be served.[1]

Service in the New Testament In English versions of the New Testament, "service" usually translates the Greek word *diakonia*. Frequently, however, *diakonia* is translated "ministry." Thus ministry and service in the New Testament are essentially synonymous. *Dia-*

konia is a common New Testament word, related to the verb *diakoneō*, "to serve," and the noun *diakonos,* "servant" or "minister" (from which comes the word *deacon*).[2]

Five things stand out in the way the New Testament speaks of service.

1. Service is the basic word for Christian ministry of all kinds. The New Testament speaks of various kinds of specific service: the ministry of the Word, the ministry of testifying to the gospel, serving people in their physical needs and so forth. Acts 6, in a section often mistakenly called the institution of deacons, speaks both of the ministry (service) of the Word and the ministry (service) of waiting tables. Paul says we have been given both the message and the ministry of reconciliation (2 Cor 5:18-19). We are told there are various kinds of ministries, but one Lord (1 Cor 12:5).

2. The New Testament word for service, *diakonia,* has a distinctly personal reference. It specifically means service rendered *for* some person or *to* someone. The idea is not impersonal or mechanical service, or the blind obedience of a slave. The Greek language has several other words for service, but the special word used for service in Christ's name is a personal, relational word.

3. The New Testament understanding of service is linked with the distribution of spiritual gifts. There are varieties of service because there are varieties of gifts (1 Cor 12:4-5). Sometimes, in speaking of gifts, the New Testament speaks of service itself as a gift, but it includes the working of all gifts as service or ministry. Paul says the leadership gifts are given in order to equip all believers for service or ministry (Eph 4:11-12). Peter says if we have received a gift for ministering, we should perform our service "by the strength which God supplies," as "good stewards of God's varied grace" (1 Pet 4:10-11 RSV). This connection with spiritual gifts means that God gives us his special grace and empowering in order that we may serve him with supernatural results.

4. In the New Testament, service is always tied to Jesus' servant role. As Jesus was a servant, we are to be servants. Jesus took upon himself the form of a servant, or slave (Phil 2:7). Many times he acted out the role of a servant with his disciples—symbolically in washing their feet at the Last Supper, and supremely in bearing their sins (and ours) on the cross. And Jesus was clear that the

meaning of what he did was not merely to purchase our redemption, but also to show us how to serve. Jesus said that greatness in his eyes will be measured by the standard of his example of living to serve rather than to be served (Mt 20:26-28; 23:11).

5. Because of this connection with Jesus Christ, service or ministry in the Bible is tied to discipleship and to our life in the body of Christ, the Christian community. By definition, service and ministry for Christians mean following the example of Jesus, submitting to his lordship, being his disciples and living out his lordship in the community of Jesus. Only in this way will Jesus' statement be fulfilled that his disciples would do the same works he did, and even greater (Jn 14:12).

These facets of the New Testament understanding of service underscore the fact that *all believers are called to the Christian ministry.* Gifts and ministries may vary, but every Christian is called to be a servant of Christ, to minister in a Christlike way in his name. Therefore, when we talk of the servant church, we are not primarily talking about services which the church as an organization may offer. Rather we are speaking of the service of each individual believer, and especially the ways the whole Christian community serves by following the lead of Jesus.

The Jesus Model   Jesus is the model for ministry. Christians are servants of Christ. For this reason, we may speak of the church as servant.

It is not wrong to think of Jesus as our model and example, for he himself asks us to see him that way. Jesus was not only born to die; he was born to live the perfect human life, giving us a model for our individual lives and for our life together in community. To be a Christian, then, means not only to believe in him but also to follow his example. In the words of B. T. Roberts,

One condition of our being the disciples of Christ is, that we follow him. We may bear his name, but he does not acknowledge us on that account. The church will class us as belonging to it, if we subscribe to its creed, live up to its rules, and contribute to its support; but to have Christ reckon us as belonging to him, we must, according to our ability, walk in his footsteps, and take him for our example. We must devote ourselves to doing good.

If we are really following Christ, we shall observe his precepts where they

come in conflict with the customs of the day. No one can be a follower of the fashions, and a follower of Christ. If we go with Christ only so far as the proud and the worldly go, and leave him where they leave him, then it is the world that we are following, not Christ. [3]

A genuine servant church is a community of persons radically committed to following Jesus, particularly where Jesus' way conflicts with the world's way.

We are called to be disciples and servants of Jesus. Jesus Christ, as Karl Barth reminds us, is the Lord who became Servant and the Servant who became Lord. We are called to follow his footsteps in paths of service to the world and to our Christian sisters and brothers.

Viewing the church as servant, and considering the state of the church today, we need to stress that Jesus is our model in spirituality and in servanthood.

A Model for Spirituality. Evangelical Protestant, Orthodox and Roman Catholic Christians have often been especially concerned with spirituality, though in quite different ways. For many evangelical Christians the important thing is to "be spiritual." And yet the spirituality sought is often set off from the economic, political and social affairs of life. On the other hand, many contemporary Christians who advocate radical discipleship are now insisting that authentic activism must be based in spirituality. The important thing is that spirituality be tied to the life and example of Jesus Christ. This is essential for the church to be a servant as God intends.

Spirituality has often been lifted out of its biblical context and given a bad press. It has come to mean otherworldliness or mysticism, being out of touch with the so-called real world. Obviously, no sensible Christian today wants that! And yet recent fascination with Oriental religions, transcendental meditation and the occult shows that this is precisely what many people today do want.

In any case, spirituality is a legitimate concern for biblical Christians. The Bible says we are engaged in a spiritual warfare and that our weapons are not fleshly but spiritual. Lack of a proper biblical spirituality therefore means much more than being less devotionally oriented than might be desirable. It means possibly losing the struggle for justice because of a misunderstanding of the nature of the battle. We live in a world where the most fundamental reality is spiritual, and we are less than fully human if our lives do not reflect this fact. And a lack of this awareness will eventually short-circuit redemptive servanthood.

The church has always found it hard to keep spirituality tied to Jesus Christ as a real person. Too often spirituality has become a thing in itself. Then some unbiblical yardstick of spirituality is applied, and the church ends up in a swamp of subjectivism. Spirituality has at times been measured by physical separation from the world, time spent in prayer, obedience to a rule, attendance at church, good works or how one feels when singing hymns. But these are all false measures of spirituality.

How easy it is to miss the most fundamental question: How was Jesus spiritual? All that God wants us to be is summed up and modeled for us in Jesus' life. Jesus' death and resurrection provide the basis for our salvation, but his life shows how that salvation should work out day by day.

To be spiritual means to be like Jesus. God's will is that we be "conformed to the image of his Son" (Rom 8:29 RSV). "He who says he abides in him ought to walk in the same way in which he walked" (1 Jn 2:6 RSV). We are to follow the example of Christ in our daily lives, especially in suffering for righteousness and justice (1 Pet 2:21). We must seek no other spirituality than that of Christ. We can aim no higher than to be like Jesus. We should aim at nothing less. If we are like Jesus, then we are spiritual in the sense God intends. If we are *not* like him, any other spirituality or holiness we may claim is mockery and hypocrisy.

To say spirituality means to be like Jesus doesn't entirely solve the problem, however. We are left asking what Jesus was really like. The answer should be simple, for the Gospel records are clear enough. But it is hard for us to take in the whole picture and keep it straight. We cut out little pictures of Jesus from the Bible, paste them up on the wall, and say, "There! *That* is what Jesus was like." In the early Greek church, Jesus on the Mount of Transfiguration was taken as the true picture of spirituality. Sometimes the picture has been an ethereal, otherworldly, cosmic Christ. Or Jesus has been seen exclusively as the Good Shepherd living harmlessly in pastoral tranquility with his little flock, more like a character in a nursery rhyme than the Lord of peace and justice.

Probably the greatest danger of the church has been to paint an overspiritualized Christ. People have not *really* believed Jesus had a flesh-and-blood human body, even if they said he did in their creeds. Much of this is still around. Too often Christians see no significance to Jesus' earthly life except as a source of stories illustrating his divinity and his work of atonement. They leap from the manger to the cross as though nothing in between mattered.

In this view of Jesus, spirituality means living in a spirit world divorced from this world. Only Scriptures about heaven, eternal life, the judgment and so forth are important. Spirituality becomes an excuse for noninvolvement in this world and focuses narrowly on religious feelings, peace of mind or the next life.

This is one danger. But there is the twin danger of an overhumanized Jesus. His life on earth becomes the measure of all things. Jesus comes to be seen as a political revolutionary or a dropout from society or a wandering philosopher. Or he may be pictured as a man with extraordinary insight into the nature of God who shows us what it means to be fully human. Here Christ's atoning work on the cross is largely eclipsed, and a sort of reverse metaphysical alchemy draws the spirit world entirely into space and time. Obviously, this tendency comes in reaction against an overspiritualized Christ.

A Model for Servanthood. Jesus is the model for the servant community both in his life in society and in his death on the cross. The cross, in fact, casts its shadow backward over the life of Jesus. Discipleship is tied to the cross, and the cross defines our discipleship.

Jesus asked his disciples who the crowds thought he was. The crowd had the usual wrong answers. But Peter said, "You are the Christ of God—the promised Messiah!"

Notice Jesus' response to Peter's confession. He didn't say, "Good for you, Peter! You've finally got it right. You know who I am. Now you've got your doctrine straight." Rather Jesus says, in effect, "That's a good start, but you've got a lot to learn." He says to Peter, "The Son of Man must suffer many things and be rejected by the elders, chief priests and teachers of the law, and he must be killed and on the third day be raised to life." Then Jesus says to everyone: "If anyone would come after me, he must deny himself and take up his cross daily and follow me" (Lk 9:22-23).

Jesus is telling us, "If you want to be my disciples, recognizing *who*

I am is not enough. You must *follow* me. And that will mean a cross."

The road of discipleship is marked by crosses. First we face the cross of renouncing all claim to our own lives, turning them over to Jesus. Then we face the daily cross of choosing to be like Jesus, of making the Savior our model and master as well. So the cross defines the dimensions of our discipleship. Its stark directions—up to God, down to the earth and out to the world—give us the dimensions of our own pilgrimage as followers of Jesus. The cross lifts us to God, joins us together as Christ's body, and points us to the world after the model of Jesus.

1. *We have no access to God except through Jesus Christ.* But through Jesus' sacrifice of himself, we now have access to the very holiness of God. "Therefore, brothers, since we have confidence to enter the Most Holy Place by the blood of Jesus, by a new and living way opened for us through the curtain, that is, his body, and since we have a high priest over the house of God, let us draw near to God with a sincere heart in full assurance of faith, having our hearts sprinkled to cleanse us from a guilty conscience and having our bodies washed with pure water" (Heb 10:19-22).

Our greatest need is to be lifted to God. We cannot reach him on our own. But Jesus, the Word, became flesh and lived among us. He identified fully with us, then gathered up all our guilt and pride and powerlessness and died in our place on the cross.

The cross defines for us this dimension of servanthood. In Jesus we see that servanthood and spirituality go together. Truly redemptive servanthood, servanthood that makes a difference for the Kingdom, is grounded in our union with God through Christ. And spirituality that truly knows God and breathes the spirit of Jesus follows the servant model of Jesus. The cross joins these two together.

2. *The cross also unites us as Christ's body.* In being lifted to God we are made like Jesus. This means living a shared life, as Jesus did—life in Christian community. Life in community is a dimension of our servanthood just as it is an element of true spirituality.

Things come together at the cross. Meaning emerges as we begin to understand God's economy and what he has done for us. In the cross heaven and earth come together through the sacrificial death of the God-man who not only humbled himself to take on human form but humbled himself further by stretching that form on a cross so that we might live. The cross is where Jew and Gentile, rich and poor, man and woman, black and white, slave and free come together in reconciled community. Through the cross, God in Christ is reconciling the world to himself. He is calling very diverse people to himself and to his body, the community of God's people.

This is the biblical vision of the church and the basis for authentic servanthood. We have to admit with anguish, however, that it is neither the vision nor the experience of much of the church today.

We are coming to a time of sifting in the church, however. The subtle corrosion of technological materialism has tarnished our vision of the Kingdom of God. We know well enough that the prayer "May your kingdom come" does not mean "May I have my dream house, two cars, economic security and an unlimited expense account." Still, most Christians seem to have no lively hope or even desire that the Kingdom of God come soon in space and time. It's going to be a long ride from here to the future, we think, so we may as well sit back and enjoy the scenery, indulging in all the creature comforts possible. That way we can have the best of two worlds—"All this and heaven too!"

But this will not do. It is a wrong vision. It does not take seriously the Kingdom of God or the servant model of Jesus. It substitutes sentimental hope for faith and creature comfort for the cross. It fails to grasp God's word that he is *now* at work reconciling the world to himself, and that we are coworkers with him, not just spectators.

So we are coming to a time of sifting. A new but old vision is emerging—the vision of victory through the cross. A growing number of Christians today are ready to commit themselves radically to God and to his work in the world. The concern with costly discipleship is growing. Even as many Christians are perfectly content to "sleep through the revolution," spiritually numbed by materialism, many others are calling for commitment, discipleship and radical Christian servanthood.

We have to make a choice. Not simply the choice whether or not to be Christians, but the harder choice this implies: *whether or not truly to be the church.* Too many Christians are content to live as though there were no church, as though Christ had no body. They worship a disembodied Christ and so can only say to the world, "I'm very sorry about all your problems. Jesus Christ is the only one who can help. But unfortunately he doesn't live here anymore."

So we must learn to be the servant church. We must band ourselves together in cells of costly commitment to one another, cells where we can learn what fellowship in the Spirit means. If we do not do this, we will be powerless before the world of technological materialism and will find our lives constantly betraying the values we preach and the Lord we confess.

This is what the Bible is talking about. The Hebrews understood that they were the *people* of God—a distinct race called to fulfill God's purposes. The Hebrews remembered they were a people but forgot their call. Christians believe they have heard God's call but have forgotten they are a people and not just an assortment of separate saints.

3. Finally, *the cross points us to the world.* Nailed to the cross, Jesus' arms were stretched outward and his hands were open to the world. But this was not new. Jesus' arms were open to embrace the world through all his earthly ministry. He simply died as he had lived.

It is this world-embracing love of Jesus, shown supremely on the cross, that points us to the world in our following Jesus. It is the horizontal dimension of the cross that reaches out to the world and defines the life we are to live. Jesus shows us what our servanthood must be—for the sake of the world.

If we live lives marked by the cross, we will be close enough to Jesus to hear what he says to us about his Kingdom. We will see how Jesus' birth, life, death, resurrection and present reign all fit together in the economy of God.

Jesus came preaching the Kingdom of God and ended up on a cross. But this crucified Jesus rose again, triumphed over the principalities and powers and now reigns. He will come again to bring his Kingdom in fullness.

So to be marked by the cross means to seek first the Kingdom of God. It means keeping the honor, glory and sovereignty of God first in our lives while we seek to be servants in Jesus' name.

The Church That Serves The servant model of Jesus defines for us a church that serves. Joined to Jesus, the church is implicated in the incarnation, crucifixion and resurrection of its Lord. The servant church is born and breathes in worship because Jesus rose

again. It lives by the joy and power of resurrectio.
church is enabled by community. Its life is a rea.
Holy Spirit in flesh and blood. Therefore the chu
sharing in the incarnation of Jesus Christ, and ser
sacrament come together. And the servant church is   . in
the world. Therefore the church shares in the crucifixi ut Jesus.
Jesus calls us to come and die. For it is in dying that we are born to
eternal life.

We cannot view the church exclusively in terms of service. The
church as servant is a basic biblical model, but still the church remains a mystery. The idea of the church as servant is an especially
relevant model for today, however. It is easy to think of the church
as a holy club or as the company of the elect, overemphasizing the
aspect of being separate from the world. We should see the church
as a serving, ministering community, ready to sacrifice its own interests so that others may live, but never ready to betray its Lord.
Faithfulness in doctrine and life requires that we see the church in
its present history as marked more by the cross than by the crown.

The danger is that we may give only lip service to servanthood.
This happened with Israel in the Old Testament. Hermann Beyer
points out,

*Israel had the great heritage of the commandment of Lv. 19:18: "Thou shalt
love thy neighbour as thyself." This included full readiness for and commitment to service of one's neighbour. In later Judaism, however, 3 factors
tended to obscure it. A sharp distinction came to be made between the righteous and the unrighteous in the antitheses of the Pharisees, and this dissolved
the unconditional command of love and service. There arose the attitude
lashed by Jesus in the parable of the Good Samaritan. Again, the service
was less and less understood as sacrifice for others and more and more as a
work of merit before God. Finally, there arose in Judaism the idea, which is
so obvious to the natural man, not to accord service, especially service at
table, to the unworthy.*[4]

These same tendencies sometimes operate in churches today.
Under the influence of conservative political philosophy, Christians
may come to believe they are not responsible unconditionally to
meet the needs of the poor but should help only those who really
can't help themselves. This view, however, fails to recognize that no
one is "worthy" since all are sinners. God's love is shed equally on all,

and he bears special concern for the poor—deserving or undeserving by our standards. This view also ignores social power and powerlessness. We should remember that every person is both sinner and sinned against.

The early church was composed largely of the poor. It took seriously the demands of love toward those in physical or material need. The Old Testament concern about widows and orphans was carried over into early church experience, and before long large numbers of widows were supported by the church. The church ministered to the poor, first by bringing them the good news of Jesus Christ, and then by caring for their material needs whether or not they were in the church.

A great change came over the church with the conversion of Constantine in the fourth century. Ethical and moral concern was diluted as millions of people who had little knowledge of Christ or the demands of discipleship entered the church. The joining of church and state was seen as the great triumph of the Kingdom of God. But many have argued that this was rather the fall of the church.[5] The church became linked with power, prestige, pomp and politics, largely losing the vision of a serving community that takes its place with the poor and dispossessed.

Yet the vision of the church as a serving community following the Jesus model was still tucked away in the church's Scriptures. Periodically it re-emerged to spark renewal during the long centuries of the Middle Ages. Some of the early monastic orders made service a central theme. Later came Francis of Assisi, who was able to remain within the church, and Peter Waldo, who was kicked out. These men and their followers went about preaching the gospel to the poor, calling for a return to New Testament simplicity and denouncing the church's fallen condition. The result was the Franciscan order within the Roman Church and the Waldensians, branded as heretics.

Many renewal movements, bent on recapturing the New Testament expression of the church, gave themselves in service to people around them. Yet, ironically, they were often severely persecuted. Early Anabaptists cared for their own and often for others as well. The Moravians sent little servant communities to many parts of the world. Early Methodists were known for their concern and care for the poor, the stratum of society from which so many of them came. In the late nineteenth century, the Salvation Army, the Christian and Missionary Alliance under A. B. Simpson, and many other groups made service to the urban poor their special concern. Simpson said in 1895 that God's "mightiest work" had now moved "from the church to the slums and the mission fields" and that Christians should live "the Gospel of practical religion," providing "real help for human suffering as well as human sin" and making special provision for "the physical needs and the material miseries" of lost multitudes.[6] Similarly, B. T. Roberts wrote in 1870, "The primitive Christians were ready, whenever the occasion demanded it, to give up their property, and even to lay down their lives for for one another. We must have the same disposition. Without it our orthodoxy and our prayers—our strictness or our liberality—will not prove good our claims to be reckoned the disciples of Christ."[7] Roberts combined this concern for serving the poor with strong views on riches, arguing that Jesus plainly "forbids his disciples to amass wealth."

There is no class in society in such imminent danger of eternal damnation as the rich. . . . It is not merely trust in riches, that renders it so difficult to enter the kingdom of God, but their possession. Yet who ever possessed riches, without trusting in them, at least for influence and consideration, if not for salvation?[8]

So the church that serves is not a new idea. Servanthood has always been a mark of Kingdom faithfulness. But our concern is with the church as servant today.

The Servant Church Today   In what sense should the church be a servant today? I suggest the following as marks of a servant church in our age.

1. The servant church sees Jesus as example and model, not just as Savior and Lord.

2. The servant church balances a theology of glory with a theology of the cross.

3. The servant church understands itself as a distinct community committed to live here and now by the values of the Kingdom of God through the sanctifying and enabling grace of the Holy Spirit.

4. The servant church believes that lifestyle is a part of disciple-

ship and that here, too, Jesus has given us both precept and example.

5. The servant church believes that ministry is defined as service in Jesus' name for Jesus' sake and that every believer is called to this ministry.

6. The servant church places a high priority on preaching the gospel to the poor. It is especially drawn to Jesus' words "The Spirit of the Lord is upon me, because he has anointed me to preach the good news to the poor" (Lk 4:18).

7. The servant church rejects any definition of success which compromises the call to costly service. It believes in the ultimate victory of the Kingdom of God, but trusts that this victory comes through the miracle and paradox of crucifixion, the life laid down. It is convinced that acts of loving service have Kingdom significance.

Even so, not all authentic servant churches will look precisely the same. Perhaps we should expect to find different models of servant churches. We must avoid thinking, for instance, that a church has to be an inner-city or distinctly urban church to be a servant. We need urban, suburban and rural (or small-town) servant churches. We might think of these as three models of servanthood.

The Urban Servant Church. This is the church that most directly brings liberation to the poor. It does this in various ways, taking servanthood seriously in the light of the particularly complex problems of city life. Part of this service is faithful confrontation with the principalities and powers in the city.

The Suburban Servant Church. This too can be an expression of servanthood, provided the church really serves people and the Kingdom. The suburban servant church must recognize the unique characteristics and temptations of suburbia. It needs to understand urban ecology in its spiritual, economic and sociopolitical senses. This means seeing itself as part of the total urban picture and thus as standing side by side with, and not with its back to, the inner city. Living in suburbia, it must oppose materialism and consumerism and support the church in the city. It will be concerned with a responsible lifestyle, with building the family unit as a serving community, and with reaching beyond itself in tangible expressions of serving the poor and suffering in the world.

The Rural or Small-Town Servant Church. Many Christian churches are located in rural areas and small towns and will be for some time.

But the rural or small-town servant church must see that it has a strategic ministry to the city and to the world. A large percentage of people in such churches are involved in agriculture. These people produce the food that is wasted on the rich and fortunate and denied to the poor and starving. Rural and small-town churches can have a prophetic witness to the world in the light of world food problems, creating a consciousness of world hunger and finding ways to channel excess food to the urban and Third World poor. It is immoral for Christian farmers to be paid for not growing crops while people starve. Rural churches can make a crucial difference far out of proportion to their size at this point. Yet this is a type of servanthood that by and large is yet to be discovered.

The body of Christ needs all kinds of servant churches. More than that, it needs intercommunity contact and cooperation between such servant churches. Churches must learn to serve each other.

The church must hear the call today to be the servant of Jesus Christ—to be in the world, not to be served, but to serve. It must be ready to identify with "the wretched of the earth." Christians must serve the poor, widows and orphans, refugees and sojourners, remembering that we also were strangers in the land of bondage. The church must hear and heed the call to servanthood for the sake of the Kingdom of God. It is the servant church which is free for the Kingdom.

7
THE CHURCH
AS WITNESS

For Jesus, telling good news and proclaiming the Kingdom were the same. Evangelism meant enlisting people for the Kingdom of God, liberating them from themselves, their sins and their entanglements so that they would be free for the Kingdom.

To proclaim Jesus as Savior and Lord is to proclaim the Kingdom of God. By and large, however, contemporary Christianity has cut the vital nerve between evangelism and the Kingdom. Evangelism has been so totally unhitched from Kingdom proclamation that today converts can be brought into the church without their realizing that participation in the body of Christ means commitment to God's Kingdom and justice.

In Jesus we see that evangelism and the Kingdom go together. In light of the Kingdom, winning men and women to personal faith in Jesus Christ is crucial. For to win people to Jesus is to win their allegiance to God's economy and priorities, not just to assure their entrance into heaven. Being born again is the door to the Kingdom. "Unless a man is born again, he cannot see the kingdom of God" (Jn 3:3). Unless evangelism leads to Kingdom commitments, it is something less than the evangelistic work Jesus did and calls us to.[1]

The church, then, is to be a witness for Jesus Christ and for the Kingdom of God.

Evangelism Today   In an article in the November 1978 issue of the Southern Baptist publication *Home Missions,* Toby Druin attempted to gauge the effectiveness of the nationwide Here's Life, America effort and the similar statewide Good News Texas campaign sponsored by Southern Baptists in 1977. The report raises issues which provide a good starting point for considering the church's evangelistic mandate.[2]

Here's Life, America was a multimillion-dollar evangelistic effort sponsored by Campus Crusade for Christ, localized in 253 U.S. metropolitan areas. It involved over 14,500 local churches, and three-fourths of all Americans were said to have been exposed to the campaign's catchy "I Found It" slogan during the campaign.

Good News Texas was a smaller-scale but similar evangelistic effort costing over one million dollars and aimed at evangelizing 4.7 million unchurched Texans during the spring and summer of 1977. Local church campaigns were backed by a media blitz including radio and TV testimonials by famous personalities on 300 stations, 1,700 billboards and extensive newspaper advertising. A secular advertising agency helped design and carry out the campaign. Reliable estimates indicate that more than half of all Texans saw the TV spots, and one-third of those who saw them said their attitudes toward religion had been changed. Media people say this was a significant achievement.

Perhaps the unprecedented Here's Life effort signaled a turning point for North American evangelical churches. This campaign may mark the point, not where North American churches took a quantum leap forward in evangelism, but where they finally learned that evangelism fails if it does not grow out of the integrity and spiritual vitality of the local congregation.

All indications are that Here's Life was a great media success and a dismal evangelistic failure. The same is true of the Good News Texas campaign. Millions of Americans heard the message and were influenced by it. These campaigns may even have produced some good in the form of pre-evangelism. But all empirical studies so far yield the same result: thousands of "decisions," but only the tiniest trickle of new church members. And the evidence suggests that most "converts" represented Christian rededications and transfers from one church to another.

James Engel, citing Peter Wagner's study, notes that of the more than one-half million persons who claimed they had received Christ through Here's Life fewer than three per cent became church members. Further, notes Engel,

it was contended that 175 million people were exposed to the claims of the gospel. Because of media saturation, this figure could be accurate, but exposure and comprehension are very different matters. In a survey undertaken at the Wheaton Graduate School it was discovered that about eighty percent of those living in Upper Arlington, Ohio (a wealthy suburb of Columbus), indeed were aware of the "I found it" theme, but only forty percent understood the message. And at least half of this forty percent were already Christian or Christian-oriented. The great majority never comprehended what it was trying to say.[3]

The problem is compounded by the extravagant claims made for Here's Life. Campus Crusade's Bill Bright said at the outset of Here's Life that the campaign "may very well determine both the destiny of our nation and the future of all civilization." He was quoted as saying in 1976, "Here's Life, America is the greatest spiritual harvest in the history of the church—100 times, yes, 1,000 times greater than anything I have ever seen or read about. I believe one can truthfully say here in the United States the Great Commission will be fulfilled."[4]

Such statements and subsequent claims regarding Here's Life create a giant credibility gap. As studies by Win Arn and others have shown, Here's Life had virtually no measurable impact on church membership in the United States.[5] Perhaps it had some significant, less tangible results, and it may have contributed in some way to a broad-based religious consciousness in America. But its impact was primarily on some of the individual Christians and local churches which participated, not on the mass of North American pagans Here's Life was supposed to reach.

Here's Life went the way of Key '73, Evangelism in Depth and similar efforts before it. George Peters and Peter Wagner have shown that Evangelism in Depth had little real impact on church growth and that the major reason was that the effort did not grow naturally out of the normal life of local congregations.[6] This fact suggests that an ecclesiological issue is at stake.

The major justification for such intensive evangelistic campaigns as Evangelism in Depth and Here's Life is, of course, that local churches aren't getting the job done. Churches are failing in their evangelism. Therefore large-scale, broad-based, intensive efforts by some outside or overarching entity are needed to do the job, bring in the harvest and give churches a much-needed shot of spiritual adrenalin.

But the neglected issue here is the nature of the church itself. What concept of the church does our evangelism imply? The failure of Here's Life and similar efforts is not, fundamentally, a technical or programming flaw. The problem goes deeper than the matter of methods. It is time to stop talking about programming mistakes or faulty techniques and face a fundamental theological error concerning the nature of the church and therefore the nature of salvation itself. The truth is that no one can be joined to Christ the head without being joined to Christ's body. And the error is to think, first, that a person can become a Christian without being born into God's family in a visible way and, second, that evangelism can be authentic while ignoring this dynamic relationship of head and body.

We need to recover the classical doctrine that "outside the church there is no salvation"—but we must understand it biblically. Augustine was right to emphasize the close, inseparable relationship of head and body in the church. He was right to say the history of the church parallels the history of Christ, the head.[7] The problem with the classical view of "no salvation outside the church" is that it came to be understood institutionally and sacramentally rather than in terms of vital, visible participation in the community of God's people, where intimate fellowship with God is joined with intimate fellowship with the brothers and sisters who make up Christ's body.

Many reasons may be cited for our failures in evangelism, and all these should be examined.[8] My point here, however, is that evangelistic effectiveness begins with proper attention to the life and integrity of the congregation.

The Life-sharing Community Evangelism always has been and always will be an important priority of any church which takes the Kingdom of God seriously. This is so, not first of all because of a concern for growth, but because the church is called to participate in the mission of God. The Kingdom of God incorporates all things (Eph 1:10), but it centers in the allegiance of individual wills and lives to the person and lordship of Jesus Christ. The church has an explicit biblical mandate for proclamation, persuasion evangelism, informal sharing of the good news and incorporating new believers into the life of the Christian community. Biblical faithfulness means evangelistic concern. Any church which loses its heartbeat for evangelism and its awe of eternity is less than a generation away from spiritual impotence.

Beyond the biblical mandate, however, is simply the impulse of Pentecost—the motivating power of love and joy in Christian lives, which, by the agency of the Holy Spirit, impels Christians gladly to share what they have discovered with those who remain in darkness. Thus evangelism still is "one beggar telling another where to find bread."

Viewing the church as witness and life-sharing community, I would like to suggest seven propositions which are important in developing an evangelistic lifestyle. These are based on the assumption that evangelism is a proper priority for every congregation, but that this priority fits integrally into a web of intertwined priorities to be controlled by the fundamental calling of the church to glorify God and to be free for the Kingdom.

1. *The church's first concern in evangelism is to participate in the mission of God—to do the works of Christ and to work for the progressive manifestation of his reign.*

Jesus said his disciples would continue his work and would "do even greater things than these, because [he was] going to the Father" (Jn 14:12). These greater works presumably do not involve more dramatic or more powerful feats, but rather the extension of Jesus' ministry into all the world through the church. The reason Jesus' disciples would do greater works was that Jesus was going to the Father. Jesus said this in the context of repeated references to the Holy Spirit. He said, "It is for your good that I am going away. Unless I go away, the Counselor will not come to you; but if I go, I will send him to you" (Jn 16:7). The Spirit, Jesus said, "will testify about me; but you also must testify, for you have been with me from the beginning" (Jn 15:26-27).

Jesus came to do the work of the Father. While physically present on earth, he accomplished the work given him to do. With his death and resurrection came a new phase of his work. Before his resurrection Jesus was limited by space and time. The body of Christ was a physical, space-time body like yours and mine. But that body was broken on the cross so that salvation could be manifested and the church could be born. Just as the bread was broken and multiplied in the feeding of the thousands, so Christ's body broken on the cross provided for his new body, the church, which by his Spirit is multiplied into the whole world as the community of God's people.

So Jesus tells his disciples, in effect: "It is for your good that I am going away. Now I am limited by my physical existence. But in going, I will send the Spirit. I will be with you now in a new dimension. Now *you* will be my physical body, spread throughout the earth, indwelt by my very Spirit. You will do the works I have done, and even greater, for through you my presence and my operation will be spread and multiplied to the whole world. You are my witnesses! You are now my body, empowered by the Holy Spirit."

So the church's evangelistic mandate is at once Christological (tied to Jesus Christ) and pneumatological (tied to the Holy Spirit), with no divorce between the charismatic and ethical dimensions of mission. Empowered by the Spirit, the church is to do the works of Christ. "For we are God's workmanship, created in Christ Jesus to do good works, which God prepared in advance for us to do" (Eph 2:10).

There are several implications here for the church's evangelistic mission. For example:

Since the church is called to carry on Christ's mission, her main concern is not mere numbers but winning disciples and bringing disciples to Christlikeness and Kingdom involvement. By the same token, the church cannot be indifferent to numbers, for God is "not wanting anyone to perish, but everyone to come to repentance" (2 Pet 3:9).

Second, Jesus demonstrated and stated clearly that his mission was to "preach good news to the poor" (Lk 4:18). He showed special concern for the poor and oppressed. This immediately puts a biblical restriction on simply "going to our own kind" in evangelism, neglecting the poor and using homogeneous-unit thinking as the major factor in determining our evangelistic priorities. It warns us of the danger of simply going after those easiest to reach or most likely to respond.

A third implication of our calling to participate in the mission of

God is that God's mission covers all needs of all persons in all places. The mission of God is the Kingdom of God viewed as the economy of God. It is inevitably political, social and economic, even though (and precisely because) it is essentially spiritual. Therefore evangelism includes witnessing to God's truth and justice in all areas of life and society.

A speaker at the 1978 National Association of Evangelicals convention stated, "Certainly we are to be compassionate of the world's needs, and yet, our responsibility is to proclaim the Gospel of Jesus Christ."[9] But this statement already implies an unbiblical dichotomy. Showing compassion for the world's needs and proclaiming the gospel are not two different things. Every act of kindness and compassion and justice in the name of Jesus Christ *is* proclaiming his gospel, even though the gospel is not fully proclaimed until persons have been personally confronted with the truth claims of Jesus and their responsibility to accept him as Lord.

In our evangelistic lifestyle, we need a holistic witness that gives both depth and credibility to our proclamation and evangelism.

2. *Evangelism is sharing life, and the church cannot share what it does not possess.* Therefore a congregation's evangelistic fruitfulness will be in proportion to its spiritual vitality.

A major problem with Here's Life and any other form of evangelism that relies heavily on mass media is that the gospel message becomes disembodied. The truth is twice removed from reality. First, the gospel is separated from the context of demonstrated Christian community, which is already a step toward individualism and abstraction and a step away from demonstrated reconciliation between people. This creates the danger that becoming a Christian will be seen as unrelated to the whole web of relationships in one's life, that somehow one can be joined to the head without being joined to the body. This runs counter to Scriptures which say the Christian is born into the family of God.

In media evangelism the gospel is removed a second step from reality when it is presented either impersonally or in the pseudo-personal way of TV and radio. Prospective converts recognize that the TV evangelist does not really know them or their needs, so the words are hollow when the evangelist intones, "I care about *you!*" Such professions of love and concern must often come across to needy, suffering folks as utterly phony, no more real than advertising slogans such as "We do it all for you" or "You're the Boss!" We all have a built-in discount factor for such propaganda, and evangelism must reckon with this. More important, Christians compromise the integrity of the gospel when they broadcast it wholesale *as though* they were communicating directly and personally with individual persons in real-life situations. Media evangelism has a legitimate place, but only when Christians recognize its limitations and use it in a strictly secondary and supportive way.

Here's Life did, of course, attempt to personalize the gospel message through telephone and front-door contacts. But in most cases this contact either did not spring directly from the community life of the local congregation or failed to communicate the community-centered nature of the faith. "Finding it" must have been understood, in the vast majority of cases, as a purely individual, personal, mental decision, unrelated to becoming part of a distinct community of God's people or to changing one's behavior in light of God's Kingdom.

The point is not merely that evangelism must be personal or that it should be tied in with the local church. The more basic question is the authenticity and vitality of the local congregation itself. Regrettably, many churches simply have nothing to share with unbelievers.

This is true even of doctrinally orthodox churches. We may argue that as long as it has the Bible and correct doctrine, a church has the gospel to share. But gospel truths divorced from experience generally fail to communicate the intended message. The message may be received, but it is not comprehended as really being the gospel. Truth not clothed in life lacks the ring of authenticity.

A congregation must have more than correct doctrine; it must have spiritual life. It must be spiritually vital.

In other words, the authenticity and vitality of the congregation are themselves matters of evangelistic importance, and the gospel must be presented on the basis of personal relationships. The gospel is not primarily abstract truth but personal relationship with God through Jesus Christ. This will be best comprehended as we present the gospel on the basis of personal relationships and through personal relationships.

3. *Spiritual life depends on and is deepened by a vital experience of Chris-*

tian community. Genuine Christian community itself is evangelistic, and a church which is weak in community will be weak in evangelism —even though it may show "results."

Both Scripture and experience show the importance of Christian community for personal spiritual life and growth. Much of the dynamism of the early Christian church in Jerusalem was due to the fact that the believers "devoted themselves ... to the fellowship" (Acts 2:42), "were together" (Acts 2:44) and "broke bread in their homes and ate together" (Acts 2:46). They were discovering Christian community and in the process discovering more fully the meaning of the reconciliation they had received from God.

Soon the Jewish believers were to learn a deeper lesson in community and reconciliation. Gentile believers were also incorporated into the church. Later Paul was to say this was the very mystery of the gospel: both Jew and Gentile are reconciled in one body (Eph 2 and 3). Paul then went on to teach that God's plan is that the whole body of Christ, the whole Christian community, grow together and grow up into Jesus Christ, the head (Eph 4). Spiritual growth is described in terms of community, unity and the mutuality of service and gifts.

This is why the New Testament says very little about evangelism. It puts the emphasis on authentic Christian community, the reconciled life together that comes from being mutually joined to Christ and mutually growing up into him. The implication is clear: If the church is genuinely a reconciled and reconciling community, the Lord will add daily to its number those who are being saved.

The church must *be* good news in order to *proclaim* good news. It is certainly good news if ordinary men and women are growing in their relationships with God and with each other, if they are discovering new resources for everyday life, new direction and motivation for ministry, and deeper dimensions of what it means to share life and faith deeply with Christian sisters and brothers in intimate community.

This is not to say that a church weak in community will be unsuccessful in evangelism. Such a church may, in fact, show impressive gains statistically. It may see many people converted and added to the church rolls. But without genuine community, little discipleship will follow. New converts will come to church and claim allegiance to Christ, but little will change in their lifestyles. Their use of time, money and other resources will change very little. Their lives will present no real challenge to the built-in evils of oppression, prejudice and exploitation in society. Where community is weak, successful evangelism will do little more than speed the church's accommodation to surrounding society. Evangelism without community and discipleship may simply hasten the process of bringing the world into the church, rather than bringing the gospel to the world. This was true when the Roman population was nominally Christianized after Constantine and will always be true when evangelism is put ahead of the authenticity of the Christian fellowship itself.

Genuine community itself is good news. Community without Christ is not *the* good news, but *any* form of community is good news to one seeking a way out of loneliness and the depersonalization of technological society. This is the explanation of the interest and fascination today in all forms of community—communal living, sensitivity groups, false cults and other forms of groupness. People hunger for real community. Often they hunger for *structured* community. People have their defenses to keep from getting hurt, so they may shy away from chances to become involved in community. But at a deep level, all human beings yearn to be a part of a close-knit fellowship of others who know them, who care about them and with whom they can share all aspects of life. This is true because we are all created in the image of God. As meaningful family life declines, this need for community becomes increasingly pressing. So the church that neglects the understanding and experience of genuine Christian *koinōnia* does so at its own peril. And it compromises its evangelistic witness as well.

By contrast, the congregation that demonstrates deep caring and community increases the credibility of its evangelistic witness. When onlookers can say "Behold how they love one another!" they can more easily believe that God is love.

This implies that in evangelism congregations must give attention to building deep Christian *koinōnia* not only for its own sake, but as part of their evangelistic strategy.

4. *Evangelism is enriched and empowered by a vital experience of worship.* We may not often think of the link between worship and evangelism, but it is key. If nothing happens in worship, not much will

happen in the church's witness. Much of the dynamism of the charismatic renewal derives from the joy and power believers experience in worship.

I am not suggesting that churches should plan "dynamic" or "exciting" worship services so that people will feel good and visitors will want to come back and eventually join the church. This smacks too much of promotion and manipulation. I am pointing to the priority of worship itself among the church's purposes.

Worship is directed first of all toward God, and worship must lead us to encounter God—who he is, what he demands, what he offers, what the conditions of his covenant with us are. Worship is crucial for evangelism, not primarily as a way of attracting nonbelievers to God (although genuine worship will do this), but because in worship believers come to see the world from God's perspective and come to share the divine impulse for doing the works of Christ. This kind of worship both impels believers outward in witness and, by God's Holy Spirit, empowers that witness to be effective in the world (Acts 1:8).

The church that is serious about participating in the mission of God and doing the works of Christ will take seriously the priority of worship. We can accomplish the work begun by Jesus only if we have the same consciousness of God's presence and power that Jesus had.

5. *God gives some people gifts for evangelism and evangelistic leadership. Therefore effective evangelism depends on identifying, recognizing and using these gifts.* Here we must refer again to Ephesians 4:11-13: "[God] gave some to be apostles, some to be prophets, some to be evangelists, and some to be pastors and teachers, to prepare God's people for works of service, so that the body of Christ may be built up until we all reach unity in the faith and in the knowledge of the Son of God."

At first glance the role of evangelist in this passage may appear unclear or not directly related to bringing unbelievers to a knowledge of Jesus Christ. But note carefully what Paul is saying. First, God's people are prepared for ministry, and the body of Christ reaches maturity by the harmonious functioning of all leadership gifts—apostle, prophet, evangelist, pastor, teacher. The gift of evangelism functions in conjunction with other gifts. Second, an evangelist is not merely one who wins people to Christ. He or she is one who leads the people of God in evangelism. An evangelist is a person specially, charismatically gifted by God to bring others to Jesus Christ, to announce the Kingdom of God and to lead others in doing the same.[10]

As this happens, God's people are equipped for ministry and the body of Christ is strengthened. Thus "the whole body, joined and held together by every supporting ligament, grows and builds itself up in love, as each part does its work" (Eph 4:16). Here is growth coming from the proper functioning of each member and each spiritual gift.

Evangelists, then, are equippers in two senses. First, they help others become witnesses. Second, they help build the body by contributing to its normal, healthy functioning.

The congregation concerned to witness effectively will therefore give attention to the matter of spiritual gifts. It will identify those with the gift of evangelism so that the evangelistic witness of the church can be extended. And it will be concerned with the exercise of other gifts as well, understanding that the proper functioning of all the gifts together allows the church to become the growing, functioning body described in 1 Corinthians 12—14, Romans 12:6-8 and Ephesians 4:11-16.

How can the church make this teaching about spiritual gifts practical for its evangelistic witness? First, the church should understand what the Bible teaches concerning the gifts of the Spirit. Solid biblical teaching in this area is important. With this can be joined a study of the outreach of the church as recorded in the book of Acts.

Second, the church should expect God to awaken various gifts in the congregation and should watch for these, looking for sparks of interest or initiative which may indicate spiritual gifts.

Third, gifts grow out of the community life of the church. In community, gifts are awakened, discovered and facilitated. Therefore the church needs to involve its members in various forms of small-group structures so that community can be fostered and spiritual gifts can spring forth.

Fourth, those who appear to have evangelistic gifts should be encouraged and trained to use their gifts effectively. This means helping them understand their gifts, giving them training and experience in evangelism, and freeing them from other responsibilities so that they can concentrate on the gift-ministry God has given them. (Peter Wagner suggests that in most congregations, about ten per cent of the members normally have the gift of evangelism.)[11]

Fifth, since evangelism needs to be joined with nurture and discipleship, the congregation must also work to develop gift-ministries —teaching, exhortation and others—that will help new converts become growing disciples.

Finally, the congregation should provide partial or full-time economic support for people with demonstrated gift-ministries. We should rid ourselves of the automatic "pastor equals full-time salary" equation and think rather in terms of multiple charismatic ministries in the congregation. If the congregation employs anyone full-time or part-time, it should be those whose ministries have become so crucial to the life and witness of the congregation that the church decides to provide for the full-time exercise of these ministries. Such forms of service may be pastoral, evangelistic, missionary, social or of other varieties, depending on the life, needs and opportunities for ministry of the particular congregation. The point is that the church should put its resources behind the ministries that are most crucial to its life and most significant for the Kingdom.

Through thus recognizing and facilitating the exercise of spiritual gifts, the alert congregation will discover widening possibilities of outreach and ministry.

6. *Conversion begins a lifelong process of spiritual growth, discipleship and sanctification toward the restoration of the image of God in the believer. Therefore, evangelism must lead into this growth, and the congregation should make provision to facilitate it.*

Biblically-based evangelism does not focus exclusively on the death and resurrection of Jesus Christ. Rather, it sets these crucial events in the context of Jesus' earthly life and of his present reign. The fact that in Jesus "we have redemption through his blood, the forgiveness of sins" (Eph 1:7) is part of God's economy "to bring all things in heaven and on earth together under one head, even Christ" (Eph 1:10). Or, as Paul says similarly in Colossians, God has "rescued us from the dominion of darkness and brought us into the kingdom [or reign] of the Son he loves, in whom we have redemption, the forgiveness of sins. . . . For God was pleased to have all his fullness dwell in him, and through him to reconcile to himself all things, whether things on earth or things in heaven, by making peace through his blood, shed on the cross" (Col 1:13-14, 19-20).

In this Colossian passage, Paul goes on to say that God wills "to present you holy in his sight, without blemish and free from accusation" (Col 1:22). So he says, "We proclaim [Christ], admonishing and teaching everyone with all wisdom, so that we may present everyone perfect in Christ" (Col 1:28). As "in Christ all the fullness of the Deity lives in bodily form," so "you have been given fullness in Christ, who is the head over every power and authority" (Col 2:9).

Focusing on Jesus' life and reign, as well as his death and resurrection, we see that God's concern is not only to rescue us from hell and redeem us for heaven. It is also to re-create within us, and in the life of the congregation, "the fullness of Christ." It is to restore the image of God in our lives and relationships. Bringing all creation to harmony and order under the headship of Christ begins with bringing all believers to harmony and Christlikeness through the discipling and sanctifying work of the Spirit of Christ in the church.

For the church as witness, this means evangelism is never an end but always a beginning, or rather, part of a continuing cycle of life and growth in the body of Christ.[12] Therefore the congregation must be as concerned with those processes and structures in the body which bring spiritual growth and maturity as it is with the work of evangelism itself.

We may discern a three-step process here: (1) Individual persons must be brought to the lordship of Christ, *so that* (2) the church can grow up into Christ, experience his fullness, be formed in his image and acknowledge his reign, *so that* (3) the whole creation can be freed from its bondage to decay and be set free in joyful subservience to the God of the universe. So we keep our eyes on the larger goal, and we join evangelism to the larger work of acknowledging Christ's lordship in every area of society and culture. Thus evangelism is crucial for the church's Kingdom work and witness.

7. *A congregation's structure reflects the actual priorities of the church and its leadership. Thus, if evangelism is a priority in the congregation, this will be reflected in church structure.*

A church's structure is a clear indicator of what the congregation considers important. It is an illuminating exercise to examine church structures, including official and unofficial patterns of operation and organization, leadership, budgets and financial policies, and church property and facilities. We cannot guarantee vitality or renewal by the way we structure a church. But a church can be structured, actively or passively, in ways that nearly guarantee that it will have little life or witness.

We can identify both a negative and a positive side to this matter of structure. On the negative side, we are faced with the effect of human fallenness on all our structures. Structure is always an adaptation to the space-time context in which we find ourselves. Just as architecture partakes of and reflects the culture of its period and place, so organizational and doctrinal structures are rooted in their historical-cultural setting. This is not bad; it is simply true.

Structures become obsolete or restricting for at least two reasons. First, because of their roots in past culture, structures tend to be static even though culture is dynamic. Second, because of human sinfulness, structures have a warp that subverts the very purposes they were intended to serve. These two factors are inseparably linked because the culture that forms the context for all structures already is fallen and, at important points, demonic.

This whole problem can be reduced in seriousness, however, if we pay attention to the kind of structures we create and the fundamental models or images on which structures are built.

Here the difference between an institutional/organizational or organic/charismatic model of the church becomes important. If we understand the church primarily as an institution, we will probably adopt (often unconsciously) structural patterns which presuppose that the church should operate as other institutions do, on the basis of formal structures, hierarchy, delegated authority and impersonality. But if we see the church organically as a functioning body, our structures will tend to be more flexible, informal, person oriented and useful for mission. A basic source of confusion and frustration in the church today is that many of us give lip service to an organic/charismatic understanding of the church while in fact our structures presuppose an institutional/organizational understanding.

On the negative side of this problem of structure, we need to look carefully at structure to see whether it is helping or hindering the life and witness of the congregation. Do our structures tend to choke off whatever life the congregation has? If so, we need to dismantle those structures. On the positive side, we need to ask ourselves whether we have appropriate structures to carry out the witness we claim to believe in. If structures reveal our priorities, we need to develop structures which really help the congregation accomplish the goals we consider important.

I do not mean to betray the principle that form follows function. We do not necessarily move closer to effective ministry just because we create structures intended to extend our witness. Our rationale for putting up a worship center in a growing community may be that we hope to minister to the community. But the structure may instead become a barrier between us and other people, and thus between us and ministry.[13] We very easily get the structural cart before the ministry horse. Witness and service spring from the effervescent life of the Christian community. If the life is not there, our structures will only entomb our deadness. But where ministry and outreach are already happening, we can extend that outreach by appropriate structures, conducive to the nature of the church as the community of God's people.

This happened in the New Testament church. Three examples are the pattern of home meetings referred to in Acts 2 and 5, the "Acts 6 principle" of differentiating between different kinds of ministry based on priorities and recognized gifts, and the appointing of elders in local congregations. These patterns were appropriate to the community life of the church, compatible with the culture of the day and functional in the church's life. Ministry was already beginning to happen; Christians were worshiping, witnessing and serving. And as growth continued appropriate structures were, with differing degrees of self-consciousness, adopted.

The implication here: Existing structures need to be examined for their appropriateness for evangelism. Do our structures propel us into ministry or insulate us from it? Financial, architectural, organizational and even doctrinal structures all should be examined with this question in mind.

At this point we question the heavy involvement of most churches in property and buildings. Here is a major blind spot in the life of the contemporary North American church that seriously compromises the church's credibility, vitality and witness.

With little or no questioning of basic priorities, many churches move quickly into major commitments in real estate. In a society where church property is not taxed and where substantial financing is often available through ecclesiastical or other sources, it is all too easy for a congregation to tie itself so heavily to property and buildings that its sense of mission and of being a pilgrim people is seriously compromised. The church mortgages not merely its property; it mortgages its ministry and future.

Consider this: A church of some five hundred members decides it needs a larger worship facility. It is growing slowly, mainly by transfers from other churches. The congregation features a dynamic pastor and excellent programming in many areas, although they have almost no outreach either in evangelism or in social witness and very little *koinōnia*. But since they are seeing some growth and are financially prosperous, they decide to build a new facility. Options such as double worship services or starting a second congregation are not even considered. The congregation votes to launch a multiphase building program with an eventual price tag of over one million dollars.

My purpose here is not to throw stones at sacred cathedrals, crystal or otherwise. It is simply to raise the question of priorities. To emphasize my point, let us consider the following hypothetical situation.

A congregation of some five hundred members becomes concerned about the problem of famine and spiritual darkness in the world and its own affluence in an age of poverty and hunger. What can be done? A group is appointed to study the matter. After careful consideration, the group proposes that the congregation launch a major fund drive, mortgage its property, and ask for cash and pledges in order to raise one million dollars for famine relief, evangelism, and technical and agricultural assistance to increase food production in needy countries. What happens? It is not hard to guess. The sanity of those advocating such a course would be seriously questioned. Go into debt by hundreds of thousands of dollars to take care of people halfway around the globe? Preposterous! Impractical! Poor stewardship!

And yet, without blinking an eye or examining a priority, the same congregation will tie up its resources and determine its focus for years to come by launching a major building program with dubious justification from the standpoint of God's economy. Such realities raise deep questions about the sense of mission and awareness of priorities of our congregations. They point us back to Matthew 6:33.

These are matters of the church's authentic witness. The church's fascination with buildings and property today, so reminiscent of the Middle Ages, reflects the materialism and comfort-orientation of the majority of North American Christians. It testifies to the shallowness of our experience of community as well as our misunderstanding of the church and the Kingdom. And of course, when it comes to *church* buildings—often mistakenly called "houses of God" —whatever critical faculties we have are further blunted by a sacralist mentality which says expensive buildings are justified because they are dedicated to religious purposes or "God's glory." Surely God deserves the best! We forget that God does not live in temples made with hands (Acts 7:48), but in the lives and relationships of the Christian community; that Jesus left heaven itself to live and serve among the world's poor, preferring suffering people to celestial palaces or terrestrial temples. The community of God's people is the temple of God (2 Cor 6:16), not our fine structures of glass and concrete. Kingdom priorities dictate that we bend our efforts and our faith toward turning the world into God's temple and house (*oikos*), not in building little sanctuaries where we wall off God from the world.

A fundamental issue of ecclesiology is at stake here: *How is the church visible?* If the true church of Jesus Christ is visible at all, it must be as Jesus and the early church were visible: through people, through demonstrated community, and through deeds of love and service. Significantly, whenever the church has had its greatest impact on society, it has been visible to the world not through buildings or institutions but through people and community—just as was true of Jesus.

When the church is visible mainly through buildings, it faces at least three problems: (1) its buildings become a barrier between the world and life-giving Christian community, masking the true nature of the church before the world; (2) the church is therefore faced with the task of convincing the world that the church really is something more dynamic than buildings and institutions; and (3) the church is almost forced to some kind of theory of the "true, invisible church" to explain the discrepancy between its profession and its visible manifestation. When the church is understood and visibly embodied as the community of God's people, these problems are largely resolved.

I see no way of softening this seemingly radical critique and yet remaining faithful to the biblical vision of the church existing for the liberation which springs from and signs forth God's Kingdom.

Again, the point is not to criticize buildings but to raise questions about structural priorities. What we do with buildings is merely a sign of our attitude toward structure in general and our understanding of the economy and ecology of the Kingdom.[14]

As the congregation comes alive to witness in the world, the question of appropriate structures for evangelism needs to be asked. Identifying and encouraging spiritual gifts for outreach will go far toward answering our structural questions and suggesting viable forms. The place to start is with provisions that will help those gifted in outreach carry out their ministries.

Here's Life, America was one major attempt to provide an effective structure for evangelism. In that sense it was a good idea. The problem, as we have seen, was that it did not grow out of the community life of local congregations. Further, it failed to zero in on identifying and using spiritual gifts, it was not sufficiently based on communicating the gospel through personal relationships, it was overoptimistic about what could be accomplished through mass media, and it was divorced from the proclamation of the Kingdom. In short, the problem was an ecclesiological one.

Structures for evangelism, do, however, have their place, as we saw in examining the ecology of the church in chapter three. Even large-scale mass evangelistic efforts are useful, provided these are conceived and carried out with integrity, are tied functionally to the life of local congregations, and are not oversold. We need a healthy dose of modesty regarding just what can be accomplished through large-scale efforts, especially those which rely heavily on mass media. And we need a clear perception of the dangers and superficialities of creating a mere media church.

We must stress once again what the church of Jesus Christ is: the community of God's people, the body of Christ, Jesus' disciples who continue his work, God's chosen agent of the Kingdom of God in the world. We must learn what it really means to think spiritually-ecologically and what the real environmental impact of the church is. How often we forget or betray the essence of the church in the ways we attempt to minister! Though it sounds trite, it still remains true that the evangelistic effectiveness of the congregation is based on its truly being the living and growing community of the people of God. This is the church which is free for the Kingdom.

True, the church's witness is broader than evangelism, as I have noted throughout this book. Much could be said here about the church's witness on questions of justice, peace and other Kingdom priorities. But if the church today is the Kingdom community, basic to these concerns is the priority of evangelism. Understood from the perspective of the economy and Kingdom of God, evangelism means freeing people and the church for God's work in the world.

three

THE CHURCH
FOR THE KINGDOM

8

THE MINISTRY
OF ALL BELIEVERS

Call it revolution or reformation—the church's understanding of ministry is changing radically.

Ministry is in crisis today. Seminarians say they don't feel called to the traditional pastoral role, and young men and women in pastoral service tell me, "I feel I don't fit here." A young man with an M.Div. degree, two years out of seminary, wrote, "My wife and I just don't feel at home here. We have lots of questions about the traditional pastoral role we're placed in, and we feel isolated." He was serving as assistant pastor, working closely with the senior pastor and with a group of people who know and love the Lord. But he felt something was out of focus and out of gear. He felt he was spinning wheels instead of building community.

This is not an isolated example. Several currents are combining to challenge and undermine the traditional pastoral role. The cultural consensus that perched pastors on a pedestal and made them useful chiefly for "taking the curse off" social gatherings, as one pastor friend puts it, is now fortunately breaking down. While most seminaries still operate on a professional school model (the religious counterpart to a legal or medical school), here and there that model is being challenged. Biblical images of pastors as equippers and disciplers are beginning to yeast their way into the church. On the other hand, in many local churches the expectation, both official and unofficial, is that the pastor is the professional religionist, the expert, not the equipper and catalyst. The pastor is the one who does the religious work for the people, not the one who turns "laymen" into ministers.

Often we fail to feel the force of our models. We expect doctors to treat us, not to train us to treat others. We expect lawyers to give us expert advice, not to admit us to the secret fraternity of those who understand how the legal system works. Likewise, we want pastors to serve us, not to build and train us. But this is the wrong model, biblically speaking. Jesus explicitly rejected the religious and legal professional model of his day when he talked about ministry (Mt 23:1-12).

Some Examples from History   When people hear that someone is a minister or is "called to the ministry," they automatically think of the ordained pastoral function. In this kind of thinking, the worst thing that can be said of a pastor is that he has "left the ministry." In some cases, however, that person has in fact just entered the ministry.

Protestants have always held, at least theoretically, to the doctrine of the priesthood of believers. For the most part, however, this doctrine has been understood soteriologically rather than ecclesiologically. That is, it has been understood to mean that all Christians have direct access to God without the mediation of a human priest. But the implications of this doctrine for Christian ministry have seldom been drawn out. Perhaps the reason is that these implications radically call into question the clergy-laity split by asserting that all believers are priests and therefore ministers.

And yet, if we trace centuries of church history, we find that renewal has often accompanied a widening understanding and practice of Christian ministry. As the church institutionalizes, it narrows its view of ministry to the point where only certain people at certain times with certain training can perform God's real work. But in renewal movements, both pre- and post-Reformation, ministry that was restricted to a certain place, time and people often broke through those barriers and was given anew to the whole body of Christ.

One example is the Franciscan revival. When Francis heard that he should go and preach the gospel, he thought that's what he should do. So he went about, unordained, preaching the gospel to the poor. He touched both a raw nerve and a deep hunger. Soon thousands of young men and later young women were actually ministering Jesus' love, following Francis's example. They did this within the church, and yet knowing that their practice was in part a judgment on the church.

Many other examples could be cited, ranging from early reform and monastic movements in the church's first several centuries to the evangelical revivals of recent centuries to the Confessing Church in Nazi Germany and many house fellowships and Christian intentional communities today. When the Holy Spirit softens the church, he breaks down the barriers to ministry.

My purpose here, however, is to set the ministry question in a biblical framework. What would a biblical understanding of Christian ministry really look like? It certainly starts with the fact that all Christians are the people (laity or *laos*) of God. And it therefore cannot avoid questioning the clericalism and professionalism that have encrusted the church's understanding of ministry for centuries.

If we take our questions concerning ministry to the Scriptures, we find rich material from several perspectives. It seems to me that three of these perspectives interlock into a threefold basis for Christian ministry. This basis has been valid ever since the institution of the new covenant and is especially significant for the understanding and practice of the ministry of God's people today.

The three foundation stones for the ministry of God's people are the priesthood of believers, the gifts of the Spirit and the servanthood example of Jesus.

The Priesthood of Believers　　The key passage here is 1 Peter 2:4-9. Peter says that believers are "being built into a spiritual house to be a holy priesthood, offering spiritual sacrifices acceptable to God through Jesus Christ." The church is "a chosen people [*laos,* or "laity"], a royal priesthood, a holy nation, a people belonging to God," called to "declare the praises of him who called [it] out of darkness into his wonderful light."

In coming to know Jesus Christ, believers became part of the body of Christ, the church. Under the high priesthood of Jesus the church itself is a priesthood. In 1 Peter, the author refers to Exodus 19 where Moses was about to go up the mountain to receive God's law.

God said to Israel, "Now if you obey me fully and keep my covenant, then out of all nations you will be my treasured possession. Although the whole earth is mine, you will be for me a kingdom of priests and a holy nation" (Ex 19:5-6). The whole nation of Israel, not just the tribe of Levi, was to be God's priesthood. God's plan was that his people would represent him to the world. They would be the channel of his revelation and his salvation purposes. This was God's commission to Israel. Although Israel often was unfaithful and the commission was only partially fulfilled, God's purpose was clear.

This background gives us a fuller understanding of New Testament references to the priesthood of believers. The meaning of priesthood in the Old Testament was narrowed finally to Jesus Christ, the Messiah who has become our great high priest (Heb 3—8). But in Jesus Christ the priesthood has been expanded to include the whole people of God, fulfilling God's original intent. With the birth of the church, the old clerical priesthood was set aside, for a new high priest had come. Jesus, king of justice and king of shalom, came as God's Son, not through the Levitical priesthood (Heb 7:1-10). And the whole church, the whole people of God, is his priesthood. So the church is a kingdom of priests, a priestly kingdom. The church is a priestly people set free for the Kingdom of God.

This spiritual priesthood means at least three things for the ministry of God's people today. First, it means, as the Reformers said, that *all believers have direct access to God.* We may "approach the throne of grace with confidence" (Heb 4:16). Since Jesus is our high priest, we don't have to go through a human priest to come to God. The way to God has been opened directly through Jesus Christ.

This, however, is only part of the meaning of the priesthood of believers. An overemphasis on this point can lead to excessive individualism. The priesthood of believers then is taken to mean that since we each have direct access to God, we don't need each other. This is a distortion which fails to see the full meaning of priesthood for the church.

A second, balancing truth is that *we are priests to each other.* We are not just individual priests; we are a *priesthood,* just as the church is a body, a people and a nation. The church is a fellowship in which each person serves as a priest to the others.

I am thankful for brothers and sisters in the church who have been priests to me. Some were pastors, but many were not. Archie, who ran the grocery store and always greeted people at the church door on Sunday mornings, was a priest to me. So were many friends, teachers and ordinary saints in the body of Christ. They probably didn't realize it, but they were priests to me personally. They represented Christ to me.

As a priesthood, then, the church is not a collection of isolated priests, each going separately to God, but is a community of priests. We have this ministry together, to be priests to each other.

A third truth, however, is equally important. *Priesthood is not just for the internal life of the church; it is for the world.* As priests, Christians are God's missionaries and servants for others. The job of a priest is to represent God to the people and to represent the people to God. So the church is Christ's body in the world, charged and empowered to represent God to the world and to bring the world to God. This again traces back to the Old Testament, where Israel was to be God's agent before the nations.

The church, then, is God's priesthood in the earth. It is commissioned to be heralds and servants to the world, and to gather up the world's burdens and concerns and present them to God in prayer and intercession.

Biblically, this is the first foundation stone for understanding the ministry of God's people. From the perspective of the priesthood of believers, every believer is a minister. Every believer is a priest, with access to God, responsibility to others in the body and a ministry in the world. This is not the full picture, however. One foundation stone is not enough. We must join the priesthood of believers with the fact of spiritual gifts.

Gifts of the Spirit The key passage here is Ephesians 4:1-16. The passage speaks of the unity of the church—one faith, one Lord, one baptism. Throughout the passage the themes of unity, diversity and mutuality intertwine. After the initial stress on unity, a contrasting theme is introduced in verse seven: "But grace was given to each of us according to the measure of Christ's gift" (RSV). The context indicates that Paul is not referring here to the grace by which believers are saved, but rather to the particular grace God gives his people for ministry.

In chapter three of Ephesians Paul says he had been given a particular grace, a special gift, for ministry. Now in chapter four he says this is true of all believers, although our ministries vary. He is saying, in effect: Now that you have been saved by grace, you need to understand that God continues to give you grace—grace for ministry. The principle and power by which you were saved is the principle and power by which you serve. The church operates by grace *(charis)* through the gifts of the Spirit *(charismata)*.[1] The church is charismatic because it is *saved* by grace and *serves* by grace. As believers, we are all one in Christ, all part of the body, the community of God's people. God shares his grace with us from the fullness of Christ. God's fullness in Christ is not exhausted by the new birth; it includes abundant resources for ministry through the charisms or gifts given to the body. As John Arndt wrote, "Christ lives and works in all the members of his body so that each one might receive of his fullness (Jn. 1:16), for he as the head has all the fullness of all and each gift."[2]

Paul says that God intends the church to "grow up into him who is the Head, that is, Christ." The church "grows and builds itself up in love, as each part does its work" (Eph 4:15-16). And each part does its work, to some extent, through the exercise of the full range of spiritual gifts.

What does it mean to attain "to the whole measure of the fullness of Christ"? (Eph 4:13). Note that this passage is addressed to the whole body, not to individual Christians. No Christian can grow into the fullness of Christ except as he or she is part of a growing, maturing body. It is the whole believing community, not the individual believer, who reaches Christ's fullness, and the individual believer reaches that fullness only in the environment of a maturing community of believers. Such is the ecology of the church.

This is where spiritual gifts come into proper focus. As gifts are recognized and exercised, each part does its work in the body. When each believer discovers God's particular manifestation of grace in his or her life for ministry, then the body grows and builds itself in love. Paul plainly teaches that spiritual gifts are basic to the healthy life of the church and to redemptive ministry in the world.

We learn by looking at Jesus when we consider spiritual gifts. In Jesus we see almost all the gifts mentioned in Scripture. Jesus Christ was an apostle, a prophet, a pastor, a teacher, a healer. He called and pastored his flock of disciples, the embryonic Kingdom community. Many of the gifts specifically mentioned in the New Testament are exemplified in Jesus. Why? Because Jesus Christ is the fullness of God. All gifts are found potentially in Christ, and from him flow spiritual gifts as the Spirit animates the body of Christ. No one believer is going to have all the gifts, for only Jesus is the fullness of God. Most believers will have one or two gifts, or however many God wants to give. Paul says in 1 Corinthians that the Holy Spirit determines the distribution of gifts (1 Cor 12:11). It is not up to a general conference or church council to give or restrict gifts. "Now to each one the manifestation of the Spirit is given for the common good" (1 Cor 12:7). No one can exercise all the gifts, but in community all the necessary gifts will emerge through the Spirit's work. And through all the necessary gifts working and mutually supporting each other, the whole body grows into the measure of the stature of the fullness of Christ.[3]

More is involved in the fullness of Christ, and in growing in him, than simply the exercise of gifts. Sanctification, discipleship and growth in Christlikeness are all involved. This discipling, perfecting emphasis balances the stress on spiritual gifts within the ecology of the church. In Scripture the gifts of the Spirit are not divorced from the fruit of the Spirit. Christian character is not divorced from charismatic power. In the past some have emphasized the gifts, particularly the more dramatic ones, without a sufficient corresponding stress on sanctification and the building of Christian character. In contrast, others have insisted that gifts were for the early church only, that the important things now are love and sanctification, with no emphasis on gifts. But Scripture holds the charismatic and discipleship dimensions together. And they belong together, both logically and practically, for in God's economy gifts assist the body to grow in Christlikeness, and increasing maturity helps gifts function more effectively and redemptively. This is precisely what Ephesians 4 is all about. The church quenches the Spirit when it fails to make enough space for the exercise of the gifts God gives.

Regrettably, this is all too often the case. For the church to quench the Spirit would seem to be a contradiction in terms. But apparently it is not, for Paul warns against it (1 Thess 5:19).

The contemporary church does not believe profoundly in the biblical doctrine of the gifts of the Spirit. Such a broad generalization obviously requires significant qualification to fit the various branches of the church, but as a general description of contemporary Protestantism, especially in Europe and North America, it fits quite well.

According to the New Testament, the Holy Spirit gives various specific, useful gifts to the church—apostles, prophets, evangelists, pastors, teachers, and other gifts such as healing, administration, tongues, and so forth. This is clear from 1 Corinthians 12, Romans 12, Ephesians 4 and other passages. Much of the church has long functioned, however, on the implicit assumption that these passages have no real importance today. At least this is the impression one gets in comparing these passages with present-day corporate-style Christian churches, organizations and denominations.

In many local churches one sees little evidence that it is the Holy Spirit who has appointed various persons to specific ministries. Too often we do not find every joint working together so that nothing is lacking and the whole body is built up in love. Why?

There is a reason, and it is crucial. The New Testament assumes *certain preconditions,* and where these preconditions are lacking, New Testament results will not follow. Paul's teachings about the gifts of the Spirit assume a New Testament view of the church. Those teachings make little sense when transplanted into a highly institutionalized concept and practice of the church. Today, the Holy Spirit is often hindered in his ministry of distributing and igniting gifts among the members by traditional church structures. And so church structure quenches the Spirit. For example:

The Spirit-led church chooses its leaders according to each member's gifts. The institutionalized church chooses leaders according to how many positions it takes to run the organization.

The Spirit-led church chooses those who are spiritually most mature and qualified. The institutionalized church chooses some of questionable spirituality in the hope that more responsibility will help them grow spiritually.

The Spirit-led church involves all to the limit of their capacity and according to their gifts. The institutionalized church piles responsibilities on the few with special gifts for organization or promotion and considers others as incapable of significant service.

The Spirit-led church enlists all who can make a contribution to the Kingdom, while the institutionalized church enlists only those who can maintain or extend the church's institutional life. And so, whatever its dynamism, it is not free for the Kingdom.

In the church for the Kingdom, the motto is not maintenance but mission, not survival but service. In the institutionalized church, the Kingdom dynamic has been domesticated, and the saints have lost the ability to see a difference between Kingdom service and organizational self-preservation.

How do institutionalized church structures quench the Spirit? In the following ways, at least:

☐ By defining *service* and *ministry* in organizational terms.

☐ By splitting the body of Christ into "clergy" and "laity."

☐ By a building-centered program.

☐ By organizational, instead of personal, ministries.

☐ By institutional, rather than spiritual, goals, rewards and measures of success.

☐ By the evangelism-social action split which blinds believers to many potentially crucial Kingdom ministries or calls those ministries into question.

☐ By insensitivity to the fundamental ecology of the church.

As a second foundation stone for the ministry of God's people, the gifts of the Spirit suggest three important things. First, *all ministry is by God's grace.* This truth is fundamental in the New Testament, and it is beginning to dawn on the church in new ways today. Redemptive ministry for the Kingdom is not a matter of training, intelligence, experience or ordination, even though all these have their place. These considerations are secondary to God's ministering through human agents by his own grace. The importance of other considerations may vary widely according to the context, but ministry by grace is the normative and constant reality.

Second, *God gives a wide variety of ministries,* all of which are important for the Kingdom. The early church understood spiritual gifts as meaning a variety of ministries, as we see from 1 Peter 4:10-11 and Hebrews 2:4. With gifts, diversity and mutuality are the point. We see here how the gifts and the fruit of the Spirit go together.

All Christians are to manifest all the fruit of the Spirit, but not all believers are to have the same gifts. We are all to have love, joy, peace, patience, self-control. It is not right for me to say that I have no love but plenty of joy, or that I have no peace but much patience. But with gifts, the matter is different. I may be a prophet but not an apostle, or I may have the gift of evangelism but not of healing. The point is Spirit-given diversity and functioning mutuality in the body, not uniformity. The picture is that of the human body. The body is not all hands or all feet. The church is to be like a human body, not a centipede or an octopus. The Christian community is a functioning, balanced body of different gift-ministries, all according to God's intentions and the manifestations of his Spirit.

Third, *every believer has some ministry.* Every believer has at least one spiritual gift which is to be put to work for Kingdom purposes. The biblical understanding of the church is revolutionary. It tells us that every person in the church is created in God's image, every person is a gift, and God gives every person gifts for eternally significant ministry. When even one God-given gift fails to operate, to that degree the Kingdom of God is diminished and the church's ecology is twisted. In Christ, individuals are not cogs in a great machine or boxes in an organizational chart, but living, God-imaged *persons* capable of showing forth something true and lovely about God. A person may be warped, twisted, sick, retarded, handicapped, oppressed or dispossessed. But the church for the Kingdom is a healing, helping, lifting, liberating community where the Spirit shines through our twistedness and lights the way to the Kingdom.

In the institutional view, people have value because of what they can do. Talented people are worth more because they can do more; others are worthless because they perform less. But in the biblical view, everyone has value because each person is created in the image of God. Through the work of Christ and the healing life of Christian community, God makes ministers of us all. What about the handicapped and the mentally retarded? God knows how to take those warped and impaired by circumstances or sin and how to use them as instruments of grace in his Kingdom. All of us have been warped by sin, both our own sin and the accumulated sins of society. Yet God knows how, in the body of Christ, to take even those who are worthless to society and make them instruments of his grace. This high view of personhood is basic to the scriptural understanding of who God is, who we are and, therefore, what the church is.

Linking the priesthood of believers with the gifts of the Spirit, we find they clarify and reinforce each other. Both point to the same truth: Ministry is for all believers. All are priests; all are gifted. But spiritual gifts add a complementary truth. While priesthood tells us all believers have a priestly ministry, it does not tell us how believers' ministries vary. Here gifts help. Believers carry out their ministries differently, according (in part) to the gifts they receive from God.

Servants of Christ   The third foundation stone for the ministry of God's people is the call to be servants of Jesus Christ. To be a minister in the church means to be a servant. This underscores the practical significance of the church as servant, the model we explored in chapter six.

A key passage here, though many others might be cited, is Matthew 20:25-27. "You know that the rulers of the Gentiles lord it over them, and their high officials exercise authority over them. Not so with you. Instead, whoever wants to become great among you must be your servant, and whoever wants to be first must be your slave— just as the Son of Man did not come to be served, but to serve, and to give his life as a ransom for many."

Jesus says, in effect: If you are going to be my disciple, you must function differently from the world's way. The model is not hierarchy but servanthood. Ministry is service, and greatness is Christlikeness.

This foundation stone also suggests three things for the ministry of God's people. First, *Jesus is the model for ministry*. We do not have to look elsewhere, and anything we learn elsewhere must be corrected by Jesus' example.

Jesus shows us the spirit in which ministry for the Kingdom is to be carried out. When we follow Jesus, priesthood does not become professionalism and gifts do not become self-gratification. In our ministry we are to have the mind of Christ, following his self-emptying, serving example (Phil 2:1-16). Like Jesus, we are to take the form of a servant. Christ's body is to be the servant church for the sake of the Kingdom.

Second, *success is measured by faithful service.* It is required of servants that they be found faithful (1 Cor 4:2). The standard in the church is not faithfulness *instead of* success. Rather, in the ecology of God's plan, faithful service is the only way to Kingdom success. Jesus illustrated this in his parables of the Kingdom.

The standard of success is different in the church from that in the world because God's Kingdom operates fundamentally by grace, not by technique, and through the building of community, not empires. God the King is the source of both the power and the wisdom which bring the Kingdom. As we serve him in the spirit of Christ, we serve the Kingdom. He has given us the secret of the Kingdom, and the secret is service.

Third, servanthood suggests that *we are to do the works of Christ.* As we saw in chapter seven, doing Jesus' work is an essential part of the church's Kingdom witness. As Jesus, empowered by the Spirit, did the works of the Kingdom, so the church today, empowered by the Spirit, is to do the works of the Kingdom. And the works will be even greater than those Jesus did; for God's Spirit now works in the church, and the church is spread throughout the world.

We are not, then, left with blind faithfulness. We are not to do our will but God's will. We are not to build human empires but God's Kingdom. We are not to serve earthly powers but God's power. We are not to do simply whatever seems good to us but to discern the mind of Christ. What we see Jesus doing in the New Testament, this we are to do as servants of God and his Kingdom today.

These, then, are three foundation stones for the ministry of God's people. They fit into the overall ecology of the church which we have been exploring throughout this book. Christians are priests of God and servants of Christ, gifted by the Spirit.

Note the shift here from the Old Testament to the New. In the Old Testament, *some* of God's people were priests; now *all* are priests, fulfilling the original design. In the Old Testament, *some* people were special servants of God; now *all* believers are servants of Christ. In the Old Testament, *some* people were occasionally gifted by the Spirit for special tasks; now *all* God's people receive gifts of the Spirit. The drift of church history has often been to reverse this: to restrict ministry and charisms, and certainly authority, to a select priesthood or clergy. But in the ecology of the Kingdom all believers are priests, servants and gifted ministers.

These three foundation stones form an interlocking basis for Christian ministry today. They all say the same thing: *Ministry is for all believers.* Every believer is ordained for the ministry. To be a member of the body of Christ is to be a minister.

This does not, of course, answer all questions about Christian ministry. But it provides a basic perspective from which to deal with specific questions. It suggests the direction any valid reformulation of the church's understanding of ministry must take. Some further implications and applications of this fundamental perspective will be explored in the last section of this book.

The basic point is that God wants us *all* for his Kingdom. In a church of one hundred members he wants one hundred ministers, not one, five or ten. And this will be a functioning reality if we see what Kingdom ministry is and agree with Scripture that the church is a ministering community in which every believer is gifted, called and empowered.

Just how far does liberating all God's people for ministry extend? It reaches even to doctrine, lighting the fuse for the liberation of theology. To this we now turn.

9
THE LIBERATION
OF THEOLOGY

The fundamental crisis of the church today is a crisis of the Word of God and of Christian community—the Word and the church. Conservative Protestantism needs as radical a recovery of the Word of God as liberal Protestantism needed at the turn of the century. But it also needs a radical recovery of the experience of the church—a recovery of genuine Christian community lived in the light of God's Kingdom. In short, the church must become a community of the Word in a way it has never been before.

I am not speaking here primarily about the crisis of Scripture or the battle over the Bible, though this is important and is part of the picture. I refer rather to the crisis of the Word of God which goes beyond Scripture. Together with other branches of the church, evangelicals need to recover—or rather, be recovered by—the Word of God in a way that will dynamically combine a high view of Scripture with a compelling view of Jesus Christ, the living Word, in the context of a fundamental experience of Christian community—the Word lived out in the light of the Kingdom. Here is a key to liberating the church.

The church must be liberated through the Word to be free for the Kingdom. Part of this liberation concerns theology. The church is a theological community, a people who seek to understand and obey what God is saying. This involves a theological task.

But how can Christians do theology without betraying, rather than serving, the church? More basically, how can the church reflect theologically in such a way that it moves toward, not from, faithfulness to God's Word?

Theology and Community The church has a theological task. Scripture itself shows that Christians should and must reflect carefully on the nature of God and his work in the world. The point is that this task is given to the church *as a community and a people*. This means at least five things.

1. *Theological reflection is a necessary and proper fruit of the church's life together.* This is true because of the nature of God, creation and Scripture.

God is beyond reason but not irrational. The world has order which reflects reason and balance. The creation of man and woman in God's image accounts for the remarkable human capacity to think, reflect, theorize and conceptualize, to order phenomena and mental processes. Seen as the recovery of the image of God in human personality and relationships, salvation necessarily involves growth in our mental comprehension of God, his plan and his activity in the world. So Paul speaks of his "insight into the mystery of Christ" (Eph 3:4) and prays that the Ephesian Christians might not only be rooted and grounded in love but might also have "the Spirit of wisdom and revelation" (Eph 1:17) so that they can comprehend the whole economy *(oikonomia)* of God (Eph 3:16-19). Scripture both endorses rational theological reflection and insists that God's truth is not known truly and fully unless put into practice.

Traditionally, the church has viewed theological reflection as a highly individualistic enterprise. Theology has been understood as the work of individual theologians reflecting on their own faith and experience of God. Frequently it has had little connection with the actual community life of the church. Properly understood, however, theological reflection is the work of *the Christian community*. This is so because people experience God most fully in Christian community and are called to carry out their obedience in community. While each person has his or her own personal encounter with God, we come to know him most fully through the communal experience of the body of Christ in worship, *koinōnia* and ministry. To be born again is to become part of a new people, a new community, a new social reality—the body of Christ. The reality and depth of community experienced by individual believers largely determine the reality and depth of their experience of God. The tradition of solitary saints is not the Christian ideal. Perhaps a person can maintain a kind of spiritual life and growth all alone. But the whole biblical emphasis on the church teaches that Christians are a new people, a new community that lives the life of the Kingdom and does the work of God in ways that would be impossible on a purely individual basis.

Since believers experience God in Christian community, it follows that the Christian community *as community* ought to be engaged in theological reflection. The Christian community should be the matrix where mind, will and emotion join in harmonious balance. Part of the church's worship, *koinōnia* and witness should be a conscious probing of who God is, what he has done and what his revealed plan is for the church and the world. We should stretch our minds and creativity to the limit in attempting to understand and articulate the nature of Christian faith and life.

Acts 2:42 says the early believers in Jerusalem "devoted themselves to the apostles' teaching and to the fellowship, to the breaking of bread and to prayer." Whatever else was going on, this must have been a fruitful time theologically. The believers heard and explored the apostles' doctrine. We can see from Acts something of what this doctrine or teaching was. It must have been the repetition of what Jesus had taught the Twelve, but it was more. It explained Jesus' life, death and resurrection in the light of Jesus' own teaching, the Old Testament Scriptures, and the fact and experience of the church as it was coming into being. Peter combined these elements at Pentecost, giving meaning to the Pentecost events by referring to Old Testament prophecies and God's action in raising Christ from death. So the apostles' teaching naturally involved biblical revelation; the life, death and resurrection of Jesus; and the continuing experience of the Christian community, the church.[1]

As the experience of the early church illustrates, theological reflection is both inevitable and legitimate. The theological task of the Christian community is summed up in Peter's statement, "This is that..." (Acts 2:16). *This,* our present experience of God's reality and our perception of his activity, is to be understood in the light of *that,* God's previous revelation of himself.

The church needs to recover the ecclesiological bearing of theology. Theology must be seen not as an esoteric science to be practiced by those academically initiated into theological knowledge but as the normal reflective activity of the Christian community, part of its normal spiritual life and growth, as the church seeks to understand its place and mission in God's world. Theology is the *church's* activity of faith seeking understanding.

2. *The theological task is entrusted to the whole Christian community,* not just to professional theologians. The church is the body of Christ, not a corporation with a theological R & D department. The constant tendency in the church is to fall back into what John Howard Yoder calls the "professional religionist" mentality—to reduce the essence of the faith to a hidden, special *gnosis* open only to a special class which then dispenses this knowledge to the unenlightened.[2]

This mentality has unfortunately become widespread in the church. It is the counterpart in theology to the professional clergy mentality in the church's pastoral ministry. Just as we continue unbiblically to split up God's people into clergy and laity, so we unbiblically distinguish between "the teaching church" and "the learning church." We forget that Christ himself, and Christ only, is the head of the church, and that he has promised to be with the church in the continuing presence of the Holy Spirit guiding us into all truth. The promise of the Spirit's guidance was given to the whole Christian community, not to professional theologians.

The entire Christian community, including each local Christian assembly, should be theologically aware. Each community of believers should be engaged in theological reflection, not necessarily formally or in learning the jargon and subtleties of academic theology, but in becoming aware of God's overall plan for creation and in seeing conceptual growth as part of spiritual growth. We need more "lay" theologians, rank-and-file Christians who understand and can share profoundly about God and his work in us, preferably in simple language. Here theology and evangelism come together.

3. *God calls some believers to a special ministry of theological leadership.* This is a balancing truth that qualifies to some degree what I have just said. The Christian community should recognize and encourage members who have special gifts for theological work and leadership.

Theological leadership may be understood in terms of spiritual gifts. Paul's statement that the church is "built on the foundation of the apostles and prophets" (Eph 2:20) has theological implications, and both apostle and prophet are identified as charismatic gifts. Doubtless other gifts also have significance for theological leadership.

Theologians, then, should be those who are spiritually gifted for this task. Whatever other preparation and training they may have, they must be men and women of God who have the needed charism for theological work—a charism not synonymous with office, but based on God's action through his Spirit and confirmed by the Christian community. As a "gift-bearing and gift-evoking community," to borrow a phrase from Gordon Cosby, the church watches for signs of God's charismatic graces in its members and encourages and enables each individual to find the ministry God intends. In the words of Peter, "Each one should use whatever gift he has received to serve others, faithfully administering God's grace in its various forms. If anyone speaks, he should do it as one speaking the very words of God. If anyone serves, he should do it with the strength God provides, so that in all things God may be praised through Jesus Christ" (1 Pet 4:10-11). Only in this way does the church "reach unity in the faith and in the knowledge of the Son of God and become mature, attaining to the whole measure of the fullness of Christ" (Eph 4:13).

4. *The nature of the Christian community itself must be a fundamental consideration of theological reflection.* This is part of what I mean by the "ecclesiological bearing" of theology. Just as the theological task is committed to the whole church, so the nature of the church should be a basic concern of theological thought.

This, again, is so for at least two reasons. In the first place, the church is the special place of God's activity in the world. Despite its unfaithfulness, we are still confronted with the mystery of the church. God is working through it (Eph 3:10). Theology arises because the church must give an account of itself. So it was at Pentecost, and so it has always been when the church has significantly shaken surrounding society with gospel power.

Second, the church must seek to understand itself biblically and theologically because of its life in history and culture. Part of the mystery of the church is its existence at the very intersection of space and spirit, time and eternity, the invisible and visible worlds. In a strange way, the church appears as a time-bound, social institution even while it is the body of Christ. For this reason, the church is always uniquely faced with the challenge of infidelity. It is always in need of reform, always in need of being called back to biblical faithfulness.

Although the church is more than community and the communal nature of the church could be overemphasized, it is crucial that we recover an understanding of the church *as community*. Like other humans, Christians are social beings. Their views and behaviors are largely socially determined. We are influenced and formed by the culture around us. Church members will quite predictably be squeezed into the mold of the world unless the church is such a dynamic community that it can withstand the pressures of society. We have seen a massive accommodation of the church to the world simply because the church is not a sufficiently intense countercultural community to maintain biblical fidelity. And evangelicals and fundamentalists are certainly not immune here. Fundamentalist political activity and priorities often breathe more the spirit of the world than the atmosphere of the Kingdom—just as is true of the liberal side.

5. *Theology takes its place among other functions of the church's life, activity and creative expression.* Theological reflection is only one way of comprehending reality, and for some aspects of the church's life it is not the best way. I am thinking here of the role of art, music, drama, various forms of literature and other kinds of creative expression. Some truths about God or about human life can be comprehended through music or visual art in ways that theology is incapable of. This, again, underscores the need for theological reflection to be woven into the community life of the church, intimately and dynamically joined to the whole worshiping, sharing, serving ecology of the Christian community. Theology will be enriched and made more useful and biblically faithful through continuing fertilization by the total creative life of the church. At the same time, theology thus enriched can add meaning and depth to other forms of creative work. And in the process, theologically gifted persons may learn new and better ways to do theology. Biography, story and

other forms of narrative will be used more extensively as modes of theology. Theology will breathe more the spirit and atmosphere of Scripture itself and will be less an arid and abstract theoretical science.[3]

The church is in the world as the agent of the Kingdom of God. Since God is working through the church to reconcile all things to himself, all things are properly the concern of the body of Christ. Theology can help the church live up to its calling if Christians will see and experience theological reflection as the necessary and legitimate fruit of the community life of the church.

Theology and Scripture   If the fundamental crisis of the Christian community is a crisis of the Word of God, then Scripture must be a fundamental concern for the church. Since God has spoken uniquely and authoritatively through the Bible, the church's theological reflection must be based on Scripture while being open to all truth.

In the introduction to his *Gnomon,* the German Pietist scholar J. A. Bengel wrote,
Scripture is the life of the Church: the Church is the guardian of Scripture. When the Church is strong, Scripture shines abroad; when the Church is sick, Scripture is imprisoned. Thus Scripture and the Church exhibit together the appearance of health, or else of sickness; so that the treatment of Scripture corresponds with the state of the Church.[4]

If Bengel is right, the health of the church and the power of Scripture in the church are linked. Scripture fails to play its proper role in the church's life to the extent the church is not truly the community of God's people. I have argued that the church is a theological community, a fellowship of believers who endeavor not only to do the work of God but to understand what that work is. But the church can do this only if it is faithful to the Word as revealed in the Bible.

The church has tended both to individualize and to intellectualize the Bible. That is, it has seen the Bible too narrowly as a repository of doctrines concerning individual Christians' relationship to God. In so doing the church has often overemphasized rational belief and underemphasized corporate fidelity to God's Word.

The Bible itself suggests a viewpoint that underscores the corporate nature of God's people and the key role of the written Word in forming and sustaining the church. This is the perspective of Scripture as the book of the covenant. From this perspective (which we will discuss further in the next chapter) may arise a fuller understanding of the proper function of the Bible in the life of the church. Two affirmations need to be made in this connection.

1. *The Bible functions as the normative authority in the church's life, but in conjunction with reason, experience and tradition.* The Bible—not reason, experience or tradition—establishes the church's covenant relationship with God and determines what fidelity to God means. But God also reveals himself in creation and on the plane of history. Therefore reason, experience and tradition also become useful tools in understanding and interpreting Scripture. Given the unity and consistency of the divine Being, we confess a fundamental consistency between Scripture and other sources of knowledge. On the basis of the biblical testimony itself, however, we confess that reason, experience and tradition all bear the marks of sin in a way that Scripture does not, so that our fundamental faithfulness to God must be on the basis of Scripture. The Bible must be the judge of human reason, experience and tradition.[5]

The church lives by the Spirit and the Word. The Word of God is not dead or static, even in its written form (Heb 4:12-13). The Holy Spirit remains alive and active in the church. In the life of the church it is not Scripture alone which is the Word of God, but Scripture interpreted to us by the Holy Spirit. The living and active Word cannot be confined to a book. But God wondrously reveals himself in such a way that, by the action of the Holy Spirit, the written Word both is and becomes to us the very Word of God.

Here again, we are brought back to the reality of the Christian community, the church. The Christian community experiences God's action. It seeks to live in fidelity to the Word of God, and in so doing creates a tradition. It reflects on and reasons about God and his action. All this is part of the life of the church. And in the midst of this life, the church is called to remember the covenant God has made and recorded with his people. The final question is whether the church has lived in obedience and fidelity to that covenant.

2. *Because of the nature of God and his creation as revealed in Scripture, theology must recognize all truth as God's truth.* Theology seeks and claims all truth for God. No truth frightens it. We have seen that

in the real ecology of God's plan, every dimension of reality is interconnected. So every truth, properly understood, is part of the larger
Truth of God. Challenge and adventure come in sorting out the
strands and connections that make up the economy of God.

Here theological reflection should follow the pattern already revealed in Scripture. Many of the biblical writers recount God's action
in creation and history and then show how this action fits into God's
overall plan. The psalms speak of God's entire creation and describe
all things as expressing God's glory. The Revelation sees the whole
realm of nature, and even evil itself, as finally fitting into God's
scheme of things. All that *is* says something about God, and all things
are to be claimed for God and his Kingdom.

Here again, it is important that theological reflection be carried
on as a function of the church *as community*. The body of Christ includes artists, musicians, scientists, engineers, doctors, lawyers,
sociologists, psychologists, historians, astronomers and many other
specialists. Often the church and its theology do not benefit from
these vast resources of knowledge and expertise. All these resources
need to be brought into the Christian community and should feed
into the church's theological reflection. The work of Jacques Ellul
shows how fruitful a sociological and legal perspective can be in pur-
suing creative theological work. How enriched the church would be
and how much more likely it would avoid the obscurantism that has
often plagued professional theology, if it would truly become a theological community! This is true at the local level, but it also applies
to the church worldwide as an international, multicultural community of believers.

The perennial danger, of course, is that the church may take a
particular philosophical, scientific, psychological or other perspective as the key to interpreting Scripture and the church's life and
witness. There is no final safeguard against this danger. But a variety of perspectives feeding into the church's self-understanding
tends to minimize the danger. As the church genuinely becomes the
community of God's people, living in real *koinōnia* and depending
daily on the Spirit and the Word, it is more likely to use the world's
resources of knowledge to enrich, rather than undermine, its theological reflection and covenant fidelity.

In the final analysis, the church's greatest resources for theological reflection (beyond the Spirit and the Word) are the persons who make up the Christian community and their experience of life together. Resources of knowledge and expertise gained through education are useful, but often the greatest and most practical wisdom comes from simple, plain folks who have little formal education. Here we must affirm again the priesthood of believers. The church especially needs the simple, the unlettered and the poor in its theological work. Often their wisdom is what makes theology fly. Even, or perhaps especially, in theology, it seems true that "God chose the foolish things of the world to shame the wise; God chose the weak things in the world to shame the strong. He chose the lowly things of this world and the despised things—and the things that are not— to nullify the things that are, so that no one may boast before him" (1 Cor 1:27-29).

The glory of the church is its being a reconciled community of diverse persons, gifts, cultures and experiences, melded together by the Holy Spirit. Out of this mix, out of this praxis and life together, creative and redemptive theology comes.

Theology and Fidelity *Theological reflection in the Christian community seeks the fidelity of the people of God.* The primary aim of theological reflection is that the church be faithful to God and faithful in its Kingdom tasks, that it be true to the covenant and economy of God.

1. *Theology must speak both to the world and to the church.* Theology is by nature comprehensive and will have something to say in both directions. The renewing power of the Word of God in the world often depends first, however, on the church itself being called back to covenant fidelity.

The church has nothing to say to the world—and no power to change it—unless it has spiritual power within. As Clark Pinnock observes,

In the realm of the Spirit the critical factor is spiritual power, not human intelligence. We are often attracted by the novel theology which comes up with a brilliant fusion between the Bible and something contemporary. But this is not what God is after. He desires us to be faithful stewards of his Word, who do not seek glory in this age, and do not value what man thinks above what God has said, but open ourselves to his Spirit, walk by faith and not by sight, and proclaim the Gospel with fearlessness and undiminished power.[6]

We may think here of the Old Testament prophets or of the letters to the churches in Revelation. The church always carries the seeds of its own renewal through the presence of the Spirit and the Word. Though obscured at times, the Bible is a continuing seed of renewal in the church, a ticking time bomb that once enlivened by the Spirit's new action shakes the church and calls it back to covenant fidelity. So it was when the book of the Law was rediscovered during Josiah's reign, and when Ezra read the book to the people and renewed the covenant with Israel's remnant. So it has been down through the long ages of church history when a fresh discovery of the Word has launched renewal in the form of new orders or other renewing movements such as Anabaptism, the Reformation, Pietism or Methodism.

The theological task of the Christian community is to live continually by the Word in its total ecology of worship, *koinōnia* and witness. Theology is truly prophetic in the church and in the world only when it is based on renewed faithfulness to the Word of God on its own terms, not on a capitulation to the world's perspectives.

2. *Theology must, however, engage the mindset of the age.* It will not do this with biblical fidelity simply by formulating new theological speculations. Rather it will do this, if at all, by repeatedly opening up a new perspective the world does not see—or rather, revealing a divine perspective the world has lost.

Jacques Ellul writes, "The Church should always be the breach in an enclosed world."[7] Jesus Christ ripped a huge hole in the veil of human philosophy and speculation. The church at its best has always opened an expanse before humanity's view of the world. When faithful to God, the church has been a window on a supramaterial world—in other words, a window on reality and the full ecology of God's plan.

Christian theology should be to the world as Christian worship is to the church. In worship the Christian community sees through the temporal mists and is reminded of the greater reality of God and his creation. In engaging the mind of the world, Christians must be able to point out false gods and open breaches in an enclosed world. The church must repeatedly rip the fabric of space-time materialism and show the larger, truer reality which alone gives final meaning to physical existence. Every real act of love does this, and so does true theology. This is part of what it means to think ecologically.

The church, however, can do this only as the Holy Spirit is at work in and through the Christian community. The church cannot sustain or reveal a perspective it does not see. If the life of the Christian community does not demonstrate that Christians actually know and live by a fundamentally different view of reality than that of the world, whatever words it proclaims will fall to the ground like hollow shells.

Since the days of the early church the experience of Christian community has both nurtured and verified the truth of the church's proclamation. Genuine human community has an appeal all its own. It exercises a fascination on the mind and inflames the fires of idealism.[8] But the only basis for truly human, truly loving community is the gospel of Jesus Christ. Only the demonstration of this kind of Christian community will grab the world's attention long enough to engage its mind. To win the world the church must capture both its heart and its head, and this requires theology born of and ratified by visible Christian community.

3. These considerations suggest, finally, that *theology must grow out of and call the church to faithful discipleship.* If biblically faithful, theological reflection will call the Christian community to discipleship and will be deepened by the experience of discipleship.

Throughout Scripture God's people are warned of the ills that will befall them if they violate the covenant with God, and of the blessings that will be theirs if they are faithful to the covenant. And throughout biblical history God sent his prophets to recall his people to covenant fidelity. So also today, faithful reflection on revealed truth and on the present experience of God's people will recall the church to discipleship—to covenant obedience.

It is no accident that calls for more radical discipleship are issuing precisely from those Christians who are discovering more radical forms of Christian community and *koinōnia.* Many of the most disturbingly prophetic voices today come from the growing number of Christian intentional communities. And some communities, such as Sojourners Fellowship, Reba Place Fellowship and the Missionaries of the Common Life, have discovered that the earnest effort to be prophetic in the world has led them to a deeper understanding of the nature of the church as community.

But this is nothing new in church history. To think of people like Thomas Merton or Avery Dulles is to recall the long history of Christian communities and the great thinkers and prophets who have discovered new depths in the Christian tradition from within the experience of religious orders or communities of various kinds. Men like Augustine, Aquinas, Gregory of Nyssa, Richard of St. Victor and many other creative thinkers and writers, women as well as men, worked in the context of close community.

This is not, of course, to agree with everything such people wrote nor to endorse any one style of Christian community as the necessary form for Christian *koinōnia* or theological reflection today. The point is that many expressions of intentional community in the history of the church have been attempts at more radical discipleship, and from these attempts have often come fresh and vigorous theological work which has sparked wide-ranging renewal in the church. We could add as well the experience of the early Anabaptists, the Moravian communities, or the fresh voices and perspectives that arose from the recovery of deeper *koinōnia* and discipleship in the Pietist, Quaker, Methodist and similar movements. So also much of the creative theological work of Dietrich Bonhoeffer grew out of the intense experience of the Confessing Church under Hitler.

My point, again, is not to hold up any one form of Christian community as a norm for the church. Doubtless there are many faithful styles of discipleship, and any style is acceptable that brings people into vital contact with God and each other and that is able to sustain Christian life and witness in biblical fidelity. My concern is the frequent lack of truly biblical community in the church today. We must discern the dangers of accommodation to the surrounding society which a lack of biblical community raises for the church. We face the likelihood of the betrayal of the church and the prodigality of its theology unless more radical and intense forms of Christian community and discipleship are recovered by the church at large.

A Critical Choice Modern culture presents the church with a choice. It is not an easy choice, for the (North) American way of life is still very attractive. It is still quite possible to make it, to succeed handsomely by looking out for number one. It is relatively easy for evangelical Christians to reach and maintain a way of life marked by affluence, consumption, comfort and status if this is their goal. And it is quite as easy for the church to be nothing more than the institutional religious reflection of such a lifestyle.

The church faces a difficult choice: To follow the way of easy affluence that leads almost inevitably to spiritual poverty or to take seriously the demands of the gospel and become a covenant community that risks taking a countercultural stand at every point where Christian faithfulness is at stake. My concern is that Christians choose the second option. Unless we do, our theology as well as our life will finally betray the Lord we profess. We will be found working against the very economy of God.

Through the resources of the Word, the world and Christian life together, the church can be a dynamic theological community that continually offers a new but faithful word to the world and to itself. This is an important part of liberation for the Kingdom. Today every believer needs to be part of a dynamic, alert, caring, reflecting community of believers that faithfully speaks and signs forth the promise of the Kingdom of God.

10

THE BOOK
OF THE COVENANT

The church that is free for the Kingdom is subject to Scripture. Biblical authority, however, is mired in controversy today. Donald Bloesch speaks of "the present impasse in evangelical circles concerning the authority of Scripture."[1] While most Christians subscribe to biblical authority in some form, definitions of what this means vary widely.

Discussions about biblical authority are bound to go awry if they do not focus on the Bible as *the book of the church*. Western culture has tended to make the Bible either a private devotional book or a textbook of doctrines rather than the book that defines, establishes and sustains the church's life together. Regardless of how high a view of Scripture one holds, if the Bible is not seen in its primary function in the life of the church, it will fail to truly be the Word of God as God intends.

My thesis in this chapter is that seeing the Bible as the book of the covenant both clarifies the function of Scripture in God's plan for the church and provides a way around the current impasse over biblical authority.

The Language of Sacrament Donald Bloesch proposes a way of understanding Scripture that is quite similar to what I am suggesting when he speaks of "a sacramental understanding of revelation." Bloesch distinguishes three basic approaches to Scripture in church history: the scholastic, the liberal-modernist and the sacramental.

The liberal-modernist view sees revelation as "inner enlightenment or self-discovery" and represents a compromise with modernist presuppositions that undermines biblical authority. The scholastic approach "understands revelation as the disclosure of a higher truth that nonetheless stands in continuity with a rational or natural truth" and sees the Bible as "a book of revealed propositions which are directly accessible to reason and which contain no errors in any respect." Bloesch, however, argues for the sacramental approach. This view "sees revelation essentially as God in action and regards Scripture as the primary channel or medium of revelation. Here Scripture is thought to have two sides, the divine and the human, and the human is the instrumentality of the divine." Bloesch contends that such a sacramental understanding of Scripture was common to Augustine, Calvin, Luther, Spener, Jonathan Edwards and others.[2]

In applying the language of sacrament to Scripture, Bloesch uses a way of speaking that makes it possible to affirm the Bible's full authority and infallibility without locking oneself in to exclusively rational and propositional categories. A sacramental understanding leaves room for mystery—a recognition that the Bible both is and becomes God's Word in a way we cannot fully explain—precisely because it is *God's* Word and not merely human words. "We need to recognize anew," Bloesch argues, "the element of mystery in revelation, which was generally acknowledged by the church fathers and Reformers. . . . Our language about God can be at the most analogical, not univocal, for there can be no direct or exact correspondence between human ideas and the veritable Word of God. It is also imperative for us to reaffirm the mystery of the accommodation of the Holy Spirit to the deficiencies and limitations of human language."[3]

Bloesch maintains that Scripture is infallible because in Scripture "all the words are selected by the Spirit of God through his guidance of human authors; and . . . the truth of God is enshrined in and mediated through these words. The Bible is the Word of God in all that it teaches, though this teaching is not immediately self-evident but must be unveiled by the Spirit."[4] Thus Bloesch's emphasis is on "the infallibility of Word and Spirit" rather than the infallibility of original manuscripts.

The written word partakes of divine infallibility because it is grounded in the incarnate or revealed Word, Jesus Christ. Moreover, it is an effectual sign of the revealed Word in that it serves to communicate the significance of this revelation through the power of the Spirit. There is a union, but not a fusion, between the written word of Scripture and the divine word of revelation.[5]

In sum, a sacramental understanding of revelation holds that "Scripture is a divinely-appointed means of grace and not simply an earthly, historical witness or sign of grace. . . . Scripture is inseparable from the revelation which produced it and which flows through it but . . . the words of Scripture in and of themselves are not divine revelation." Bloesch believes the current impasse regarding biblical authority could be overcome if the church returned to such a sacramental understanding.[6]

Such an approach is appealing because it is rational without being rationalistic. It upholds the authority of Scripture finally on the basis of faith in who God is, not primarily on the basis of faith in Scripture itself. It affirms all that the Bible affirms about itself without having to claim more than this. In using the language of sacrament it maintains both the authority and the mystery of Scripture. The Bible is the Word of God in the way sacramental bread and wine are the body and blood of Jesus. More than simply symbolizing God's revelation, Scripture is actually a means of grace, an "effectual sign" through which God authoritatively speaks to us.[7]

It was essentially this understanding of scriptural authority for which the Pietist scholar J. A. Bengel argued, partly in reaction to Lutheran scholasticism. As we noted in the last chapter, Bengel saw Scripture as intimately tied to the life of the believing community: "The treatment of Scripture corresponds with the state of the Church." Bengel also comments regarding the Bible, "It follows that those who have been intrusted with so great a gift, should use it properly. Scripture teaches its own use, which consists in *action*. To *act* it, we must understand it, and this understanding is open to all the upright of heart."[8] In other words, God's Word is available to all sincere believers, and their proper understanding and use of it will result in obedient action. This thrust cuts against both an elitist and a purely intellectual or theoretical understanding of Scripture.

Another aspect of the sacramental understanding of Scripture is particularly important for the church today. Sacrament is a connecting concept. In a way that the scholastic and liberal-modernist approaches do not, the sacramental understanding links the Bible to the church. In this view Scripture is a means of grace in the church, not primarily a repository of doctrine (though it is that) or a mere testimony to God's acts in history. In the sacramental approach the Bible is the book of *the life* of the church.

Precisely for this reason, it is helpful to think of the Bible as the book of the covenant. Scripture functions as a means of grace when it serves as an instrument for the church's faithfulness, when it constitutes and upholds the church as the people of God. Here we return to the Old Testament and to the way Scripture originally functioned in the life of God's people.

The Bible as Book of the Covenant   The Bible gives us the basis for the covenant relationship between God and his people. This was true with ancient Israel, and it is true for the church today.

Note how the writing down of God's law functioned in the time of Moses:

When Moses went and told the people all the LORD's words and laws, they responded with one voice, "Everything the LORD has said we will do." Moses then wrote down everything the LORD had said.

He got up early the next morning and built an altar at the foot of the mountain and set up twelve stone pillars representing the twelve tribes of Israel. Then he sent young Israelite men, and they offered burnt offerings and sacrificed young bulls as fellowship offerings to the LORD. Moses took half of the blood and put it in bowls, and the other half he sprinkled on the altar. Then he took the Book of the Covenant and read it to the people. They responded, "We will do everything the LORD has said; we will obey."

Moses then took the blood, sprinkled it on the people and said, "This is the blood of the covenant that the LORD has made with you in accordance with all these words." (Ex 24:3-8)

Here the book of the covenant is the written record of the agreement between God and his people, the basis upon which Israel is constituted a people and on which this people will be either blessed or cursed.

This, by extension, is the way Scripture functions in the life of the Christian community. The Bible witnesses to God's action and

promises in history. It records the basis upon which God has cove-
nanted to be *our* God and upon which we may faithfully be his people. The Bible is God's contract with the church.

Viewed from this perspective, the primary consideration regarding Scripture is not its inerrancy but its authority in the church and
the church's response in obedience. To use the analogy of an employment contract: The primary concern is not accuracy in detail
(though that is important) but whether or not the contract faithfully
records the basis for agreement and the commitment of the two
parties. So it is with Scripture. As the book of the church, the Bible
faithfully records for us who God is, how he has acted in history,
and what his faithfulness will mean for the church in face of the
church's fidelity or infidelity to God.

The church confesses that the Bible *is* a faithful record of God's
action and self-revelation in history, and it is encouraged to find that
as time passes the historical accuracy of Scripture is more and more
attested by extrabiblical evidence. But this is secondary. The primary conviction of the church is that God has constituted a people
for himself on the basis of his action throughout history and supremely in the life, death, resurrection and reign of Jesus Christ.
Thus the concern of the church must be to *be* the covenant community of God in faithfulness to Scripture.

This is not to imply, however, that it is unimportant how we understand scriptural authority, or that it is fruitless to deal apolo-
getically with the questions of biblical inspiration and authority. The
point is, we should understand Scripture on its own terms and in the
light of the function for which God has given it.

From the perspective of the New Testament, the Bible is the book
of the new covenant—the covenant through which God's word
is written not merely on stone or paper, but on the heart by the
Spirit. The issue today is that the church understand and heed
what God is saying to it. Because God has seen fit to create the material world (and thus history), and because he has seen fit to work
out the economy of redemption on the plane of history, it is reasonable and appropriate that he has given us a book, written by human
hands, which records his actions and reveals his character and will.
The Bible is a genuine mystery and miracle of both divine and
human action.

Authority and Historicity From this perspective, the question of fidelity or infidelity to the covenant is a more fundamental consideration than the question of inerrancy. Questions concerning the inspiration and infallibility of Scripture are inescapable and must be dealt with. But in the perspective of the book of the covenant, these issues appear rather as the problems of *authority* and *historicity*.

At heart, Christians affirm the authority of the Bible, not on the basis of its inerrancy, but on the basis of God's being and character as disclosed in Scripture. The fundamental presupposition for the Christian is not, or should not be, that the Bible is true. That is to begin with a bibliology from which one then derives a theology. This runs the risk of making God dependent on a book and one's faith in God dependent on one's view of Scripture. Rather, the Christian begins with the conviction that God is and acts. "In the beginning God created," Scripture says. This we believe—not just because the Bible says it, but because we have met God in Christ, and the Scripture's testimony is consistent with what we have learned of God through Christ. Our confidence rests in God, not on the authority of a book or on any one theory as to how the book was inspired.

Biblical authority, then, derives from God's authority. It is not too much to say that the Bible has no authority *in itself.* That would be superstition. The Bible's only authority is God's authority. The Bible is authoritative for us because God has chosen to speak through it. God has chosen to communicate his character and will to humankind through the written Word and through the incarnate Word. We need claim no other authority for the Bible.

This line of thinking by itself could, however, lead to a mere existentialist understanding of Scripture, which says the Bible is the Word of God only in the sense that it provides the situation or circumstance through which one actually encounters God. This can become a subjectivist morass with no basis for any rational understanding of biblical authority. One may be left with no solid criteria outside one's own personal experience for taking the Scriptures seriously in all they affirm.

The affirmation of authority must therefore be tied in some way to the question of history and historical accuracy. The question of historicity or facticity is important. Christians take history seriously, and therefore they must take the historical character of the Bible seriously. A strong inerrancy position may be as unhistorical as a strong existentialist view if it fails to take Scripture on its own terms as a product of divine-human cooperation down through history and as the record of historical happenings. Far from fearing the historical character of the Bible, biblical Christians should delight in it! We rejoice that God has revealed himself historically, both in historical events and in the recorded witness to those events.

Since the Bible is a historical book, the question of historicity is important and is tied to the question of authority. Something is wrong if the Bible does not bear truthful witness to God's real activity in history. It would be contradictory if, on the one hand, certain historical happenings had salvation significance but, on the other hand, the Bible gave an unreliable account of those happenings. We must recognize, of course, that the Bible uses phenomenological language; we must take into account differences in cultures; we must not apply modern conceptions of historical or scientific accuracy to biblical times. But with these allowances, we must expect the essential historical accuracy of biblical accounts. Only an unhistorical understanding of Scripture could affirm its authority on the one hand and its historical unreliability on the other.

Fact and Faith   Historicity and authority correspond to the concerns of fact and faith. Ultimately the church affirms biblical authority by faith. But this faith is not cut off from or inconsistent with fact.

The way God speaks to us through Scripture is illustrated in the way Jesus spoke to his followers. To the Jewish crowds—the uncommitted, curious ones wondering whether Jesus was the Messiah—Jesus spoke parables. He didn't answer all their questions; in fact, he raised more questions in their minds. Through his parables and discourses, as well as his acts, he gave people enough information and insight to kindle the spark of faith. But he never so proved his identity as to make faith unnecessary. He *under*whelmed his hearers. The reason is clear: Jesus wanted commitment, not just assent; changed hearts, not just changed minds. Jesus could have bombarded the crowds with facts and powerful acts so that they would virtually have *had* to believe him. Instead, he spoke parables and performed signs. Likewise, after his resurrection he could have given overwhelming proof to everyone that he was the risen Messiah. But he didn't.

The book of the covenant is something like that. God has revealed himself in history, in space and time. Much of the Bible is historically verifiable. No "fact" of history can ever be proved with total scientific certainty, but by the normal canons of historical investigation we can verify much of what is written in Scripture. Significantly, even in this modern, scientific age of archaeology, historiography, astronomy, geology, linguistics and biblical criticism, no fundamental problems have been found with the history recorded in the Bible. We have seen more confirmation (if confirmation were needed) of biblical history in this century than ever before. The historicity of major portions of the Bible has been confirmed within accepted standards of historical investigation.

Does this *prove* the Bible is true? Not in the least. This is not the point. The point is that the Bible speaks to persons much as Jesus did to the crowds. It gives enough information and carries enough plausibility to ignite faith, but it never says so much as to make faith unnecessary or inevitable. Thus the Word of God in both its incarnate and written forms "penetrates even to dividing soul and spirit" and "judges the thoughts and attitudes of the heart" (Heb 4:12). It draws a line between those who are genuinely seeking truth and those who are not. For the true seeker (the truth-seeker), the Bible's plausibility is sufficient basis for faith to take hold. But to others, the Bible becomes a rock of offense, a stumbling block or laughing-stock, just as Jesus' parables did.

We may note a kind of parallel between Jesus, the incarnate Word (the God-man), and the Bible, the written Word, the issue of divine-human cooperation at a different level. This parallel is helpful because it reminds us of the high biblical view of human personality, even in its fallen state. God does not compromise his sovereignty when he invites human cooperation in the great work of redemption. But this parallel also suggests something else. God so worked in the Incarnation that Jesus Christ was born and lived without sin. He was perfect. Does the same hold for the Bible? Did God so work in the biblical writers that the resulting written Word was perfect in the sense Jesus was? Not really, for when we look at Jesus we see living, morally responsible personhood, not a book. And so we look to Jesus first, and then to the Bible, interpreted to us by the Spirit, as the witness to Jesus. A book of words, written over many centuries by fallible men and women, even under the inspiration of the Holy Spirit, can never be perfect in the sense Jesus was and is. The very nature of history and language precludes this. The essence of personhood and the image of God, which can never live in paper and ink as it can in a living being, precludes this. But by faith and with rational consistency Christians can affirm the full authority of the Bible as the Word of God, as witness to the incarnate Word and as the book of the covenant. We affirm everything Scripture does concerning itself. We affirm biblical authority by faith, and we find its historicity borne out by facts. This is all we need.

Perhaps we can do no better than the statement of Bengel: "Scripture was divinely inspired not merely while being written, God breathing through the writers, but also while it is being read (and expounded), God breathing through the Scripture."[9] In this sense the Bible is always the Word of God which reveals the Word of God.

The Book and the Community   In sum, the Bible should be seen as the book of the covenant between God and the church. The written Word and the incarnate Word go together. The church needs both. There is no salvation without Jesus Christ, but Scripture is the essential testimony to Christ.

The paradox of the church's liberating role is that it is a truly liberating force only when it stands under the authority of Scripture. The tragedy today is that many in North America who uphold biblical authority fail to understand the church's liberating role because of Christianity's identification with American middle-class culture, while many who argue for liberation have an inadequate view of biblical authority, thus running the danger of undermining the church's ability to be a truly liberating force. Understanding the Bible as the book of the covenant may be one way around this impasse.

It is absolutely imperative that the church maintain its biblical moorings, that it stand under the authority of Scripture in both its doctrine and life. We cannot afford another split between those who stress biblical doctrine and those who advocate biblical living.[10] We must insist on the priority of Scripture over reason, experience and tradition, even while we give proper place to each of these as aids to understanding Scripture rightly. Scripture is reasonable. It proves itself true in experience. It provides the basis for legitimate tradition. But the moment we insist (or simply allow) the Bible to conform to our prior commitments, theories, philosophies, structures or experiences, the church is in trouble. The Bible, interpreted in the church through the Spirit, must correct our reason, discipline our experience and judge our traditions.

The Bible witnesses not only to the coming of Jesus himself, but to the whole range of salvation history through which God prepared a people and accomplished the essential work of Christ in history. The Bible is essential because without it we do not know what it means to be the people of God and the body of Christ. The function of the Bible is precisely to reveal this.

Scripture shows, above all, the divine economy of salvation through Jesus Christ and the church. Its primary role is to create a people who live and act in covenant fidelity with God through Jesus Christ for the sake of the Kingdom. The purpose of the Bible is to create and sustain a faithful people. And the fundamental concern of the church should be to live in fidelity to God's covenant as revealed in Scripture. This means searching the Scriptures to know, understand and live out God's Kingdom plan for the church. The proof of understanding Scripture is living the lifestyle of the Kingdom.

11
THE LIFESTYLE
OF THE KINGDOM

The gospel is as much a way of life as a walk of faith. This is not because action is more important than belief but because lifestyle is determined by one's faith commitments. Not to *live* the gospel is not to *believe* the gospel. Not to live for the Kingdom is not to take seriously who Jesus is and what he taught. A consideration of Scripture leads naturally to the question of lifestyle.

Paul says repeatedly, "Live a life worthy of the calling you have received" (Eph 4:1; note Col 1:10, 1 Thess 2:12 and similar passages). Virtually all New Testament writers sound the same note. Jesus himself says, "Not everyone who says to me, 'Lord, Lord,' will enter the kingdom of heaven, but only he who does the will of my Father who is in heaven" (Mt 7:21).

In other words, how we live as Jesus' disciples is a central concern of God's Kingdom. Are we free to live the liberating lifestyle of the Kingdom?

Lifestyle has become a pressing Christian concern for both good and bad reasons. Positively, many Christians are coming to greater world-consciousness. We are beginning to see ourselves as neighbors not just to the family next door but also to forgotten old folks in urban slums and homeless thousands in the streets of Calcutta. Expanding consciousness of the world is enlarging our heart of compassion.

Negatively, we feel the pressure of shrinking resources. The problem is not just oil, gas and mineral reserves, but, even more basically, the growing threat to fresh air and water and the serious decline in good farm land worldwide. Both development and growing deserts are gobbling up thousands of acres of precious land annually, virtually guaranteeing massive famines in the future. Longer range, the greater problem may be the shortage of fresh water.

While these problems raise many issues, almost all the issues trace back to lifestyle in one way or another. The connection with lifestyle is inescapable once we start thinking ecologically. The growing concern with stewardship of dwindling resources is prodding Christians everywhere to re-examine how they live. This reassessment is especially needed in North America where the postwar economic boom has created an artificial, short-term island of abundance, affluence and prosperity. As we see things more realistically on a worldwide scale, perhaps we will find ourselves more at home with the lifestyle values of the frontier or the depression than with those of suburbia in the fifties and sixties.

In many ways, today's North American Christians are a generation "out of time." Products of a brief flash of affluence, we have forgotten or rejected the values of simplicity, plainness and frugality held by our mothers and fathers and most of the world's peoples. Affluent Christians are out of sync with the times, and especially with the future. Unless we develop greater sensitivity to the *ethics* of the way we live—how our lifestyles affect others worldwide—we will in fact find ourselves out of phase with the Kingdom of God.

Spiritually and theologically, lifestyle is important because it goes to the heart of an incarnational understanding of the gospel. As we saw in chapter two, how we live lies at the heart of an ecological understanding of the Kingdom. Lifestyle, however, is a thorny subject. North Americans are heirs to generations of individualism. We have been taught that our mode of life, and especially anything having to do with money, is a highly private matter not to be questioned by others.

As heir to this tradition, I also find it difficult to deal faithfully with the matter of responsible lifestyle. Integrity demands consistency between what we profess and how we live. You have a right to ask me, and we must ask each other, whether we are practicing what we preach, whether our lives are consistent with convictions we have or are coming to. So I speak as one who wants to be consistent, who has deep convictions concerning the kind of life we as Christians must live in today's world, but who in some areas is still struggling to find ways to translate convictions into specific actions and patterns of life.

Simplicity   Both secular and Christian discussions of lifestyle have focused on the value of simplicity or the simple life. One of the most significant statements in the 1974 Lausanne Covenant reads, "Those of us who live in affluent circumstances accept our duty to develop a simple life-style in order to contribute more generously to both relief and evangelism."[1] But those who take such questions seriously find responsible living is not always simple either to reach or to practice. Even so, affirming the value of simplicity in the way we live makes sense—simplicity not as ultimate goal but as a way of testifying to the Kingdom of God.

Simplicity has often been seen as a Christian virtue. Commenting on the phrase "in simplicity and godly sincerity" in 2 Corinthians 1:12, John Wesley wrote:

We are then simple of heart, when the eye of our mind is singly fixed on God; when in all things we aim at God alone, as our God, our portion, our strength, our happiness, our exceeding great reward, our all, in time and eternity. This is simplicity; when a steady view, a single intention of promoting his glory, of doing and suffering his blessed will, runs through our whole soul, fills all our heart, and is the constant spring of all our thoughts, desires, and purposes.[2]

Our concern with lifestyle, however, and our understanding of simplicity must be grounded in God's revelation in Scripture. And here several concerns stand out.

Paul says in 2 Corinthians 1:12, "For our rejoicing is this, the testimony of our conscience, that in simplicity and godly sincerity, not with fleshly wisdom, but by the grace of God, we have had our conversation in the world, and more abundantly to you-ward" (KJV). The word translated "conversation" here in the Authorized Version literally means "manner of life" or "lifestyle." As a noun (*anastrophē*) it occurs some thirteen times in the New Testament in passages which underscore the biblical concern for Christian lifestyle (for example, Eph 4:22; 1 Tim 4:12; Jas 3:13; 1 Pet 1:15, 18; 2:12; 3:1-2, 16; 2 Pet 3:11). Often in the New Testament holiness and lifestyle are tied together.

Christians are to live a holy and godly life in the world. But what does this mean? Six biblical realities put the question of lifestyle in clearer perspective.

1. *Human stewardship of the inhabited world.* Man and woman were created to be faithful stewards of the created world. In the past five centuries, especially, this creation mandate has been twisted to mean exploitation. But today many Christians are beginning to reaffirm the original intention of the biblical mandate. A stewardship was given the human family which was distorted by sin. The human race has been unfaithful to its ecological responsibility, but the duty remains. It is Jesus, however, who puts things right (Heb 2:5-9). And because the church is Jesus' body, Christians have a special stewardship in the world. We must first of all be Jesus' servants and good stewards of God's grace (1 Pet 4:10-11) so that as his body we may begin to fulfill the stewardship of the inhabited world which has been committed to us. All this means the church must set the example of what it means to be proper stewards of the earth's resources *in the way Christians live.*

2. *Jesus' teachings in the Sermon on the Mount.* Jesus' words about giving to others, being merciful and being relatively unconcerned about food and clothing form the charter for our lifestyle today. Most basic is the teaching that we should seek above all the Kingdom of God and its justice. If the Kingdom of God is really first in our lives, lifestyle will follow along in proper perspective.

3. *The servant role of Jesus Christ.* In today's world, it comes close to blasphemy to say that God wants us to live like kings or that "the desires of our hearts" refers to material accumulations. Through Christ we are rich, but Jesus, being rich, chose to become poor—for our sake. So we must follow his steps. For the sake of those who suffer, for the sake of those who are nearly as without Christ as the world was before Jesus came, we must empty ourselves and take up the servant towel, even if this means becoming obedient to death.

4. *The gospel to the poor.* The Old Testament insistence on justice for the poor, the fatherless, the widow and the refugee forms the

basis of Jesus' statement that he came to preach the gospel to the poor. As B. T. Roberts noted one hundred years ago, preaching the gospel to the poor was "the crowning proof" that Jesus was "the One that should come." Roberts said, "In this respect the Church must follow in the footsteps of Jesus. She must see to it that the gospel is preached to the poor."[3] As Jim Wallis notes, "By his relationship with the poor, Jesus establishes their value. So must the church. The Christian point of view must be that of those at the bottom. Their rights and needs should always be the most determinative element of the church's social stance."[4] Wallis adds, "In a world where most people are poor, a rich church is living testimony of idol worship. The mere possession of such wealth is proof of serving money." "Accumulating wealth while brothers and sisters are in poverty is evidence of sin in the church's life."[5] All who have ever effectively been Christ's servants among the poor teach us the same thing: To preach the gospel to the poor with integrity, our lives must be marked by simplicity and transparency.

5. *The biblical concern with justice.* In Scripture, justice is not egalitarianism, but it certainly includes economic sharing. Justice involves lifestyle—not merely restraint from "grinding the face of the poor," but restraint from the accumulation of wealth or worldly power. As Richard Foster notes in *Celebration of Discipline,* "The biblical injunctions against the exploitation of the poor and the accumulation of wealth are clear and straightforward. The Bible challenges nearly every economic value of contemporary society."[6] Foster goes on to say, "Jesus spoke to the question of economics more than any other single social issue. If in a comparatively simple society our Lord would lay such strong emphasis upon the spiritual dangers of wealth, how much more should we who live in a highly affluent culture take seriously the economic question."[7]

6. *The simplicity of God and his plan.* There is a profound simplicity to God himself. Plato's notion that God is the only supremely simple being has a seed of truth in it, as Christian theologians have often affirmed. The profound simplicity of God's nature is reflected in the simplicity of the gospel, which even a child can grasp, and in the mysterious simplicity of the atom which, in its coherence of light and energy, reflects the creative simplicity of God himself.

Our very speech and manner are to mirror the simplicity of the creation and of God himself. Jesus did that. In remarkable ways, Francis of Assisi and the greatest of the church's saints did that. And so our lives and faith today must reflect the profoundest simplicity —the simplicity of life drawn together around the one integrating purpose of serving God and his Kingdom. In a complicated world, life centered in God is the only hope for genuine simplicity.

Contemporary Concerns Biblical teachings on lifestyle take on special urgency today because of the pressure of world events. Several contemporary concerns underscore this urgency for the church. These are the concerns of world hunger, the energy and environmental crises, technological materialism, and nutrition and health.

1. *World hunger.* In its starkest form, the point here is simply that millions of human beings in the world today have little or nothing to eat, while most North American Christians have too much. We live in a world community where differences of geography and culture are irrelevant in the face of such disparity. The question of lifestyle is no less pressing for a middle-class American or Canadian in North America today than it is for a North American missionary working among the poor in India. Biblically, our neighbor is the person we can reach, not the person we cannot avoid. We do not have to answer for past generations, but God will not hold our generation guiltless if we continue to lead affluent lives while others starve for lack of either spiritual or physical food.

2. *The energy crisis.* Today's energy crisis is much more than a matter of gasoline shortages, lower thermostats or higher fuel bills. The energy crisis is the firstfruit of a fundamental shift in the world's economy. It will not get better; it will get worse. A major crisis is probably just a short distance down the road. The energy issue is multifaceted and highly explosive. What will happen—socially, economically and politically—when massive shortages of energy, or of the rare minerals necessary for producing energy, develop?

As Christians we have a choice. We can wait and react with the majority, or we can begin now to set an example and learn creative ways to live in a world of shrinking resources. As a start, we can learn how to conserve more and consume less. And we can go on to find new ways of dealing with energy shortages that will help us as Christians make a creative contribution to society.

3. *The environmental crisis.* Discerning the economy of God and the ecology of the Kingdom, Christians should set an example of living harmoniously with the environment. We must be those who work *with* nature, not against it. This is part of our stewardship. It will lead us to greater simplicity and harmony in the way we live. Simple foods, energy-efficient and ecologically sound homes and church buildings, and patterns of life that put us close to nature should increasingly be part of the way we live.

4. *Technological materialism.* We are all victims of the technological society which Jacques Ellul has so profoundly described. As Ellul has pointed out, technology is not amoral. It tends to create its own morality of pragmatism, a morality of means. Our response must be not only a rejection of materialism, but also a rejection of ever-increasing and ever more massive technology in the service of material consumption. We need to develop or rediscover those simple techniques, the minitechnology which works with nature and not against it. This means opting out of the booming technological gadget market and affirming a lifestyle in which people are more important than things and community more precious than technology.

5. *Nutrition and health.* One fallout of technology over the past decade or so has been the growing awareness of the insanity of the health and nutrition habits of North Americans. We are the generation which is learning that eating and breathing are dangerous to our health! Of all people, Christians should be most concerned with the stewardship of our health and bodies. Here again, faithfulness lies in the path of simplicity.

All these issues interlock to form a clear pattern for Christian stewardship. They all point the same direction. Added to the biblical perspective outlined earlier, they constitute an overwhelming constellation of concerns which say that responsible Christian living is not an option for the body of Christ. It is a mandate.

Kingdom Living Today   But what is a responsible lifestyle? What does it mean to live for the economy and Kingdom of God? Here are some basic definitions which may help us work with our brothers and sisters toward greater Kingdom faithfulness.

1. *Kingdom living is life centered in God.* Genuine simplicity is, first

of all, an inward and spiritual thing. Here the Christian parts company with secular views of simple living. Kingdom living begins with the calm centering of the soul in God, total dedication and openness to him, and continuing growth in godliness and the Spirit-led life. Kingdom living recognizes and revels in the profound simplicity of God's design. Growing from daily encounter with Scripture, it rests in the assurance of God's plan and purposes and the certainty of the Kingdom of God. It is able to be very active because it first of all recognizes who is in control. "The closer you are to the kingdom of God, the more gentle and humble, the more simple you will become. Christ will be your life."[8] The simple life is centered in God, following the example of Christ.

2. *Kingdom living sees the world from the perspective of God's rule.* God is Lord of the nations. He has the whole world in his hands. He wants his glory declared among all peoples. He has revealed his glory in creation. He shows his glory in the plan and plane of redemption. He is forming a people for himself so that he can reconcile the world to himself. He is especially the God of the poor and the oppressed, as Scripture shows. If we see the world from God's perspective, we will be a people marked by signs of God's Kingdom.

3. *Kingdom living sees the value of the created order.* It does not affirm a mere asceticism or a withdrawal from the world, denying human materiality, sexuality or transience. Rather it affirms that matter itself is good, an expression of God's being and kindness. It understands that "nothing will be revealed in the hereafter that is not already grounded here."[9]

4. *Kingdom living seeks to live in harmony with God's design.* It seeks to cooperate with every good process which God has given and to deny every process which works for destruction and chaos. The direction of evil is always toward annihilation and suicide. But God's plan leads to life, fulfillment, harmony and completion. When our lives are marked by careless and wasteful consumption, we are cooperating with death and are "kicking against the pricks" of God's design for a world of harmony, health, beauty and ecological balance.

Because of this, Kingdom living is concerned with conservation rather than consumption. It denies the myth of unlimited progress and economic development, recognizing that we live in a finite world where the accumulation of wealth necessarily means the impoverishment of the poor. We are right to think of God's Kingdom coming on earth, as well as in heaven, but we are wrong to associate the Kingdom of God with material affluence and unlimited economic growth. We must be the generation which affirms that God's commission to Eve and Adam was not exploitation but rather the care and keeping of the created order. Unlimited *spiritual* development is possible because God is infinite and we live in a vast, spiritual universe. But unlimited economic and material expansion in a finite, material world is finally impossible and can only lead to a giant blowout. Kingdom living means learning to conserve and preserve —which means living, eating, traveling and clothing ourselves as good and careful keepers of the good earth.

5. *Kingdom living identifies visibly with the poor.* Psalm 112 says that as God looks down on his created world, he especially sees the poor. God's intervention in the world in behalf of the poor comes especially through Jesus Christ and through us, his body. Like Jesus, we must become poor (and not just "willing" to become poor) so that others may be rich (and not just live off the promise of future riches). The more our lives and churches are involved with poor and suffering folks, the more we learn the meaning of Kingdom lifestyle.

6. *Kingdom living raises signs of the Kingdom of God.* Jesus sent John the Baptist's disciples back to him with the report that the blind were seeing, the lame walking, the deaf hearing and the poor receiving the gospel. These were signs of the Kingdom!

What are the sure signs of the Kingdom today? We raise signs to the Kingdom whenever we show concretely in our lives that we believe what Jesus said in the Sermon on the Mount, when we truly are seeking first God's Kingdom and righteousness. Faithful living for Jesus' sake is itself a signal of the Kingdom of God, for it shows where our treasure is and where our confidence and resources lie. The simplicity and beauty of genuine Christian community are the most profound visible demonstration of the presence of the Kingdom, just as community is the spring for other signs of the Kingdom in the present world. As was true in the New Testament, however, God often calls attention to the power of the Kingdom through "signs and wonders" as well as through selfless service. As Peter Wagner comments, such signs function "to draw public attention to the power of God in order to open unsaved people's hearts to the message of the gospel."[10]

7. *Kingdom living is life in community.* From a Christian standpoint, the simple life is the shared life. This is part of the fundamental ecology of the Kingdom. We are good at insulating ourselves from each other. Things, money, time, distance, titles, education and position all make excellent insulation. Jesus would blow out the stuffy insulation and bring us together in love. We will never fully learn simplicity in lifestyle and in material things until we learn the simplicity of intimate Christian community. This is fundamental to Kingdom living.

8. *Kingdom living is life in tension with the world.* The Jesus way is not necessarily a secure or tranquil way. When we begin to live by God's standards, we strip the gears of the Great American Dream Machine. We become not cogs but clogs in the great machine. To choose simplicity and Kingdom faithfulness in a materialistic and sophisticated age is to enlist in a counterculture which is in conflict with surrounding society. Look at Jesus! He shows us the simplicity we should seek and the tension which results.

9. *Kingdom living is a life of discipline.* Since Kingdom living places us in tension with the world, we must choose discipline if we would choose simplicity. In our world, the simple life is an ordered life. We choose joyful disciplines and laugh at legalism because we know where the source of our simplicity lies. Prudential disciplines will not lead to legalism if our existence is truly centered in Jesus Christ and in the community of his people. We must adopt shared disciplines for careful use of time and other resources, and we must learn to check up on one another in love and tenderness. Both individually and corporately we must "be very careful" how we live, "making the most of every opportunity, because the days are evil" (Eph 5:15-16).

Making It Practical As individuals we can all make some limited progress toward faithful Kingdom living. But both Scripture and history teach that responsible living is possible only in the context of community. The church must be such a community. We must commit ourselves as the church, and as small cells within the church, to a journey into discipleship and Kingdom faithfulness. Here are some beginning steps we can take, and these may suggest others.[11]

1. *Committed discipleship groups.* The church needs to recover the dynamic of discipleship groups or covenant cells. We must recapture the life of the church meeting in small committed groups in homes. This is part of the function of community in the ecology of the church. Every Christian should be part of a small cell of eight to twelve persons—a group of believers to whom she or he is accountable and which helps each one grow into a biblically faithful lifestyle. This is fundamental to translating good intentions into good actions.

2. *An instructed lifestyle conscience.* North American Christians need to develop a lifestyle conscience—not a new legalism that attaches itself to a few items of dress or behavior, but a profound conscience of love and stewardship which sets a mood of expectations of what it means to be a people committed to Kingdom values in a materialistic, technolatrous age.

3. *The graduated or incremental tithe.* Ron Sider has popularized the "graduated tithe" in his important book *Rich Christians in an Age of Hunger.*[12] Essentially the graduated tithe, like the graduated income tax, uses a formula based on amount of income. As one's income increases, the tithe percentage goes up at an accelerated rate. This is intentional bracket creep for the sake of the Kingdom! The more one earns, the more one gives—not only in actual amount but also in percentage. If this were followed in the United States and Canada, Christians in these countries would be giving literally billions of dollars more to the Lord's work, especially to feed the starving and shelter the homeless.

The incremental tithe is a somewhat similar idea. The formula is simply to increase one's minimum giving each year by one or two or more percentage points. Thus, if at the end of the year you discover you gave twelve per cent of your total income for the interests of the Kingdom, you might decide next year that your minimum percentage would be fourteen per cent. This may sound coldly mechanical, but at least it provides an objective look at our stewardship outside of our feelings. And it need not be a legalistic or joyless thing. The fun comes in trying to go beyond the percentage. Setting goals does make us more conscious of our resources and our giving and can be an aid toward living for Kingdom priorities. A worthy goal for most North American Christians would be to reach the point where they are giving away more than they are spending on themselves. This is obviously a more realistic goal for some than for others, since amount of income, family size, special health needs and other particulars may enter in.

4. *Fasting and prayer.* Ours must be the generation which rediscovers the historic and biblical disciplines of fasting and prayer. Jesus said *when* you pray and *when* you fast, not *if*. These are normal Christian disciplines. To fail to fast and pray in the interests of the world's poor and dispossessed when we live in an affluent age and society is to be guilty of sin. As a beginning minimum, we should fast at least one meal a week and spend the time praying for those around the world who lack physical and spiritual food. The money which we would have spent for food—which doesn't really come out of our pockets, because we would have spent it anyhow—can be given to feed the hungry. If just twenty million North American Christians would fast one meal per week and give the two-dollar cost for feeding the poor, the result would be the transfer of over two-billion dollars' worth of food annually from our bodies and the food industry to the bodies of our sisters and brothers who are starving. This is more than the total amount the U.S. government gives for nonmilitary foreign aid annually![13]

5. *Lifestyle garage sale.* Like millions of other Americans, many middle-class Christians have garage sales in the spring or fall to help unload unneeded goods. These sales may net anywhere from fifty to several hundred dollars. Why not go two steps further? First, Kingdom-conscious Christians could add to the sale a few things they are still using but don't really need, especially extra clothes and appliances which waste energy. Second, the money could be given to Kingdom interests, rather than being spent for more material goodies. If one million Christian families did this and netted an average of one hundred dollars per sale, another one hundred million dollars would become available for the Kingdom of God.

6. *Alternate celebrations.* Are our Christmas, Easter, birthday and other celebrations Christian or pagan? This old question takes on new meaning in today's world. Commercial interests do their best to manipulate the marketplace so that the chief mark of our celebrations will be more spending. The ideal of business is to have at

least one major holiday or special observance every few weeks so consumers will always have reason to buy what they don't need. Most recently we have seen the crass attempt to introduce Mother-in-law Day and Grandparents Day as gimmicks to boost sales. But Christians need alternate celebrations—Kingdom ways of celebrating our life together and what God has done for us. We can seek simpler, less consumption-oriented ways of celebrating Christmas, birthdays and other special events.

7. *Eating and dressing more simply.* In recent years we have learned not only that North Americans eat too much, but they eat the wrong things. The average American eats too much meat (twice as much as twenty years ago), plus an unhealthy mix of sugar, salt and chemicals. But we do not have to be trapped by this. We can improve and simplify our diets, at the same time learning to live more economically. We really need very little meat and should rely less on processed foods. And this need not mean sending women back to long, slavish hours in the kitchen if we learn the values and joys of shared meal preparation, closer cooperation and living in tighter community. Through publications such as the *More with Less Cookbook* we can learn how to eat better while consuming less.[14] We can form food cooperatives for ourselves and to help the less fortunate.

The important thing is to see everything in the light of Kingdom priorities. When it comes to clothing, our objective is not to be in style or out of style, but to give as little time and attention to clothing as possible—for the sake of the Kingdom. Clothes consciousness is a sign of worldliness, though color and beauty consciousness may be a sign of godliness. Genuinely attractive persons are those who are so wholly God's and who live so fully for the Kingdom that their sincerity, serenity and warmth make others forget about clothing and see how shabby the concern with style is from the Kingdom perspective. The point is not to dress this way or that, but to spend as little time, thought and money on clothing as possible. If we seek the Kingdom, such matters largely take care of themselves.

8. *Direct involvement with the poor and dispossessed.* Nothing will change our lifestyle expectations and our definitions of necessities and luxuries like sharing our lives with poor folk. This means encountering the poor as people like ourselves who have hopes and fears, family needs and burdens, mouths to feed and bills to pay—

but without many of the resources we take for granted. Spending time with the poor—letting them teach us—will help us see things from Jesus' viewpoint and will teach us the meaning of social power and powerlessness. We may experience a "conversion to the world," as Orlando Costas puts it, for the sake of the Kingdom, coming "to discover the world of the poor and the disenfranchised as a fundamental reference of the Gospel."[15]

9. *Learning the simplicity of community.* Many of these things point us back, again, to the simplicity of community. Kingdom living grows out of simplicity of heart and relationships. We must encourage and develop the depth of community in the church which will help us relate to one another with openness and transparency. The Kingdom of God is designed to work through community, and nothing else will achieve it.

Understood from the perspective of the economy and Kingdom of God, simplicity is a Christian value—even while it is a means to a more basic end. The end is to be like Jesus, to be so joined to him that we will, in fact, be his body and his presence on earth and agents of his Kingdom. Genuine simplicity in faith and life makes us both more evangelistic and more prophetic. It makes credible the claim that our treasure is in heaven, not on earth. It can help the church be the community of God's people in ways it has never been before. It helps build a Christian counterculture which demonstrates that the church really *is* putting the Kingdom of God and his justice first. Kingdom living will help liberate the church.

four

THE CHURCH
IN THE FREEDOM
OF THE SPIRIT

12

"LAYMEN"
FREE TO MINISTER

God's Kingdom means "the glorious freedom of the children of God" (Rom 8:21). The church is the community of the Spirit, and "where the Spirit of the Lord is, there is freedom" (2 Cor 3:17). God's people are to "stand firm" in the freedom Christ won for them, avoiding the twin dangers of legalism (Gal 5:1) and self-indulgence. The principle is clear: "You, my brothers, were called to be free. But do not use your freedom to indulge the sinful nature; rather, serve one another in love" (Gal 5:13).

The gospel sets people free. It transforms sinners into God's own people so that they may serve God in the freedom of the Spirit (1 Pet 2:9-10).

Yet how quickly, how easily that freedom is compromised! Often we may feel the same frustration and astonishment the apostle Paul felt when he saw how quickly the Galatian Christians were betrayed into legalism (Gal 1:6-7). How rarely do God's people live up to their privileges as the children of God!

God makes us a free people by his Spirit. In the shorter or longer run, this freedom is throttled. Like the children of Israel in the desert, we yearn for the predictable, safe bondage of institutional captivity. If we are to live the freedom Christ won for us, we must understand what that freedom is and what it means practically to *live* the freedom of the gospel in the present order. In these final chapters we will examine some of the practical implications of the liberation Jesus has won for us and what it means to be the church in the freedom of the Spirit. What does this freedom say, especially, to "laymen," women, the poor and, finally, to pastoral leaders?

Since we have already discussed the ministry of all believers, only a brief word need be added here concerning the freedom of "laymen" to minister.

The Freedom to Minister As we saw in chapter eight, all believers are ministers. The universal priesthood is a universal call to minister in Jesus' name. A high priority in seeking the liberation of the church today, therefore, must be freeing God's people for the work of ministry.

The catch phrase "liberating the layman" has seldom been understood radically enough. Generally it has meant the clergy enlisting "laymen" in various kinds of significant but clearly secondary roles. Seldom do we get to the root of the problem: the unbiblical division of God's people into an elite class of "ministers" and a vast second-class body of believers called "laymen" who make up the lower ninety per cent or so of the ecclesiastical pyramid.

Church history shows that one of Satan's key tricks is to convince Christians that only *some,* not *all,* believers are ministers. Aided by the "iron law of oligarchy" and similar sociological catches, the enemy has often been remarkably effective. Within two or three centuries of Pentecost, gospel ministry had effectively been stolen from God's people and concentrated in the hands of the priest or professional religionist.

Understandably, the restriction of ministry to an emerging clergy class was accompanied by a decline in discipling or disciple-building. As Carl Wilson has pointed out, "The decline of the disciple-building ministry and the emergence of a separation between the church leadership (clergy) and the people (laity) are directly related." In fact, Wilson argues, "a New Testament ministry that involves all the people of God and produces a normal gradual flow from layman to leadership has never been restored."[1] The only real exceptions to this pattern have come in some renewal movements, and then only partially.

I have often thought that should the apostle Peter or Paul show up in one of our Christian assemblies today, we would have much to explain. As we began to introduce the apostle to the brothers and sisters, he might note that we described some Christians as "ministers" and others as "laymen." He would be confused. We would have to stop and explain: "I know that in New Testament days you believed all God's people were ministers. But you have to understand that a few things have happened during the past couple of thousand years."

Liberating the church means restoring gospel ministry and Kingdom work to all God's people. This certainly does not mean finding new ways to draft "laymen" into church work or developing better techniques for pastors to "use their laymen" (a hot topic in many church leadership seminars). That might simply result in the diversion of more time and resources into church work rather than Kingdom work—unless the church truly understood its Kingdom mandate and its biblical ecology in God's plan.

Freeing God's people for Kingdom ministry does mean at least two things:

1. All believers should be taught that they are called, gifted and, in baptism, ordained to the Christian ministry. This requires teaching and discipling after the pattern of Ephesians 4:11-12. It means understanding that leadership grows out of discipleship, but also that ministry is much broader than what we commonly call leadership.

2. Believers also need to understand what Kingdom ministry really is. It is much more than church work, so called. On the other hand, if the church truly is the community of God's people, there is no higher nor more strategic work than nourishing the internal life and the outward witness of believers. In this sense, pastoral ministry may be thought of as the highest calling, for it involves freeing and equipping believers to be agents of the Kingdom of God.

The Work of the Kingdom   Kingdom ministry is any service carried out in the name of Jesus that serves people or nature and shows forth God's rule in the world. Christian ministry is especially seen in care for the poor, the oppressed and dispossessed, refugees and aliens, all those who suffer, and in general those with no social power. It includes witness through the arts and various other forms of creative expression as well as intellectual inquiry into the nature of the world and human culture. An especially strategic aspect of

Kingdom work today involves environmental science, in theoretical study and research and in the more applied areas of agriculture and the management of natural resources. Some of today's front-line Christian ministers are those who turn the sod, care for land and animals, and provide models of reconciliation between persons and the natural environment.

This is not to say, of course, that all work is Kingdom work. Far from it! Much human activity has been co-opted by the technological society and is in fact subverting God's Kingdom purposes. Unfortunately, many sincere and dedicated Christians, lacking Kingdom insight, give their best time and effort to jobs in business, industry, education and other fields that are directly or indirectly contrary to Kingdom interests—even while they maintain high standards of personal morality and pay their tithes. The only antidote to this paradox is for Christians to be part of a local community of believers which has faced the issue of God's economy and opted for Kingdom priorities in all areas of life. Only thus can Christians be free for the Kingdom.

The Kingdom community will be concerned to break down not only the clergy-laity fence but also the wall between "sacred" and "secular" callings. The key fact in anyone's work is not its relation to the church but its function in the Kingdom. The point is not whether someone's work is religious or nonreligious, whether it is "church work" or "secular work," but whose sovereignty and lordship are being acknowledged and served. Jesus' words are not a casual observation: "You cannot serve both God and Money" (Mt 6:24). Work which furthers the Kingdom of God—its justice and righteousness—is Christian ministry. Work which clashes with Kingdom priorities and values is of the devil, even when done by sincere Christians.

By grace and the power of God, all Christian men and women are free to minister, free to be servants of Christ in the work of the Kingdom. Liberating the church means putting this freedom into practice. This calls for discerning the economy of God and the true ecology of the church. And it underscores the need for those entrusted with leadership to *really* equip all believers for the work of ministry—preparing believers for Kingdom business, not just for church business.

13

WOMEN
FREE TO LEAD

Stop and think. Is there any good reason why women, created in
God's image, should not be allowed to enjoy the same freedom of the
Kingdom available to men? The obvious answer—which is also the
biblical answer—is no. And yet a whole forest of deeply rooted tradition has grown up, denying women fundamental freedoms Jesus
won for them on the cross.

Unfortunately, the whole subject of women in ministry has been
contorted and confused through the absolutizing of some New Testament teachings intended for specific situations on the one hand,
and on the other by an extreme, unbiblical feminism which makes
many sincere Christians shy away from any assertion of women's
rights.

Restricting full rights of ministry to men only, like restricting
them to the clergy, is one of Satan's tricks to undermine the church's
Kingdom witness. Liberating the church means removing those restrictions which keep the church and the world from benefiting
from the redemptive ministry of Christian women.

Nearly one hundred years ago, the evangelical reformer B. T.
Roberts wrote,

*The feeling against woman's being accorded equal rights with man, is old and
deeply rooted. Generally, among mankind, the law of force has been the pre-
vailing law. The stronger have tyrannized over the weaker. It is no wonder
that our prejudices against the rights of women, infused into us from early
childhood, should be strong. But reason and grace serve to overcome prejudice.*

In other words, the position accorded women in the church has often been a sign of the church's worldliness rather than its faithfulness. Roberts argued, "Though Christianity has greatly ameliorated the condition of woman, it has not secured for her, even in the most enlightened nations, that equality which the Gospel inculcates." He went on to contend,

It is impossible to estimate the extent to which humanity has suffered by the unreasonable and unscriptural restrictions which have been put upon women in the churches of Jesus Christ. Had they been given, since the days of the first Apostles, the same rights as men, this would be quite another world. [1]

The issue of women's roles is crucial to the liberation of the church for at least two reasons: (1) because of the extent and kind of ministry lost to the church through women's secondary place and (2) because of the spiritual and psychological damage done to Christian women and homes through the church's sexist understanding of ministry.

Historically the church has restricted authority and leadership to the clergy, rather than to the whole people of God, and to men rather than women. The logic in both cases is the same: insistence on "qualifications" for ministry which the Bible does not prescribe. As a result, women have become not second but third-class citizens of the Kingdom, behind clergy and lay*men*. When renewal comes to the church, however, leadership often breaks out of the clerical collar and comes to all God's people—women as well as men, "laymen" as well as clergy, and "unschooled, ordinary" folks (Acts 4:13) as well as the learned, powerful and well-to-do.

The church needs to repent for convincing women they are not really, in the final analysis, equal with men in the church and in God's sight. Sometimes, of course, men who teach woman's submission insist that women are equal. They say submission does not really mean inferiority or inequality. But that always sounds a bit hollow coming from the ones in authority or those benefiting from the submission. Christians have become at least somewhat aware of the sinfulness of racial prejudice, but many of us have yet to deal with our prejudices toward women and the poor. And yet these matters are all of one piece.

Women in the Bible   How we understand Scripture is, of course, the crucial question here. In the first place, we should start with "all that Jesus began to do and to teach" (Acts 1:1) before rushing on to Paul and other New Testament writers. We should note, for example, Jesus' respect for women, his twelve or more woman disciples,[2] and the marked prominence of women in Luke and Acts.[3] According to Luke, women accompanied Jesus as he "traveled about from one town and village to another, proclaiming the good news of the kingdom of God" (Lk 8:1-3). Was not Jesus demonstrating something about the good news of the Kingdom by taking women with him on these tours?

Second, we need to be careful in the way we interpret biblical truths. The Bible gives us clear, basic, shaping truths. The more obscure or troublesome biblical passages must be interpreted so that they do not cancel out or compromise these basic truths. For example, the teaching to be subject to political authority should not be interpreted so that it compromises our allegiance to Jesus Christ. Concerning women, this means that none of Paul's statements must be interpreted in such a way that they undercut fundamental truths, such as Galatians 3:28—in the church "there is neither Jew nor Greek, slave nor free, male nor female, for you are all one in Christ Jesus."

Scripture gives us several foundational truths which show how we should approach the question of women in the church. We may especially note four.

1. *Man and woman were created in the image of God.* Notice the careful way Genesis 1:26-27 is expressed: "Then God said, 'Let us make man in our image, in our likeness, and let *them* rule over the fish of the sea and the birds of the air, over the livestock, over all the earth, and over all the creatures that move along the ground.' So God created man in his own image, in the image of God he created him; male and female he created *them.*"

Why did God create man as male and female? When one looks at Genesis 1:26-28 with the possibility in mind that sexual differentiation may have more significance than mere biological reproduction, important as that is, two things stand out. First, sexual differentiation is intimately connected to the divine image and to the intended fellowship of man and woman with God. Second, the ruling, stewardship commission is given jointly and equally to man and woman.

This is explicit: "Let *them* rule" (verse 26). To *both* the man and woman God says, "Fill the earth and subdue it. Rule over "the fish of the sea and the birds of the air and over every living creature" (verse 28). The woman rules with the man. No hint is given that the woman is to be subordinate to the man, or to rule only under his authority. Joint rule as stewards of God is the specific commission.[4]

Man and woman were created for God and for each other. Neither one fully expresses the divine image; it takes the partnership of man and woman, and their community together, to fully express God's glory. The woman, in her personality and sensitivities, reflects something of God that the man does not, and therefore it takes both of them to express the divine image and to create the truly Godlike and Christlike community.[5]

This truth has tremendous, far-reaching implications. Would the human race have been so quick, for example, to go to war or to spoil the natural environment if woman had ruled jointly with man as God first commissioned?

2. *God intends a relationship between men and women of equality, complementarity and mutual submission,* not one of male domination.

Much of the church today adheres to the worldly doctrine of male dominance. It sees no reason to question the view expressed in "Fiddler on the Roof":

And who has the right as master of the house
To have the final word at home?
The papa!

This was the tradition in Anatevka. So it is and has been in many other places and cultures. It is the doctrine of male dominance—a doctrine being preached with new vigor and vehemence in much of the popular evangelical and charismatic church today.

The odd thing about the doctrine of male dominance is that it is so widespread in non-Christian cultures and so little supported in Scripture. We should always be suspicious when a teaching with slight biblical basis is strongly held in the church. This is a sure sign that the doctrine in question is *functional*—that it fulfills an important need or purpose for those who hold it, whether or not it is true. The doctrine of male dominance, like the doctrine of clerical supremacy, clearly does fulfill such functions. While not based on

Scripture, it is very useful. Today it provides the basis for men, instinctively feeling the threat of feminism, to hold on to a place of privilege and domination over women in society and in the church.[6]

The key principle for man-woman relationships in the church, however, is not male dominance but complementarity. Here the Genesis 2 account of the creation is particularly relevant, Genesis 1 having established the point of equality. While Genesis 1 and 2 are structured differently, they both lead to a climax expressed with particular poetic force (Gen 1:27; 2:23).[7] The climax of chapter two is the creation of Eve and her presentation to Adam. For dramatic effect, all other creatures are pictured as passing before Adam, who names them but recognizes that none is compatible with him as a partner. His response to the woman, however, is: "This one at last is bone of my bones and flesh of my flesh" (Gen 2:23 *Anchor Bible*).

Eve, according to Genesis 2:18 and 2:20, is a "suitable helper" for Adam. Literally, she is a helper "alongside him," meaning "corresponding to him."[8] The relationship implied seems best expressed by the word *complementarity*. The man and the woman fit each other —not just physically, but spiritually, emotionally and psychologically. As the perfect partner for the man, Eve is the crowning, completing work of creation, like the final piece in a puzzle. Just as the creation of man as male and female in God's image is the climax of creation in Genesis 1, so the mutual complementarity of man and woman is the climax of chapter two.[9]

Adam and Eve were equally created in God's image and equally given dominion over creation. Because of this equal status, the only way man and woman can possibly relate fully and harmoniously together as God intends is through mutual submission. While this mutuality was undercut by the Fall, it has been restored in Jesus Christ.

The relationship between man and woman can be understood in at least four ways:

Inequality/Male dominance
Equality/Male dominance
Equality/Complementarity
Equality/Uniformity

The third of these options, it seems to me, is most consistent with Scripture. Those who favor options one or two often suggest that the fourth option is the only alternative (with scary labels like "unisex"), but in fact the equality/complementarity option is both more balanced and realistic and more biblical than the others. It fits the ecology of the church and the Kingdom. Option two is, in fact, ultimately untenable; it is parallel to the "separate but equal" view of racial relations. While many contemporary Christians who argue for female subordination wish to insist that male dominance does not mean inequality, such a view has a gravitational pull in that direction. Trying to hold equality and male dominance together is like Pharaoh's dream: The lean cows end up devouring the fat ones. Equality becomes a fantasy—not to say a manipulative tool.

3. *In the church, the distinction between male and female should have no functional significance in matters of leadership* (Gal 3:28). The victory at Calvary and the Spirit of Jesus are powerful enough to transcend male-female alienation and to overcome the results of the Fall. The consistent New Testament teaching is "neither male nor female" (Gal 3:28) but "a new creation" (2 Cor 5:17). It takes constant sensitivity to the Holy Spirit in the church to keep that newness from slipping back into oldness.

Whether in the church, the home or society, women should never be excluded from leadership simply because they are women. The leadership and stewardship charge given equally to women and men at creation justifies leadership of women in any role or function open to men.

4. *The principle for all relationships in the body of Christ is mutual submission and service.* Jesus set up servanthood as the model for his followers, and Paul himself points to Jesus' "taking the very nature of a servant" (Phil 2:7) as our example. We are to serve one another (Gal 5:13; Mt 20:26-28) and, as women *and* men, to submit to each other (Eph 5:21). The various biblical passages that speak specifically of the relationship of men and women in marriage must be understood in such a way that they do not contradict or undercut these basic principles.

Problem Passages Full freedom for women in the church is the most consistent biblical view. Yet some New Testament passages seem to deny it. One of the most difficult is 1 Corinthians 11:2-16, which includes the statement, "the head of every man is Christ, and the head of the woman is man" (verse 3). Taken at face value, this passage seems to conflict with full equality for women. How should it be understood?

This passage gives Paul's view and is part of revealed Scripture. It can be taken as a normative teaching for the church, however, only when interpreted in the light of the principles discussed above.

Throughout this passage Paul's primary appeal is to custom and tradition. He wants the Corinthians to "hold to the traditions" he had passed on to them. That it is a disgrace for a woman to have her hair cut off or for a man to cover his head is clearly a cultural value, not a fundamental revealed truth for all time. The phrases "it is proper," "the very nature of things," and "we have no other practice" all reflect the customs and perceptions of Paul's day. But Paul appeals to a more fundamental truth in verse eleven: "In the Lord, however, woman is not independent of man, nor is man independent of woman." In creation we see complementarity: "For as woman came from man, so also man is born of woman" (verse 12; cf. 1 Cor 7). So how does one interpret the statement "the head of the woman is the man"? Scholars debate just what *head* means here, but still a problem remains. Some kind of priority seems to be implied for the man. The solution is to understand this statement in the light of more basic truths, such as verse eleven. The broader teaching of Scripture is equality and complementarity, meaning that the woman is not necessarily subject to the man in any sense that the man is not subject to the woman. Paul's statement here is true, but it is only one side of the truth. Verses eleven and twelve teach complementarity, which Paul had earlier stressed also in 1 Corinthians 7:2-5, 10-16, 32-34. This one statement cannot, therefore, be taken as a fundamental principle for relationships in the church today. It must be understood in the light of more basic teachings. Passages such as Galatians 3:28 interpret 1 Corinthians 11:3, not the other way around. Such an interpretation avoids the absurdity of Scripture contradicting itself.

This interpretation in no way conflicts with a high view of Scripture. Christians already accept this approach on many other issues. Good examples are the matters of dress, slavery, women speaking in church and of course many specific provisions of the Old Testament. Were we to take other individual verses as normative without considering their context and the teaching of Scripture as a whole, we would argue as well for short hair for men, head coverings for women, silence of women in the church and the moral neutrality of slavery. Even this kind of legalism does not solve the problem, however, because it forces the Scripture to contradict itself at some of these very points.

While our concern here is with liberating women for leadership and ministry in the church, a word should be added about marriage. Often the error is made of making the marriage relationship the model for the relationship of men and women generally, rather than the other way around.

Within marriage there may be a kind of leadership priority to the *husbanding role,* depending on how it is understood. But it is wrong to carry this over into the church and to say men therefore have priority over women generally. There is no biblical reason why a woman, whether married or unmarried, should not exchange or share the husbanding and wifing roles, either temporarily or permanently. *Husband* and *wife* are not the same as *male* and *female.* The latter are created sexual differences, while the meanings of *husband* and *wife* are much more culturally relative.[10]

Larger Questions   The role of the laity, the role of women and the question of slavery (or of racial differences) are parallel issues. From a fundamental gospel perspective, it is logically consistent to maintain that racial distinctions have no place in the church, that all Christians are ministers and there are no "laymen," and that women have fully the same rights as men. The very same arguments that justify superiority or "headship" of men over women can be used to justify the superiority of clergy over laity, Whites over Blacks or the institution of slavery. It is no accident that many evangelicals and Holiness abolitionists of the past century later took up the struggle for women's rights. The women's rights movement, in fact, was born in the evangelical church.[11]

Stephen Clark in his *Man and Woman in Christ* argues for a subordinate role for women and specifically contests the claim that the slavery and feminist issues are connected. His essential argument is that sexual role differences are grounded in God's intention as revealed in creation, while slavery is a human institution without scriptural warrant. To oppose slavery may be justified, but to oppose

different social roles for men and women and the subordination
of women is to be in conflict with God's revealed will. "For Paul,
the man-woman relationship and the subordination it involves is
[sic] based on the order of creation; it therefore expresses God's purpose in creating the human race." In contrast, "Paul views slavery
in a different way. He . . . never bases his teaching by appealing to
the divine institution of slavery." It is impossible to treat slavery
and sexual differentiation in parallel fashion "since slavery is a
human institution and male-female differences are biological features of the human race."[12]

This argument does not hold, however. While it is true that sexual
differentiation is biologically based and slavery is not, this is not
where the parallel is to be drawn. The more accurate parallel is between slavery (a human institution) and male dominance of women
(also, I argue, a human institution). Slavery, especially in its American form, relied on an elaborate theory of racial differences which
held that the social practice (or social roles of master-slave) were in
fact based in God's order—á la Clark's argument regarding male
dominance. That view has now been totally discredited, though not
wiped out. Those who argue for a *biblical* feminist position do not
wish to deny or do away with sexual distinctiveness or uniqueness,
but only with the injustice of the domination of one sex by another.
Clearly a parallel does exist between feminist issues and the issues
of racism and slavery.

To be valid, Clark's argument would have to show not just that
men and women are different in their constitution and social roles,
but also that God *intends* for the woman to be subordinate to the
man. This is, of course, the fundamental point which Clark attempts
to prove, but the argument advanced fails to be convincing.[13]

The view I am presenting here could be called a high view of sex
and of the meaning of sexual differentiation. It is a view which
neither overemphasizes the physical aspect nor subsumes the physical into a "higher" spiritual meaning. Rather it holds the physical,
psychological and spiritual dimensions of human sexuality together
in a way that is consistent with the wonder of our creation in God's
image.[14]

Fundamentally, this view sees sexual differentiation as *more* significant than many feminists and antifeminists do. Sexual differ-

ences reach deeply into the psyche and the spirit, and therefore into the self-identity, of each person. For this reason both the masculine and the feminine should be seen as essential to the image of God. God, far from being "sexless," incorporates within himself those qualities and characteristics that naturally bring forth, in human nature, sexual differentiation and distinctiveness. I do not mean by this to read sexuality back into the Godhead, but rather to argue in the opposite direction. The very nature and glory of the Trinity, while it cannot be understood through sexual categories, is such that it leads naturally to the sexual differences in man and woman, just as it leads naturally to human community. This is to make sexuality much more fundamentally significant than just a matter of bio-logical reproduction or, as some say, "just a matter of plumbing."[15]

Liberating women for the Kingdom has enormous practical con-sequences. Sexism in society and in the church (one face of worldli-ness) is needlessly causing or condoning suffering which Jesus died to remove. The significance of the issue can be felt in this response from a woman who had just learned that in God's Kingdom plan she was to serve where God had placed her:

I am married (eight years) and we have an eight-month-old son. The cir-cumstances of the economics in our area and a back injury have caused my husband to be at home and myself to be at work. Due to pressures from the church community, our attitudes of thankfulness and contentment have been swallowed up in depression and despair in trying to make our relationship be what others have said it has to be to be "right." Any problems we have with anything at all have been promptly attributed to the fact that I'm not home "where I belong" and my husband isn't supporting his family "like he should."

It's like sunshine after a dark, dark storm to not feel like I'm "supposed" to hate my job and I'm "supposed" to do all of the housework when I get home because it's "demeaning" to a man. It's "OK" that my husband enjoys caring for our son and cooks great meals and has a sense of pride in a stack of clean, folded diapers. He is providing for his family and is the head of it—even though the paycheck has my name on it.

I also enjoy my son and cooking and homemaking. My husband has a real desire to be working and puts in a full day every week looking for a suitable job. But the anxiety is leaving us and we are trying to "do heartily" the jobs God has given for this time.[16]

Perhaps the most indisputable argument for women's equality

and leadership in the church is that God continues to call women into pastoral and other forms of ministry. The task of the church is to let women hear God's call to them and then submit to the authority of their gifts. As B. T. Roberts argued passionately,

All restrictions to positions in the church based on race have been abolished; it is time then that those based on sex were also abolished. The church has no right to forbid the free exercise of abilities to do good which God has given. To do so is usurpation and tyranny. Men had better busy themselves in building up the temple of God, instead of employing their time in pushing from the scaffold their sisters, who are both able and willing to work with them side by side. [17]

When women are free to exercise their full, God-given rights of leadership alongside men, both the church and the family will function with new power. We will more fully understand the economy of God and see expanding evidence of God's Kingdom, fulfilling what God's Word has promised. God has yet to show what he can do when his Spirit is fully poured out on "all people," "sons and daughters," "both men and women" (Joel 2:28-29). [18]

14
THE POOR
FREE TO DECIDE

The freedom of the poor and dispossessed to be fully human is a fundamental benefit of the gospel. God lifts the poor to a position of freedom and self-determination. "He raises the poor from the dust and lifts the needy from the ash heap; he seats them with princes, with the princes of their people" (Ps 113:7-8).

Scripture makes clear that God has a particular concern for the poor. It teaches that injustice and oppression, not laziness, are the most fundamental causes of poverty, and that God acts in history to liberate the poor and the victims of injustice.[1] Further, God's people bear special responsibility for the poor. They must stand with the poor, defending the cause of refugees, the defenseless and the oppressed.

The church is *for* the poor mainly through being *of* the poor. Jesus could speak both of the "poor in spirit" (Mt 5:3) and the economically poor (Lk 6:20) without consistently distinguishing between the two. Material and spiritual poverty are often closely related. The Kingdom of God is for the poor in spirit, and Jesus knew and demonstrated that the poor in spirit were most likely to be found among the world's poor rather than among the rich.

The life of Jesus is instructive here. We need to observe not only Jesus' death on the cross, but also how he came into the world and the way he fulfilled the prophecies foretelling the Messiah.

The prophets and psalmists promised justice for the poor. They promised divine intervention for the oppressed and the suffering.

But, for the most part, what the prophets had in mind was not Jesus!

And then Jesus came—born of the poor, born in a nation oppressed, raised in despised Galilee. A likely Savior! Born of the poor, he preached to the poor, healed the suffering, freed the demon possessed. Above all, he formed a new people among the poor. In his death and resurrection he freed this people from the power of sin, freed them and empowered them—these outcasts from the religious, social and political power structure—to be agents of the very authority and rule of God! He authorized them to be his witnesses, witnesses of the Kingdom.

Instead of setting a just ruler over them to force justice from above, God sent a Savior among them to build a just community from beneath. This was a strategy not as visibly dramatic, but one infinitely more revolutionary and efficacious in the course of history.

Who were these people of the new community, these new people of the Kingdom? Mainly the poor, plus a scattering of the wealthy and powerful who became outcasts to their own class and kin by daring to identify with Jesus and his ragtag followers (not unlike what happened with St. Francis eleven hundred years later).

The Jews in Jesus' day suffered under political, economic, religious and spiritual oppression. As a nation, the Jews were under the heel of Rome, oppressed by political control, military force and taxation. In addition, the mass of the people were oppressed religiously and often economically by the Jewish power structure. Jesus especially singled out the religious leaders for their injustice and hypocrisy and for their religious and economic oppression of the poor (Mt 23:1-36; Mk 12:38-40; Lk 20:45-47).

Added to these forms of oppression were the spiritual oppression of the people's own sin and the frequent bondage of demon possession. The people suffered from evil in many forms—evil institutionalized in the religious and political power structures, the evil of direct demon attack and the evil present in their own hearts, leading to acts of sin. Jesus' public ministry is understandable only against this backdrop of oppression. What did Jesus do? He went about announcing the Kingdom, healing diseases, casting out demons, denouncing personal and institutionalized evil, preaching hope to the poor and liberty to the oppressed. Above all, he called for a commitment of faith and obedience to himself and God's Kingdom. And he formed a community of disciples, the embryonic church of the Kingdom.

All this led to the double irony of the cross. On the one hand, the cross was the ultimate culmination and inexorable logic of the forces of evil conspiring to end the political, social and spiritual threat Jesus posed. On the other hand, this very death by crucifixion atoned for all human sin. And through the resurrection it conquered the combined principalities and powers, inaugurating the new age of the Kingdom.

In Jesus Christ, God intervened to bring justice and righteousness to the poor. And the church today, if truly righteous, will be concerned with justice for the poor. The church ought to be the community of people where the oppressed are freed to decide their own destiny through the liberating power of the gospel.

Who Are the Poor? Much of the church—including Roman Catholicism, liberal and evangelical American Protestantism, and some Third World Christians—is experiencing a new awakening to the claims of the world's poor. In part, this is due to the growing awareness of the massive disparity between rich and poor in today's world. This has been dramatized by severe famine in Africa and elsewhere. No informed Christian today can fail to deal with what Scripture says about the poor, nor to avoid personal responsibility. The two key questions are: Who in fact are the poor, and what is the church's proper response?

In discussing the first question, John Stott distinguishes between the indigent poor (those deprived of the basic necessities of life), the powerless poor (the victims of human oppression) and the humble poor (those who, humanly oppressed, look to God for help). Stott's point is that "God concerns himself both with the *materially* poor and powerless, and with the *morally* humble and meek," opposing material poverty but seeking spiritual humility. "The only community in which these concepts are combined," says Stott, "is a church that is witnessing to the kingdom of God." To those who are both spiritually and sociologically poor "the kingdom of God is proclaimed as a free gift of salvation and as a promise of justice."[2]

Clearly Scripture does speak of the poor in economic and sociopolitical as well as spiritual terms, as Stott notes. To empty biblical references to the poor of their economic, social and political content is to twist Scripture. It would be just as wrong, of course, to see the poor *only* in such terms.

My concern in this chapter is especially with those who are economically poor, in part through injustice and oppression.[3] From this perspective, we may identify the poor in Scripture and in today's world in the following three ways.

First, *the poor are those who live a marginal existence,* those often called the marginalized. They are the millions who lack the bare necessities of life. They do not have the food, clothing or shelter that most of us consider necessary for survival. They include not only the physically starving but also those whose level of physical, social or psychological existence is so marginal that their lives are nothing more than a struggle for survival.

From a slightly different angle, *the poor are those with no social power.* They do not have sufficient control over their lives to adequately provide for their own welfare or meet needs beyond mere survival.

Social power is so taken for granted by middle-class Christians that they often have difficulty even understanding the concept. To have social power means to know where the "handles" are—to know where to go, whom to see or what to do to get things done. Social power is partly economic, simply having enough money. But it also depends on education, on having sufficient understanding of society and one's own situation to know how to function effectively.

Many of the poor in America's inner cities and in the world's poorer nations have virtually no social power. Even if they receive welfare they remain powerless. They have never been taught the social knowledge and skills that would open up a broader world for them. Welfare programs, in fact, merely preserve the dependency. The poor are not free to decide what their lives will be like. To operate successfully within the social and political system is not part of their experience.

Third, most often the poor are *those with little or no vested interest in the status quo.* The poor have nothing to lose. They have no vested interest in the social, economic or political state of things. Unlike the two previous conditions, lack of vested interest is not a totally negative situation. Without vested interests one may have a greater level of freedom than would be true otherwise. One may be open to change, to new things, because change is no real threat. Lack of vested interest may also be negative, however, for it usually means a situation of suffering and oppression. And even in such situations some people, out of understandable fear, hold all the more tenaciously to the little they do have.

The Church of the Poor. The church cannot respond adequately to the world's poor unless it understands the causes of poverty in today's world.[4] As in biblical times, much of the world's poverty is caused by economic and sociopolitical oppression. The major source of poverty today is human self-seeking multiplied and extended by economic systems and structures. It is personal sin compounded by social institutions. "The rich get richer and the poor get poorer," not because the rich are smarter (and certainly not because they are more virtuous), but because society is structured to reward the rich and punish the poor. Tax loopholes and interest rates on investments are but two examples. The rich are able to channel money to all kinds of tax-sheltered investments. Large investors often get twice the return on their investments that poorer folk get and yet avoid taxes. One can't begin to earn high interest unless he or she has $10,000 or more to invest. It takes money to make money.

Although capitalism sees this as "free enterprise" which gives everyone a chance, the cards are stacked against the poor. As John Perkins cannily observes, dividing the wealth of the rich among the poor would solve nothing—because by nightfall the money would be back in the hands of the rich. That's the way the system works; that's the way the money goes. This is, on a broader scale, precisely why many Third World leaders oppose gigantic transnational corporations. They are the conduits through which wealth flows from the poorer nations of the South to the richer nations of the North. No corporation invests in a poor country unless it is convinced it can get more out than it puts in.[5]

To point to socioeconomic causes of poverty is not to deny that the basic source of evil is in the human heart. It is, however, to note the broader ecology of power and wealth in the world. Most social and economic structures are controlled by the rich and powerful. No wonder then that they are geared to preserve and increase wealth for the rich and keep it from the poor. Different societies do this in different ways. In North America we have given our economic mechanisms a tinge of righteousness by blessing the profit motive and by according Adam Smith's "invisible hand" equal status with the Bible.

This situation of poverty presents a special challenge to the church today. Biblically, it is clear God's people are supposed to be on the side of the poor—the marginalized, those without social power, those without vested interest in preserving the status quo. Kingdom Christians see the present in the light of the coming Kingdom, not primarily in the light of preserving tradition or the present state of things. This is why Christians are always potential social revolutionaries and the church is always a ticking time bomb.

But the church can do Kingdom business only on a Kingdom basis. It can effectively work for God's ends only by using God's means. It must always remember that "the weapons we use in our fight are not the world's weapons but God's powerful weapons, which we use to destroy strongholds" (2 Cor 10:4 TEV). And the primary weapon of God's people is the church itself, the community of the Word, the community that lives in allegiance to the King.

What is the church's responsibility toward the poor? Is it to work *for* the poor or to be *of* the poor? It is both. But being the church of the poor is more basic. A middle-class church typically goes about helping the poor in middle-class ways. With vested interest in the political and economic status quo, it generally fails to see root causes of poverty and instinctively resists measures that really would relieve the oppressed. In the name of helping it may actually lend support to the very economic realities that grind the face of the poor.

The church can be *for* the poor only if it is *of* the poor. This does not mean the church ever will or should be composed only of poor folks. But it does mean it must make the poor its special concern in its evangelism, justice ministries and way of life. As in the Old Testament ethic, justice for the poor will be its passion. As in the New Testament, it will preach the gospel to the poor and form communities among the poor of those who seek first God's Kingdom and righteousness.

The church cannot be *of* the poor unless it is *among* the poor. This is the catch in the church's Kingdom witness today, especially in the Western and Northern Hemispheres. The church can provide freedom that allows the oppressed to be human, to decide, only if it is in touch with the poor. But in affluent nations, by and large it is not. And the churches which are in touch with the poor are walled off from more affluent churches by denominational and socioeconomic barriers.

Being *among* the poor helps the church be *of* and *for* the poor. This has repeatedly been illustrated in church history, as well as in the life of the North American church in recent years. Where Christians have begun ministering among the urban or rural poor, actually sharing their lives with them in Christian love, they have come to see social reality from the underside. It looks different when you are on your back looking up. And from that perspective they have buttressed their evangelism and social relief work with efforts to change unjust structures and to help the poor break the cycle of poverty. Evangelical leadership in abolitionism, feminism and urban social reform in the nineteenth century are some examples. Other examples can be cited from virtually every era of Christian history.[6]

More specifically, the church can fulfill its Kingdom mandate to be on the side of the poor in the following ways:

1. *The church must identify with and learn from the poor.* We can start by trying to see things from the point of view of the poor. According to Scripture, to see things from that point of view is to see them from God's viewpoint. It is not that the two perspectives are precisely the same. It is just that if we are to see things as Jesus does we must stand where he stands.

We can understand the Kingdom from the point of view of the poor because we have the Bible and millions of Christian sisters and brothers around the world and in nearby cities who are part of the suffering poor. And the Spirit is at work in the church to help us see things as Jesus saw them.

In the final analysis, the crucial point is not *our* identification with the poor but God's. "The starting point of theology is not first of all *our* identification with the oppressed, which is very tenuous, dubious, and fragile. We are compelled to begin with *God's* solidarity with the oppressed and its implication for us."[7] From there we can move both toward greater contact with the poor and a greater sensitivity to the ways our affluent lifestyles oppress the poor.

In many churches an important prophetic task is simply to comprehend the plight of the poor at home and around the world. Fortunately many resources are available for this today in the form of books, films, brochures and study packets. Good sources of such resources are Bread for the World, Evangelicals for Social Action, the Association for Public Justice and Sojourners Fellowship.[8]

In this process, the church must deal with its prejudice against the poor just as surely as it must deal with racial prejudice. Stereotypes of the poor as lazy, shiftless, immoral and greedy must be replaced by more balanced views. When Christians share such prejudiced views with their non-Christian neighbors, are they not worldly rather than biblical?

Christians often express not only prejudice toward the poor but also deference toward the rich. The worldly standard is to think it is good—a blessing—to have many prosperous or well-to-do church members. Often I have heard some church described more or less as follows: "That's a really good church with great potential. It has a lot of professionals and businessmen in it." And at times I have found myself thinking the same way.

The Bible, however, is consistent in presenting the opposite view. The church that is rich or affluent should mourn and bewail its situation, while the poor church should consider itself wealthy and blessed. Jesus' words are clear on this, as are such passages as James 1:9-11, 2:1-7 and 5:1-6. James says, "The brother who is poor may be glad because God has called him to the true riches. The rich may be glad that God has shown him his spiritual poverty" (Jas 1:9-10 Phillips). "God chose the poor people of this world to be rich in faith and to possess the kingdom which he promised to those who love him" (Jas 2:5 TEV).

Many practical avenues are open for affluent Christians to identify with and learn from the poor. These include supporting and listening to Christians who work among the world's poor (at home and abroad), forming sister relationships with poorer churches and accepting work assignments among the poor (either short-term or long-term), where one's knowledge and skills can be put to work for the poor. For the price of a trip to Israel, a North American Christian could spend several months working alongside (and learning from) the poor in a Third World nation—and probably really get closer to the living Christ. Nearer home, an affluent suburban church could become an intentional neighbor or sister to a poorer inner-city church, especially a Black or ethnic church, which would have much to teach not only about poverty but about Christian life and worship among the poor.

2. *The church must defend the cause of the poor* (Is 1:17; 58:6-7; Amos 5:14-15, 24). This is true in at least two directions: (1) working to provide relief for the poor and opportunities for the poor to improve their own lives, and (2) examining our own lifestyles, working toward greater simplicity and responsibility in the way we live. In the ecology of today's world, North American consumption directly contributes to Third World poverty. The strands of our lives run around the globe, interlacing with the lives of the world's poor. Ultimately, their history is our history and their future is our future.

For some, defending the cause of the poor will mean helping the poor gain greater control over their own lives. For some it will mean evangelism, church planting and discipleship—building healthy Kingdom communities among the poor. For some, it will mean political action—working to modify or replace laws and structures which oppress the poor, or working to elect candidates with these priorities. For some it will mean finding creative economic alternatives based on small-scale, appropriate technology in order to help, rather than undermine, the poor economically. For many of us it means examining lifestyles, giving directly to aid the poor and boycotting products of companies whose policies oppress the poor (not just the companies that sponsor sex and violence on TV). For all of us it should mean fasting and prayer for the poor, in part so that we can hear God and learn his concerns and priorities for the peoples of the world. In this respect, prayer is the key to all other action.

3. *The church must offer Christ to the poor.* The cause of evangelism among the poor has not been discredited, even though it has been complicated and distorted by First World missionaries' and evangelists' cultural baggage. When all legitimate criticisms have been leveled, it still remains true that the poor need the gospel.

I have placed this priority third, however, because offering Christ to the poor can be done with integrity only by those who take the side of the poor and learn from them. In offering Christ to the poor, the sensitive evangelist realizes that Jesus already is among the poor;

he simply needs to be proclaimed and made known as Savior, Lord and Liberator.

Whenever it has truly had the character of a dynamic movement, the church has almost always been a movement of the poor. This was true in the first century. "Primitive Christianity, alike in its leading personalities and in the prepondering number of its adherents, was a movement of the lower classes. The water of life did not filter down from the upper level to the many and insignificant. . . . The first to drink of it were fainting stragglers from the great caravan of the unknown and the forgotten."[9] And we may expect today that the truly world-transforming movements of God's Kingdom in coming decades will arise (or are now arising) principally among the world's poor.[10]

Offering Christ to the poor does not mean transmitting "verbal summaries of the gospel"; it means proclaiming and demonstrating the good news of the Kingdom. It means not only speaking the gospel but also living it, not just God-talk but also God-walk.[11] And the demonstration of the gospel of the Kingdom comes especially through a visible community of believers, a community that lives by the standard of Kingdom justice.

4. *The church must be a reconciled and reconciling community of and with the poor.* So we come again to what the church *is* as well as what it *does.* In offering Christ to the poor, standing on the side of the poor against the principalities and powers, learning from the poor, and building Christian communities among and with the poor, the church lays the basis for the Christian revolution. As in the first century, it becomes God's Kingdom people among the poor.

I come back to this fundamental point in order to stress that the unique gift of the church to the poor, and its unique contribution to the Kingdom, is what it *is* as a reconciled and reconciling community. As a new social reality among the poor, the church builds social, economic and political, as well as spiritual, relationships among people. In other words, it *builds human community,* and especially those microstructures and intermediate structures which are the glue of a culture and the strength of its stability and justice.

As a reconciled and reconciling community, the church is not to be the church of the poor against the rich or the middle class. Rather it is to be the church of all peoples that stands on the side of the oppressed. Like God's intent for Old Testament Israel, the church is to be a healthy, prospering community, living in harmony with the physical environment, with the extremes of wealth and poverty eliminated. It is to be like the church described in Acts 4:34—"There were no needy persons among them" because the rich shared with the poor.[12]

In this way the church truly becomes a liberating force. "Laymen" are freed to minister. Women are liberated to lead alongside men. And the oppressed are freed to decide their own future, freed in Christ to be conformed to the likeness of Jesus Christ (Rom 8:29).

In this process the church itself becomes free for the Kingdom. It moves beyond church business to Kingdom business. It serves not the principalities and powers of this present age, but the one King of kings and Lord of lords.

To some this will all sound too idealistic to be workable, too vague to be practical. But the point here is to sharpen the goal and to evoke a vision. I have indicated some of the specific steps toward such a goal and vision. Much of the rest is a matter of faith and obedience. God can and will reveal his Kingdom through the church if we will but see and serve his plan.

15

PASTORS
FREE TO DISCIPLE

Stressing the priesthood of believers, as I have done in this book, could be taken as an attack on leadership, authority or the pastoral ministry. Properly understood, it is not. Once the priesthood of believers, the charismatic gifts and the principle of Ephesians 4:11-12 are understood and put into practice, pastoral leadership becomes more important than ever. But it is radically redefined, and much of the traditional pastoral stereotype is stood on its head.

Henri Nouwen speaks prophetically when he describes the daily routine of the "compulsive minister" of today. As ministers, he says, *We simply go along with the many "musts" and "oughts" that have been handed on to us, and we live with them as if they were authentic translations of the Gospel of our Lord. People must be motivated to come to church, youth must be entertained, money must be raised, and above all everyone must be happy. Moreover, we ought to be on good terms with the church and civil authorities; we ought to be liked or at least respected by a fair majority of our parishioners; we ought to move up in the ranks according to schedule; and we ought to have enough vacation and salary to live a comfortable life. Thus we are busy people just like all other busy people, rewarded with the rewards which are rewarded to busy people!*[1]

This picture is all too accurate. It is a picture of pastors who are not really free to disciple. And yet I have growing respect for the pastoral role the more I understand the biblical nature of church and Kingdom. In the biblical ecology of the church, pastoring or shepherding is rescued from all triviality and is put at the center of the healthy life of the Christian community. In the community of God's people the pastor is not the head, the pastoral director, the boss or the chief executive officer. Rather, the pastor (or better, *pastors*) serves as coordinator, equipper, discipler, overseer and shepherd. This is leadership. But it is leadership for, with and in the body. It is leadership on an organic community model, not on an organizational hierarchy model.

I said in the prologue that leadership grows out of discipleship. This is one of my theses on renewal. The church has a shortage of "ministers" only when it fails to see all believers as ministers and thus fails to disciple believers into leaders. A church that does not understand itself biblically puts low priority on discipling. It makes secondary qualifications for leadership primary and so with time inevitably runs short on leaders who are truly servants of the Kingdom.

What is the pastoral role in the economy of God? This is a crucial question—perhaps *the* crucial question in many churches. For if all believers are to become ministers, the burden in most contemporary churches necessarily falls on pastors to see that the biblical ecology of the church becomes a functioning reality.

Pastoral Priorities What is a pastor? We should go to the Bible for the answer, rather than reading the modern idea of "pastor" back into the New Testament. In the understanding of New Testament writers, a *pastor* (that is, *shepherd*) was not the sole leader of a congregation. The "one church, one pastor" idea is simply not found in the New Testament.[2] The New Testament concept is plural leadership based on the recognition of leadership gifts and the appointing to leadership of those who demonstrate maturity.[3]

The pastoral function is clearly identified in the New Testament as a spiritual gift (Eph 4:11). The word *pastor* or *shepherd* is used infrequently in the New Testament, however, for the normal New Testament pattern was a range of leadership gifts exercised in each congregation. In speaking of pastoral priorities today, therefore, the strategic question is not the precise biblical meaning of *pastor*. Rather, it is this: How can modern pastors—together with others in their congregations—implement the kind of leadership which will help the church function in harmony with the biblical ecology of the church?

What, then, should be a pastor's chief role today? Some say preaching. Others say evangelism or counseling. Most pastors confess that administration takes an unhealthy chunk of their time.

Some say the pastor's first priority is to be a man or woman of God. Others see the pastor as a prophet, or else say that the pastor, like Jesus, must function as prophet, priest and king.

Certainly a pastor must be a man or woman of God and of the Word. But this is not uniquely true of pastors. The same can be said of all Christians, and certainly of all Christian leaders. While a pastor must first of all know God intimately and live by the Word, this is not a definition of the pastoral task.

Nor can pastoring be defined primarily in terms of preaching or evangelism. Many men and women genuinely called as pastors suffer confusion and frustration because they do not have the necessary gifts for preaching, evangelism or some other responsibility commonly expected of pastors. If God has given a person ability to preach, he or she is responsible to be a good steward of that gift. The same is true regarding evangelism and other gifts, and certainly the conscientious pastor will "do the work of an evangelist" (2 Tim 4:5). But if one is not gifted in these areas, he or she may still be an effective pastor—*if* the pastor zeroes in on pastoral priority number one.

The chief priority of pastoral leadership is discipling men and women for the Kingdom. Ephesians 4:11-12 says God has gifted pastors and other leaders to equip God's people for ministry. Jesus said he was sending out his followers to make disciples (Mt 28:19). Essentially, the pastor's first priority is to so invest himself or herself in a few other persons that they also become disciplers and ministers of Jesus Christ. It is to so give oneself to others and to the work of discipling that the New Testament norm of plural leadership or eldership becomes a reality in the local congregation.[4] In other words, it is to bring the ministry of *all* God's people (based on priesthood, gifts and servanthood) to functioning practical reality. God has promised to give sufficient gifts so that through the discipling process all leadership needs are met—whether in evangelism, social witness, teaching or any other area. *Only on this basis,* in fact, has God promised that the church can reach spiritual maturity, the fullness of Christ (Eph 4:11-16).

All pastoral functions should be oriented toward the priority of equipping God's people for Kingdom life and ministry. Discipling is not a specific, specialized activity. It is the exercise of all pastoral gifts, focused on the making of disciples. Discipling is *teaching*, understood from the perspective of the Kingdom, not from some other perspective, such as secular education. It is precisely what Jesus said in Matthew 28:20—teaching believers to put into practice what Jesus taught. Once the discipling priority is clear, then preaching, teaching, counseling, worship guidance and other activities can serve the priority of disciple making.

Such a perspective immediately raises hard problems for the average pastor. No pastor has the time or ability to adequately disciple an entire congregation. In fact, no one can effectively pastor more than about a dozen people, if pastoring means discipling. Jesus didn't. This very dilemma, however, may be an opportunity and an invitation to God's design.

Today's pastor still cannot improve on what Jesus did. Modern pastors should follow his example. The greatest single contribution a pastor can make to a congregation is to develop a small group of disciples who become ministers and disciplers themselves. As the pastor does this, ministry expands and needs are met. Plural leadership becomes a reality. New ministries emerge organically, and more needs are touched than even the most professional, organized, seminared or charismatic pastor could ever accomplish.

Until this happens, today's pastor is forced to be all things to all people and finds that the church is mainly marked by mediocre discipleship. Even if the church appears to be succeeding, growth outruns depth and outward success masks inward emptiness.

Pastors minister according to their gifts. They will, naturally, have to serve carefully and faithfully in some areas where they are not gifted. This is the cost of servanthood. But the defining task of pastoral work is discipleship. It is shepherding, taking care of the flock. Because Christians are human, God-imaged persons—not sheep—pastoring goes beyond feeding and protecting the flock to include transforming believers into priests, ministers and servants in their own right.

Pastoral Accountability But if the pastor shepherds the flock, who shepherds the pastor? Is the pastor the heroic "lonely leader" who never bares his soul to anyone but God? Does the pastor have a pastor? These questions touch a basic issue that often accounts for pastoral frustrations, fractured parsonage families and that most dire of all catastrophes: "leaving the ministry."

Currently there are at least four ways in which the question of pastoral accountability and shepherding is answered in the North American church. Perhaps the most common is through administrative hierarchy.

Administrative Hierarchy. In this pattern the pastor works directly under the supervision of an ecclesiastical superior. This person may be a bishop, a district president or superintendent, or some other official. The official supervises the pastor, who supervises the local church. Supervision works downward; accountability works upward. This is an administrative and accountability sequence. It can be an efficient system, but it tends to put particular stress and value on organizational performance and little stress on more person-affirming values.

While we associate this system with the episcopal form of church government, some churches which are episcopal in form are less so in practice, and some denominations with a formally congregational or presbyterian structure in fact rely quite heavily on administrative hierarchy.

Despite its benefits, this system has several serious flaws. Pastors are supposed to fit into the system rather than the system adapting to differing pastoral personalities, capabilities and gifts. One pastor (or senior pastor) per congregation is assumed. The system breaks down if there is a weak link in the hierarchy, and yet the weak link problem may really be more a reflection on the system than on the persons because of the kinds of behavior which the system rewards or punishes. Tensions in pastors' lives and homes, and the lack of freedom pastors feel to share their deepest problems with their ecclesiastical superior, are frequent symptoms of the inadequacy of this system. The fundamental problem with this system is that it is tilted toward maintaining and preserving the institution itself rather than toward building biblically-based Kingdom communities of believers.

Chain of Command. The chain-of-command concept which has

gained a certain popularity in some sectors of evangelicalism and fundamentalism in recent years is really a variation of the administrative hierarchy. It is applied to relationships both in the church and in the family on the theory that every Christian stands in a chain of command in which he or she is under the authority or "covering" protection of another Christian. The church member is under the pastor; the wife is under the husband; children are under the parents.

A whole unbiblical mythology has grown up around this theory. Actually, Scripture teaches nothing about a chain of command. Neither the terminology nor the concept is biblical. The idea is a military concept based on a rigid and impersonal hierarchy. It fits well in a military-technological society but not in a biblically faithful church. Regardless of how one modifies or adapts the concept or tries to pour Christian content into it, it is still fundamentally opposed to the biblical understanding of the church. Christians are not intended to relate to God or to each other on the basis of a chain of command. They are to relate as persons who make up an organic community. They are to relate on the basis of mutual love, respect and submission, with proper recognition of the need for good order.

Ironically, many who enthusiastically promote the chain-of-command theory seldom practice it. What Christian home, for instance, *really* practices a chain of command? What Christian husband simply issues orders and expects (and receives) immediate, unquestioning, mindless obedience from his wife? If he does, his marriage is not really Christian and is probably shot through with tensions and resentments. And yet this is precisely what the chain of command, as a military concept, teaches.

Many who contend for the chain of command share a legitimate concern for order, accountability and leadership. The problem is that they are simply unaware of more biblical and more person-affirming options. Chain of command is simply the wrong model for dealing with these legitimate concerns. Both the chain-of-command theory and the idea of "covering" with which it is often joined go beyond Scripture and can lead to presumption and fatalism.

The point of all this is that the chain-of-command theory should not be applied to pastoral shepherding and supervision. It is unbiblical and harmful to suppose that the church should function on a military model. The Scriptures do often employ military figures, but only in a limited and secondary way, and never to teach a chain of command. God's people are not primarily an army and the Great Commission is not "Onward, Christian soldiers." The primary biblical models for leadership, authority and shepherding are the same as for the church itself. These are the models of body, family, community and the people of God. The main biblical models are uniformly figures that presume a living, organic, relational ecology for the church.

Hierarchy and chain-of-command models raise the important issue of authority. While I do not here deal with this issue directly, the views I have set forth are not (as some have suggested) hostile to authority in general nor based on a kind of unbiblical democratic ideal. We must be clear that all authority is God's authority, that Jesus has been given all authority (Mt 28:18) and that in his resurrection he has triumphed over all other authorities and powers. The church is a theocracy, not a democracy. But it is not a hierarchical theocracy tracing from God down a ladder to the lay peasant. Rather it is a family in which God rules supremely, but kindly and lovingly in a way that builds and affirms each member and makes hierarchy superfluous. This is part of what the image of God is all about. God's authority, rule and sovereignty don't require a top-down hierarchy. As the Incarnation shows, God's way subverts hierarchy and builds interdependent mutual community. The church is not a chain of command but a network of love. This is, of course, supremely impractical to people steeped in hierarchical concepts. But it is the way of the Kingdom.

Nondirective Supervision. This third option is the opposite extreme. Its motto is, "Do your own thing." It holds that every pastor should have enough sense to know how to lead the flock, and that the supervisor (if any) is there only in case of emergency. Sometimes this becomes the *de facto* system in what is supposed to be an administrative hierarchy. The supervisor simply busies himself with administrative detail and lets the pastors go their own way until a crisis comes up. This is typified by the remark of one pastor who said, "Whenever I take a problem to my supervisor he just listens and says, 'Well, do the best you can!' "

This approach must be rejected because it sidesteps both accountability and discipleship. It leaves pastors wide open to frustration, on the one hand, or to going off on doctrinal or program tangents, on the other. Often it leads pastors to seek more directive counsel or discipling elsewhere. It is another route to pastoral frustration, failure or extremism.

Shepherding Sequence. A more adequate pattern is what might be called a shepherding sequence or network. This may be understood as an alternative and corrective to a strictly administrative sequence. In denominational structure where pastors function under some type of more general supervison, such a shepherding sequence calls for supervisors to *actually function* as the pastors and disciplers of those assigned to their care. Supervisors are not primarily administrators; they are primarily shepherds for their pastors. Supervision and accountability function in a pastoral rather than administrative sense.

This pattern is much closer to Scripture for several reasons. It takes seriously the matter of discipleship. Supervisors disciple those they supervise, thus enabling pastors to effectively disciple key people in their flock who in turn disciple others. This pattern also takes seriously the matter of spiritual gifts. As gifts come into focus, expectations are based less on administrative roles and more on the spiritual and charismatic strengths of persons. Finally, this pattern takes seriously the church as a family and a people who function most fundamentally on the level of interpersonal community. A shepherding approach presupposes that discipling, rather than new big part of the picture is that the church is a community requiring mutual accountability within the body.

The Accountable Community. This is not the whole story, however. A big part of the picture is that the church is a community and that there is a need for mutual accountability within the body.

Any kind of shepherding accountability comes within the larger circle of the community life of the church. Not only is a local congregation accountable to its pastors; the pastors are accountable to the flock. Pastors are not to hold themselves aloof from their people but to trust themselves to them. They must open themselves, making themselves accountable and vulnerable to the community of believers of which they are a part. Mutuality and mutual submission must extend to leadership if the church is really going to be the church under the headship of Christ. Otherwise, any kind of shepherding network or accountability can quickly turn into a rigid hierarchy which undermines spiritual vitality.

In other words, the priesthood of believers extends this far. Leadership springs from discipleship, and all believers, including leaders, remain accountable to each other under their joint accountability to Jesus Christ, the head.

One Small Example In 1974 I learned one small but important lesson in how to share leadership and work toward the biblical pattern of plural leadership.

I was pastoring a small church in a growing, working-class community on the edge of the great city of São Paulo, Brazil. It wasn't an ideal situation. I was a North American missionary living twenty miles away, clear across the city. Other responsibilities meant I could work with the church only a couple of times each week. But I learned a lesson which strengthened the church.

At planning sessions, I noticed that one brother, Andrew, always took notes on a little pad. I was surprised. Andrew was a fairly recent convert, about three years old in the Lord. He was a little older than I, perhaps in his late thirties, and had only a third-grade education. He had been a well-known alcoholic in the community before he met Christ and was carefully discipled by a former pastor.

As I got to know Andrew better, I found he had a gift for organization and administration. He knew how to bring people together around a common purpose and get a job done. He had not learned this anywhere; it seemed to be a gift of grace. He had become a trustworthy, responsible leader.

My seminary training had taught me that administration was a big part of pastoral work. I was to be the chief church administrator. But here I was with limited time, working in a church where I had to overcome language and cultural barriers. I simply couldn't do the job of administration that should be done, and I was becoming increasingly convinced that even if I could, that wasn't God's plan.

So the Lord gave me Andrew. I had sixteen years' more formal education than he did, but he had a gift I lacked. As designated pastor I still had overall administrative responsibility, but I found I could turn over many organizational tasks to Andrew. The result was threefold: Andrew found a significant ministry, many jobs got done better than I could have done them, and more of my time could be given to spiritual shepherding and teaching. And in the process other gifts and ministries came to light in the body.

Scripture teaches that the church is a charismatic community in which each person has been given one or more gifts for building the body and working to extend the Kingdom in the world. My experience with Andrew showed me that this is a very practical teaching. Some gifts are more dramatic and obvious, while others are more mundane or hidden—but no less necessary. Andrew's gift of administration was needed to supply a lack and to make my ministry more effective. It was but one of several ministry gifts which the Spirit began to awaken in our little congregation. Plural leadership began to function.

This story could be repeated many times over. It is, in fact, happening in various ways in hundreds of groups of believers around the world today as biblical teachings of church life are being recovered. When Christ's body functions in God's way according to Ephesians 4:11-12, the result is Ephesians 4:15-16: "Speaking the truth in love, we will in all things grow up into him who is the Head, that is, Christ. From him the whole body, joined and held together by every supporting ligament, grows and builds itself up in love, as each part does its work."

Discipling for the Kingdom   A discipling ministry that through the Holy Spirit turns believers into ministers is potent for the priorities of the Kingdom. This is its strength and beauty. Following the Ephesians 4 model, it liberates the church for Kingdom business and not just church business. A few religious professionals and "faithful laymen" can make the church go and grow. But it takes the full range of gifts and the priesthood of all believers to make the biblical ecology of the church function and to equip the church to participate redemptively in the economy of God.

Today the pastoral priority, as always, is discipling men and women for the Kingdom. This means developing discipled, shared leadership so that the church will be equipped to function as a balanced ecology of worship, community and witness for the sake of God's Kingdom in the world.

EPILOGUE

Jesus came preaching the Kingdom. Scripture shows us the nature of that Kingdom; it reveals the economy of God's purpose to unite all things in Jesus Christ. The question is, How will the church respond?

Here and there one sees signs that the church is being converted anew to its Lord, which means conversion to the gospel of the Kingdom. This is the only hope for liberating the church. Where the church seeks first the economy and Kingdom of God, there the Spirit has an opening for his liberating, renewing work in the world. God has given the church all it needs to be powerful for the Kingdom. He has revealed the true nature and ecology of the church, providing for the liberation of men and women, rich and poor, ignorant and educated, to be the church free for the Kingdom. I close the book focusing on discipleship and plural leadership because, given the present historical situation of the church, this is the practical and pastoral key for turning the church toward more biblically faithful models and freeing the church for the Kingdom.

Jesus spoke much about faith and was amazed that the people around him, supposedly God's people and people of faith, showed so little faith. But where people took him at his word and believed, his divine power was released to heal and free. Jesus asked some blind men if they believed he could heal them. When they responded yes, Jesus said: "According to your faith will it be done to you" (Mt 9:29). And he healed them on the spot.

Perhaps this is a parable for the church today. Jesus offers us his Kingdom. He asks us to pray for its coming. He says we should seek it above all else. But how do we respond? Too often the church responds in doubt, as though the Kingdom were irrelevant to the present world and Jesus didn't mean what he said. And if that is what we think, to a large extent it will be true.

"According to your faith will it be done to you." If we seek God's Kingdom and believe for what we pray, we will see the coming Kingdom—not just because we believe, but because our faith will, by God's grace, produce in us the hope and love that are the wellsprings of effective Kingdom life and witness in the present age. Somehow we have come to think we may believe in Jesus Christ without believing in the Kingdom Jesus himself promised and said to seek.

God, we are told on good authority, "is able to do immeasurably more than all we ask or imagine, according to his power that is at work within us" (Eph 3:20).

What power? The very power "which he exerted ... when he raised [Jesus] from the dead and seated him at his right hand in the heavenly realms" (Eph 1:20).

If God had the power to raise Jesus from the dead, he has the power to unite all things in him. If God had the power to raise up Christ right in the midst of human history, he has the power to bring his Kingdom *now* right in the midst of *our* human history.

How is it that we can believe God had the power and will to raise Jesus from the dead, but we cannot believe God has the power and will to change the world *now* through us, the body of Christ?

God is able to do far beyond all we ask or imagine. He wants and waits to do what he promises and wills. Do we believe this?

What *is* the "immeasurably more" that God wants to do? More things, more earthly goodies, better careers, more job security, more "blessings," more personal little answers to prayer? Or dare we imagine a much bigger "more"?

Could it be—dare we believe—that God is able, willing and *waiting* to grant us his greatest of all gifts, *the Kingdom of God*?

"According to your faith."

"Your Kingdom come."

"Do not be afraid, little flock, for your Father delights to give you the Kingdom" (Lk 12:32, my translation).

The glory and wonder of the Kingdom of God are that it both does and doesn't depend on us. The Kingdom is *God's* rule and reign. But our response to him *now*, and to his sovereign plan, is a key to the realization of his purposes on earth. For the sake of God's economy and Kingdom, Christians today must be about the business of building a truly faithful Kingdom community, cooperating with the economy of God.

"Now to him who is able to do immeasurably more than all we ask or imagine" *for his Kingdom purposes,* "according to his power that is at work within us, to him be glory in the church and in Christ Jesus throughout all generations, for ever and ever! Amen" (Eph 3:20-21).

Perhaps the church today, facing an urban, technological society, is like the children of Israel as they approached the land of Canaan after the exodus from Egypt. Moses sent twelve spies to investigate the Promised Land. Caleb and Joshua encouraged the people to go into the Promised Land, but the majority report was negative. Although the land was good, it was inhabited by giants living in large, fortified cities (Num 13:28). Later the people were afraid because these people had advanced military technology: chariots of iron! (Josh 17:16).

Here were God's people, promised a land flowing with milk and honey, stopped dead in their tracks by people of great size, living in large cities, possessing advanced technology. But God promised victory. The problem was that God's people failed to believe him and so disobeyed. The result was forty years in the desert (Num 14).

What about the church today? God has promised us the Kingdom. Our temptation is to say, "That will have to wait; we can't do anything until Christ returns; our enemies are giants living in great cities with advanced technology! We are small and weak—what can we do in face of the principalities and powers, in face of urban technological society?"

But God says, take possession of the land—not to destroy it but to heal it. Failure to do so is not realism; it is disobedience and lack of faith.

In the Holy Spirit, and in the body of Christ anointed by the Spirit, the church has the resources and the power to bring the revolution and produce the firstfruits of the Kingdom. The question is faith and faithfulness to God's economy for the church.

Hans Küng has said, "The Kingdom of God is creation healed." Given our faith and obedience, God can liberate the church to heal the world.

NOTES

Prologue: Liberation and Renewal

[1] Vernard Eller, ed., *Thy Kingdom Come: A Blumhardt Reader* (Grand Rapids: Eerdmans, 1980), p. 14.

[2] "Success according to Richard DeVos, founder and chief executive of Amway," *Eternity* 32, no. 2 (February 1981):23-24.

[3] On the use of models, see especially Ian C. Barbour, *Myths, Models and Paradigms* (New York: Harper & Row, 1974); Max Black, *Models and Metaphors* (Ithaca, N.Y.: Cornell University Press, 1962); Ewert Cousins, "Models and the Future of Theology," *Continuum* 7 (1969):78-91; Avery Dulles, *Models of the Church* (Garden City, N.Y.: Doubleday, 1974); Frederick Ferré, "Mapping the Logic of Models in Science and Technology," *Christian Scholar* 46 (1963):9-39; Richard P. McBrien, *The Remaking of the Church* (New York: Harper & Row, 1973); Ian T. Ramsey, *Models and Mystery* (New York: Oxford, 1964); Howard A. Snyder, *The Community of the King* (Downers Grove, Ill.: InterVarsity Press, 1977), pp. 33-41.

[4] Thomas S. Kuhn, *The Structure of Scientific Revolutions,* 2nd ed. enlarged. International Encyclopedia of Unified Science, vol. 2, no. 2 (Chicago: University of Chicago Press, 1970), p. 111. Several writers have recently employed the model of "paradigm shift" to explain change in the church. See George M. Marsden, *Fundamentalism and American Culture* (New York: Oxford, 1980), pp. 214-16; Arthur F. Glasser, "A Paradigm Shift? Evangelicals and Interreligious Dialogue," *Missiology* 9, no. 4 (October 1981):393-408; and (with a broader application) Charles H. Kraft, *Christianity in Culture* (Maryknoll, N.Y.: Orbis, 1979).

[5] For instance, in Dulles, *Models of the Church,* and Paul Minear, *Images of the Church in the New Testament* (Philadelphia: Westminster Press, 1960). More recently, see Ralph P. Martin's useful book, *The Family and the Fellowship: New Testament Images of the Church* (Grand Rapids: Eerdmans, 1979), which shows the importance in the New Testament of the models of the church

as a family and as a fellowship *(koinōnia)*. In his concluding chapter Martin discusses several other models and how these relate to Catholic and Protestant conceptions.

1 Justice, Liberation and the Kingdom

[1] William K. McElvaney, *Good News Is Bad News Is Good News* (Maryknoll, N.Y.: Orbis, 1980), pp. 3, 5.

[2] The use of Platonism and Neo-Platonism by Augustine and the early Greek church fathers and of Aristotle by Thomas Aquinas shows both the values and dangers of employing non-Christian philosophical systems in Christian theology. Since it is impossible to avoid some interaction with contemporary intellectual systems of thought in doing theology, it is best to make any use of and dependence on such systems explicit so that they can be adequately evaluated by Scripture. Unfortunately, the degree to which evangelical theology and capitalist ideology have been blended in North America is often unperceived, which makes evangelicalism particularly susceptible to cultural blindness. Further, it is clearly a myth that capitalism is not an ideology and that it provides "the vitally important separation of economic power from political power" (as argued by Gerhard Niemeyer, "Structures, Revolutions and Christianity," *Center Journal* 1, no. 1 [Winter 1981]:79-80). On the other hand, Latin American liberation theology has not yet demonstrated that it is willing or able to provide an adequate biblical critique of Marxism, rather than accommodating the biblical revelation to Marxist presuppositions.

[3] W. A. Visser 't Hooft, *The Renewal of the Church* (London: SCM Press, 1956), p. 17.

[4] The first priority of the church's witness in the world should be to bring persons into personal, saving relationship with God through Jesus Christ (the new birth) and into the fellowship of the Christian community. This objective must never be ignored. Evangelism must always be grounded, however, in love for the person and respect for each person's self-identity and right of self-determination. This means, among other things, that in particular contexts the first priority of ministry (in point of time) may be meeting needs for food, clothing, shelter, emotional support or other less obviously spiritual needs. Such ministry is truly and authentically the proclamation of the gospel and thus part of evangelism. But evangelism is never complete until the individual comes to personal faith in Jesus Christ and active participation in Jesus' body, for only through such faith and participation does one receive the assurance of forgiveness and the capacity, through the Holy Spirit, to be a whole, integrated person who can in turn seek first God's Kingdom and justice.

[5] The connection between righteousness and justice (with reference both to

God himself and to his people) is clear from such passages as Ps 9:8; 11:7; 33:5; 36:6; 72:1-2; 89:14; 97:2; 99:4; 103:6; Is 1:27; 5:7; 9:7; 11:4; 16:5; 28:17; 32:1; 33:5; 59:14; Jer 4:2; 9:24; Amos 5:7; 5:24; 6:12.

[6]Combining the RSV and NIV translations of this verse.

[7]See Snyder, *Community of the King,* pp. 45-46.

[8]Frederick Herzog, *Justice Church: The New Function of the Church in North American Christianity* (Maryknoll, N.Y.: Orbis, 1980), p. 3.

[9]I have hinted at this in *The Problem of Wineskins* (Downers Grove, Ill.: Inter-Varsity Press, 1975), pp. 152-54, 202-3.

[10]Herzog, *Justice Church,* pp. 22, 11.

[11]Ibid., pp. 26-27 (emphasis Herzog's).

[12]For a fuller discussion of these and related issues, see Howard A. Snyder, "Why the Local Church Is Becoming More and Less," *Christianity Today* 25, no. 13 (July 17, 1981):66-70.

[13]Richard N. Ostling, "Let a Hundred Churches Bloom," *Time* (May 4, 1981), pp. 54-55.

[14]Peter Wong, ed., *Missions from the Third World* (Singapore: Church Growth Centre, 1973); Ralph D. Winter, "The Planting of Younger Missions," in *Church/Mission Tensions Today,* ed. C. Peter Wagner (Chicago: Moody, 1972), pp. 129-45; Marlin L. Nelson, *The How and Why of Third World Missions: An Asian Case Study* (South Pasadena, Calif.: William Carey Library, 1976); Marlin L. Nelson, ed., *Readings in Third World Missions: A Collection of Essential Documents* (South Pasadena, Calif.: William Carey Library, 1976). According to the World Evangelical Fellowship, Third World churches sent out a record 13,000 missionaries in 1981 (*Christianity Today* 26, no. 6 [March 19, 1982]:37).

[15]Howard A. Tyner, "Main Chicago Immigrant Groups," *Chicago Tribune,* 26 April 1981. *Assyrian* is a common description for Palestinian and other related Middle Eastern peoples in Chicago.

[16]George Gallup and David Poling, *The Search for America's Faith* (Nashville: Abingdon, 1980), p. 57.

[17]Bertram Gross, *Friendly Fascism: The New Face of Power in America* (New York: M. Evans and Company, 1980), p. 3. Gross's book was published before the advent of the Reagan administration.

[18]Ibid., p. 2.

[19]Ibid., p. 42. Much of Gross's book is a detailing of the intricate mechanisms which hold such complexes together.

[20]Ibid., p. 161.

[21]These two models in some ways parallel the Troeltschian church/sect typology, but in the present context that distinction is sufficiently misleading to be unhelpful.

[22]Jürgen Moltmann, "A Seed of the Kingdom to Come," *Sojourners* 11, no. 3 (March 1982):36.

2 The Economy of God

[1]Mark Hatfield, "Finding the Energy to Continue," *Christianity Today* 24, no. 3 (February 8, 1980):20-21.

[2]Jeremy Rifkin with Ted Howard, *The Emerging Order: God in the Age of Scarcity* (New York: Putnam's, 1979), p. 9. For a much more optimistic assessment of some of these trends based largely on the assumption of unlimited technological breakthroughs, see Herman Kahn, *World Economic Development: 1979 and Beyond* (New York: Morrow Quill Paperbacks, 1979). Kahn views the gap between rich and poor nations as "a basic 'engine' of growth. The greater the difference in relative income between the the Rich and the Poor countries, the greater the ability of the Poor countries to 'take off' and the greater their potential growth rate" (p. 64).

[3]Vithal C. Nadkarni, "The Coming Water Crisis," *World Press Review* (September 1981), p. 55. Cf. "Ebbing of the Ogallala," *Time* (10 May 1982), p. 98.

[4]There is a growing consensus concerning the meaning and gravity of these and related economic-ecological issues among people who are ecologically aware. For good summaries, note, among others, Rifkin's *The Emerging Order*; E. F. Schumacher, *Small Is Beautiful: Economics As If People Mattered* (New York: Harper, 1973); Ronald J. Sider, *Rich Christians in an Age of Hunger* (Downers Grove, Ill.: InterVarsity Press, 1977); Loren Wilkinson, ed., *Earthkeeping: Christian Stewardship of Natural Resources* (Grand Rapids: Eerdmans, 1980); Ron Elsdon, *Bent World: A Christian Response to the Environmental Crisis* (Downers Grove, Ill.: InterVarsity Press, 1981). I am well aware, however, that this general perspective is vigorously disputed by many economists and futurologists as being needlessly pessimistic (for example, Adrian Berry, *The Next Ten Thousand Years* [New York: New American Library, 1974]; Herman Kahn, *World Economic Development*). Kahn's generally optimistic future projections, based on a positive view of technology, affluence and economic development and a down-playing of environmental constraints, clash at several points with perspectives presented in this book. Kahn's projections, however, are based on (1) consistently ruling out "bad luck or bad management," (2) a long-range time frame within which Kahn admits that things may get much worse before they get better and (3) a number of philosophical or quasi-theological assumptions which are largely unarticulated but which render the author's claim to objectivity suspect. While Kahn believes the fears of environmentalists are "wildly exaggerated," he admits that among "potentially disastrous" future problems may be "complicated, complex,

and subtle ecological and environmental issues" (p. 69). My analysis would indicate that the environmental issues are already clearer and much more serious than Kahn allows and therefore render his projections unreliable.

[5] Warren Johnson, *Muddling toward Frugality* (Boulder, Colo.: Shambhala Publications, 1978), p. 88. Even though nuclear fusion is a supposedly "clean" technology, it still produces some wastes, requires tremendously high temperatures and depends on nonrenewable minerals.

[6] For example, Richard A. Underwood, "Ecological and Psychedelic Approaches to Theology," and Kenneth P. Alpers, "Starting Points for an Ecological Theology: A Bibliographic Survey," both in *New Theology No. 8*, ed. Martin E. Marty and Dean G. Peerman (New York: Macmillan, 1971), pp. 139-72 and 292-312. See also Eric C. Rust, *Nature–Garden or Desert? An Essay in Environmental Theology* (Waco, Tex.: Word Books, 1971).

[7] This is the fundamental problem with Underwood's otherwise helpful essay, noted above.

[8] Two qualifications are in order here. First, I am speaking of ecological realities, not evolutionary theories. While ecology does necessitate a long-range view, it does not require assuming time spans of hundreds of millions of years unless one is philosophically committed to evolutionary hypotheses rather than divine creation (though long time periods are not necessarily contrary to Scripture and the geological record must be taken seriously). Second, some ecologists also argue for a "catastrophe theory"—that not all ecological development occurs gradually but may be punctuated by periodic sudden change. Recognizing this possibility does not substantially alter the fact, however, that the ecological time frame is fundamentally a long-range one.

[9] Walter Brueggemann, *The Land* (Philadelphia: Fortress Press, 1977), pp. 2-3, Bruggemann's emphasis.

[10] Ibid.

[11] Brueggemann's book merits careful study by Christians sensitive to ecological thinking and categories.

[12] Alpers, in *New Theology No. 8*, p. 305.

[13] "Inhabit" and "live" in this verse are *oikos* words, forms of the verb *katoikeō*.

[14] Jeremy Rifkin, *Entropy: A New World View* (New York: Viking, 1980).

[15] Rifkin's *Entropy* is a fascinating and provocative study. It relies heavily on earlier work done on the entropy question by physicists. The basic questions, it seems to me, are whether the earth is truly a closed system in the sense the entropy paradigm presupposes; whether entropy can be legitimately applied (as Rifkin does) to social institutions; and whether it is legitimate to use entropy as a world-view model. While a number of

scientists object strenuously to the "reification" of the entropy paradigm, the opposition appears to me to be more philosophical or emotional than scientific. In any case, the matter will require extensive further research and debate, both theologically and scientifically, and ought especially to be the focus of investigation in interdisciplinary groups of Christian thinkers (such as suggested in chapter nine of this book). See *A New Pattern for Understanding Economics: The Entropy Paradigm* (Glassboro, N.J.: Glassboro State College, 1980).

[16]This seems to be the sense of Romans 8:20-21, a fundamentally important passage with echoes of Genesis 3:17-19 and the book of Ecclesiastes. See William Sanday and Arthur C. Headlam, *The Epistle to the Romans, International Critical Commentary,* 3rd ed. (New York: Scribner's, 1897), pp. 204-12. The idea that the environment in its present state is disordered but would in the future be restored in a universal *shalom* was part of the Jewish messianic hope.

[17]Note especially, for example, Jn 1:1-3; Col 1:16-17; Heb 1:3.

[18]See, for example, Is 32:16-20; 55:12-13; 65:17-25; 66:12-13.

[19]J. Philip Wogaman, *The Great Economic Debate: An Ethical Analysis* (Philadelphia: Westminster Press, 1977), p. vii. The debate over economics is now becoming active in the Christian community, as evidenced by such recent books as Bob Goudzwaard, *Capitalism and Progress: A Diagnosis of Western Society* (Grand Rapids: Eerdmans, 1979); Michael Novak, *The Spirit of Democratic Capitalism* (New York: Simon & Schuster, 1982); Harold Lindsell, *Free Enterprise: A Judeo-Christian Defense* (Wheaton, Ill.: Tyndale, 1982); and several others. Some of this debate was foreshadowed in lectures given in 1891 by Abraham Kuyper, published as *Christianity and the Class Struggle* (Grand Rapids: Piet Hein Publishers, 1950).

[20]Wogaman, *Great Economic Debate,* p. ix.

[21]Schumacher, *Small Is Beautiful,* p. 45.

[22]Schumacher notes that economics "deals with goods in accordance with their market value and not in accordance with what they really are. The same rules and criteria are applied to primary goods, which man has to win from nature, and secondary goods, which presuppose the existence of primary goods and are manufactured from them. All goods are treated the same, because the point of view is fundamentally that of private profit-making, and this means that it is inherent in the methodology of economics *to ignore man's dependence on the natural world*" (ibid., pp. 43-44; italics Schumacher's).

[23]Johnson, *Muddling toward Frugality,* p. 26. See also Rifkin, *The Emerging Order* and *Entropy.*

[24]Wogaman's *The Great Economic Debate* is helpful in this regard. He dis-

cusses in turn the economic options of Marxism, laissez-faire capitalism, social market capitalism, democratic socialism, and what he calls economic conservationism, applying an ethical analysis to each. Wogaman ends up favoring democratic socialism, arguing that economic conservationism has not yet emerged as a viable economic option. It is becoming increasingly clear, however, that some form of ecologically responsible economic system is the only valid option for the future. Such a new economic orientation can and will emerge if ecologically-minded economists give sufficient attention to its development. It is crucial, however, that the perspective of the biblical economy play a key role in this development. Some of the most creative thinking along this line is being done by the economist Herman Daly. See especially his essays in Herman Daly, ed., *Economics, Ecology, Ethics: Essays toward a Steady-State Economy* (San Francisco: W. H. Freeman and Co., 1980). Daly sees "an emerging paradigm shift in political economy toward steady state economic thinking" (p. 1). He observes that "politic economics tries to buy off social conflict by abolishing scarcity —by promising more things for more people, with less for no one, for ever and ever—all vouchsafed by the amazing grace of compound interest" (p. 7).

[25]Helge Brattgard, *God's Stewards: A Theological Study of the Principles and Practices of Stewardship,* trans. Gene J. Lund (Minneapolis: Augsburg Publishing House, 1963), p. 22.

[26]Note Is 66:1-2 and Acts 7:44-50 in this connection.

[27]Although not developed here, the motif of the habitation of God is significant throughout Scripture and dovetails with the perspective outlined in the present chapter. For a partial development of this theme (with reference to the nature of the church only), see Snyder, *Problem of Wineskins,* pp. 57-68.

[28]Note especially 1 Chron 17:1-14; 22:5-10; 29:10-13; Hag 2:6-9; Is 66:1-2. Speaking of Solomon but even more of Jesus, the prophet Nathan tells David, "I will set him over my house [*oikos* in the Septuagint] and my kingdom forever; his throne will be established forever" (1 Chron 17:14). And David later praises God, saying, "Yours, O LORD, is the kingdom; you are exalted as head over all" (1 Chron 29:11). Here is the basis for the Kingdom and economy of God now being realized through Jesus Christ.

[29]Lk 16:2-4; 1 Cor 9:17; Eph 1:10; 3:2, 9; Col 1:25; 1 Tim 1:4. In Eph 1:10, 3:9 and 1 Tim 1:4 the word seems to refer to the overall plan of God.

[30]Oscar Cullmann, *Christ and Time: The Primitive Christian Conception of Time and History,* trans. Floyd V. Filson (London: SCM Press, 1951), p. 33.

[31]"The Greek word *oikonomia,* found in the New Testament, is... very close to what, for lack of a better expression, we call 'salvation history.'

Even in its secular usage it includes the thought of a plan, of an administration of a 'household' "—Oscar Cullmann, *Salvation in History*, trans.
Sidney Sowers (New York: Harper & Row, 1967), p. 75.

[32]John Reumann, "Oikonomia-Terms in Paul in Comparison with Lucan
Heilsgeschichte," *New Testament Studies* 13 (1966-67):150. In addition to this
significant study, see the same author's "Oikonomia = 'Covenant'—Terms
for *Heilsgeschichte* in Early Christian Usage," *Novum Testamentum* 3 (1959):
282-92, and "*Oikonomia* as 'Ethical Accommodation' in the Fathers, and Its
Pagan Backgrounds," *Studia Patristica* 78 (Berlin, 1961):370-79. On the
practical meaning of *oikonomia* as household management see E. A. Judge,
The Social Pattern of Christian Groups in the First Century (London: Tyndale
Press, 1960), pp. 30-39.

[33]Reumann, "Oikonomia-Terms," p. 153.

[34]G. L. Prestige, *God in Patristic Thought* (London: SPCK, 1952), pp. 61, 67.

[35]In somewhat parallel fashion T. F. Torrance observes that in the emergence of the new Einsteinian world view "we have a radical reorientation
in knowledge in which structure and matter, form and being are inseparably fused together, spelling the end of the analytical era in science. This
involves the restoration of a genuine ontology, the replacing of the mechanistic universe with a dynamic universe conceived in onto-relational
[or we might say spiritual-ecological] terms, and the replacing of the old
forms of causal connection and natural law with field-structure and field-
laws. . . . The revolution of science that must come about will result in an
understanding so far transcending our present inadequate concepts that
our present science, even in its most sophisticated aspects, will appear
as primitive and naive. . . .

"Nothing like this has ever appeared before in the whole history of science, philosophy and culture, except in the theology of the pre-Augustini-
an Greek Fathers, who had to carry through the same kind of revolution
in the basis of their culture as modern science is engaged in carrying out
today. For the first time, then, in the history of thought, Christian theology finds itself in the throes of a new scientific culture which is not anti-
thetical to it, but which operates with a non-dualistic outlook upon the
universe which is not inconsistent with the Christian faith, even at the
crucial points of creation and incarnation. This also means that the theology most relevant to the post-Einsteinian world is that of classical Patristic theology, although of course it needs to be recast in the idiom and
style of our own ear" (T. F. Torrance, *Theology in Reconciliation* [London:
Geoffrey Chapman, 1975], p. 270). Put another way, early Greek Christian theology is of particular interest today because it was profoundly
ecological. The Patristic uses of the word *oikonomia* illustrate this.

[36]See Carl Kreider, *The Christian Entrepreneur* (Scottdale, Pa.: Herald Press, 1980), especially chapter seven, "Creative Christian Alternative Forms of Business."

[37]Ecological realities are recognized by Herman Daly's economic thinking in a way that is untrue of most economists today.

[38]This is not a call, however, for the total autonomy of small communities (or other economic units). Economic reality today is largely dominated by giant transnational conglomerates which control more wealth than do most national governments, and Kingdom economics must therefore deal with mechanisms for controlling or transforming, if not dismembering, such corporations. And it must similarly deal with means for ensuring greater equity in economic and political relations among nations.

Whether transnational corporations could ever operate for the benefit of the common good, or whether they are inherently unjust, is a question deserving intense study. In any case, their transformation requires more than simply being operated by Christians, for such corporations take on a semi-autonomous nature which seems to transcend the control of decision makers within the corporation. Thus substantial structural modifications would seem to be necessary.

On the other hand, some have suggested that several of the large international, Western-based, corporation-style Christian outreach and service organizations such as World Vision and Campus Crusade for Christ operate, in effect, as transnational corporations.

3 The Ecology of the Church

[1]Christian camps and campuses could learn much from what is being done ecologically at Au Sable Trails camp and environmental center, Route 2, Mancelona, MI 49659.

[2]The church is sometimes described rather in terms of proclamation *(kerygma)*, service *(diakonia)* and worship *(leitourgia)*. Any conception of the church which does not see *koinōnia* as basic to the church's life, however, is a distortion of the New Testament picture. Also, I prefer *martyria* to *kerygma* as suggesting a more inclusive conception of the church's witness, one which includes *diakonia*. On the tendency to overwork the idea of *kerygma*, see Michael Green, *Evangelism in the Early Church* (Grand Rapids: Eerdmans, 1970), p. 48. Heeding Green's caution that "it is all too easy to be beguiled by particular words into building a theological superstructure upon them which they were never designed to bear" (ibid.), I am suggesting worship, community and witness as basic components of the church's life, not primarily on the grounds of the technical use of these terms in Scripture, but as general categories that cover the biblical revelation and narrative about the church. Still, it is instructive to note some of the Greek

counterparts to the English words and the way the three words are used in the New Testament. For a helpful brief discussion of *leitourgia* and other New Testament words used for worship, see Ferdinand Hand, *The Worship of the Early Church*, trans. David E. Green (Philadelphia: Fortress Press, 1973), pp. 32-39.

[3]Visser 't Hooft, *Renewal of the Church*, p. 97.

[4]The incontrovertible biblical basis for this model is found in Ezekiel 10:10.

[5]For recent discussion of the Christian year in the context of evangelical worship, see Robert E. Webber, *Common Roots: A Call to Evangelical Maturity* (Grand Rapids: Zondervan, 1978), pp. 108-11. Webber has a very helpful section on worship which can serve as a healthy antidote to the shallowness of much contemporary worship and to what Webber calls "a kind of evangelical amnesia" concerning historic Christianity. On the other hand Webber does not, it seems to me, provide sufficient justification for taking second-century Christian worship as the primary model for worship today.

[6]The need for and use of small groups is further developed in Snyder, *Problem of Wineskins* (pp. 89-99, 139-48), *Community of the King* (pp. 143-58), and, with particular reference to discipline, in *The Radical Wesley and Patterns for Church Renewal* (Downers Grove, Ill.: InterVarsity Press, 1980), pp. 149-50, 160-63.

[7]Richard Foster, *Celebration of Discipline* (New York: Harper and Row, 1978), pp. 1-9.

[8]Snyder, *Community of the King*, pp. 107-16.

4 The Church as Sacrament

[1]Augustine *Epistle* 54. 1. 1, quoted in F. van der Meer, *Augustine the Bishop*, trans. Brian Battershaw and G. R. Lamp (London: Sheed and Ward, 1961), p. 278.

[2]"A Catechism," *The Book of Common Prayer* (Greenwich, Conn.: Seabury Press, 1952), p. 581.

[3]Tertullian *Apology* 39.

[4]Mystery and economy are associated also in Eph 3:2-4 and Col 1:25-26. In 1 Cor 4:1 Paul and his associates are called "stewards of the mysteries" (*oikonomous mystērion*) of God. The association of *oikonomia* and *mystērion* in Paul's writings is certainly more than coincidental and is highly fruitful theologically, particularly in the context of the church as the Kingdom community.

[5]See Dulles, *Models of the Church*, pp. 58-59; Eric G. Jay, *The Church: Its Changing Image through Twenty Centuries* (Atlanta: John Knox Press, 1980), pp. 325-27.

[6]Karl Rahner, "Sacramental Theology," in K. Rahner, ed., *Encyclopedia of*

Theology: The Concise Sacramentum Mundi (New York: Seabury Press, p. 1486. The sacramental understanding of the church has been explored by Edward Schillebeeckx, Thomas O'Dea, Richard McBrien, Gregory Baum, Henri de Lubac, Yves Congar and others. It can be argued that both Augustine and Thomas Aquinas saw the church essentially in these terms, but not in a developed sense. Augustine wrote much about the church, but before sacramental ideas were highly developed; Aquinas wrote in a time of highly developed sacramental theology, but wrote little about the church.

[7]Quoted in Jay, *Church,* pp. 325-26.

[8]Dogmatic Constitution on the Church *(Lumen Gentium),* in Austin P. Flannery, ed., *Documents of Vatican II* (Grand Rapids: Eerdmans, 1975), pp. 407-8.

[9]Jay, *Church,* p. 326.

[10]Karl Barth, "La nature et la forma de l'Eglise," in *L'Eglise* (Geneva: Éditions Labor et Fides, 1964), p. 119. Barth, however, makes almost no use of sacramental language in discussing the church. He uses the visible-invisible distinction and tries to hold the two together, but in a way which is finally ahistorical. The sacramental model is more helpful precisely at this point. Barth does, however, locate the church's primary visibility in its gathering as a community, not in its institutional structures.

[11]See the discussion in Dulles, *Models of the Church,* pp. 67-70. As a disadvantage, Dulles notes that the sacramental model "has found little response in Protestant thought" (p. 70). This is understandable but does not attest to the inapplicability of this model to Protestant ecclesiology. The key is maintaining the normative role of Scripture and scriptural models. Dulles seems to prefer the sacramental model because it is useful in relating the institutional model to a more community-centered model; it "supports the best features" of these models "while solving problems that prove intractable on either of these other two, such as the relationship between the invisible institution and the communion of grace" (p. 68). It is important, however, that the sacramental conception not be applied in a way that uncritically justifies or simply overlooks the problem of the church's institutionalism.

[12]In this connection a friend suggests that to abstain from the Lord's Table because it is so sacred is like a married couple's abstaining from sexual relations because sex is so special.

[13]Karl Barth, *Church Dogmatics* (Edinburgh: T & T Clark, 1956), IV/1, p. 666. Barth so closely identifies Christ's physical body and the church as "body of Christ" that he can say the identification church-body is not to be taken merely symbolically or metaphorically. "As His earthly-historical

form of existence, the community is His body, His body is the community" (ibid.). While Dulles suggests that herald is the primary model in Barth's ecclesiology, it can be maintained that Barth's fundamental model is really the church as community, with herald as a secondary model (Howard A. Snyder, "The Doctrine of the Church in the Theology of Karl Barth" [unpublished manuscript, 1977], pp. 20-22).

[14]The church in fact betrays its identification with Jesus if it fails to be a church of, with and for the poor—for Jesus has made it clear that he has radically decided for the poor and is present in a special way among them. He stated plainly that service to the poor is service to him (Mt 25:31-46).

5 The Church as Community

[1]All biblical figures for the church point to or are compatible with the church as the community of God's people. This is the fundamental view and model for which I have argued in *The Problem of Wineskins* and *The Community of the King*. Everything in the present book presupposes this model, and nothing here should be understood as contradicting what was said in the earlier books. I have attempted in this book to show that community is not the only lens through which to see the church, even though (I believe) it is a primary one.

[2]On the other hand, many people seem to have absolutely no interest in or need for community. This is true even among the young. Also, many who may have some interest in community have deep fear of human intimacy. My belief is that the drawing toward intimacy is fundamental to human personality and one aspect of God's image in us. Hunger for community is a natural appetite. But in our present society many people avoid community because they fear it or simply have never really experienced it.

[3]See Jacques Ellul, *Propaganda: The Formation of Men's Attitudes* (New York: Alfred A. Knopf, 1971; original French edition, 1962), especially pp. 6-9.

[4]Most of the proposals for interactive TV suggest that the new technologies and developments will scarcely build community. Rather they will be used primarily for selling products and services—in other words, for the promotion of technological materialism. On the other hand, these developments and the increasing spread of cable TV may provide some strategic opportunities for Christian witness and the articulation of Christian values in art, music, education and other areas.

[5]I am aware that some data, such as the Gallup polls, suggest a rather high level of residual orthodox Christian belief in America today. They also show, however, a split between professed belief and religious practice. (See Gallup and Poling, *The Search for America's Faith*.) Americans may have a high degree of general (and even orthodox) religious belief and feeling, but in the main this appears to be a rather vague abstraction from

an Americanized Christianity that was already heavily compromised and diluted in comparison to biblical Christian faith.

[6]Sider, *Rich Christians*, p. 193.

[7]This is a key verse in Karl Barth's ecclesiology. Barth quotes or refers to the verse over a dozen times in his discussions of the church. The verse seems to have appealed to Barth because it suggests the weakness and humility of the church while also stating its glory: Jesus Christ is there. And, especially, it emphasizes the central fact of the church's being: its gathering together in Christ's name.

[8]On the synagogue pattern see *Problem of Wineskins*, pp. 197-98 n. 6, and *Community of the King*, pp. 151-52.

[9]See Robert Banks, *Paul's Idea of Community: The Early House Churches in Their Historical Setting* (Grand Rapids: Eerdmans, 1980).

[10]Visser 't Hooft, *Renewal of the Church*, p. 54.

[11]Theodore Roszak, *The Making of a Counter-culture* (New York: Doubleday Anchor Books, 1969).

[12]John R. W. Stott, *Christian Counter-Culture: The Message of the Sermon on the Mount* (Downers Grove, Ill.: InterVarsity Press, 1978), p. 10.

[13]Isaiah 60 is the background here. Note especially verse 11.

[14]Jim Wallis, *The Call to Conversion* (New York: Harper & Row, 1981), p. 117.

[15]Jim Wallis, "Rebuilding the Church," *Sojourners* 9, no. 1 (January 1980):12.

[16]By "building community" here I mean building the total Christian community, including the aspects of worship and witness. As I noted in introducing the concentric circle model in chapter three, the basic elements of worship, community and witness are ecological, influencing each other. In this section I am not speaking specifically of the three aspects of community (discipline, gifts and sanctification), but more broadly of the total life of the church, including all aspects of the model, viewed from the perspective of community.

6 The Church as Servant

[1]This model of the church has found its place in the ecclesiology of a number of contemporary theologians, including Hans Küng and Karl Barth. Much contemporary Roman Catholic ecclesiology, inspired in part by the documents of Vatican II, combines the themes of sacrament and servanthood. (Jay, *Church*, pp. 325-31.)

[2]*Diakonia* occurs thirty-four times in the New Testament, *diakoneō* thirty-seven times, and *diakonos* thirty times. In the New International Version, *diakonia* is translated "ministry" fourteen times, "service" (or "serve," "serving") fourteen times, plus once each by the words "preparations," "distribution," "provide help," "mission," "task" and "work."

[3]Benjamin Titus Roberts, "Following the Lord," *The Earnest Christian*

(June 1878).

[4]Hermann W. Beyer, διακονέω, *Theological Dictionary of the New Testament*, ed. Gerhard Kittel, trans. Geoffrey W. Bromiley, 10 vols. (Grand Rapids: Eerdmans, 1964-74), 2:83.

[5]See Snyder, *Radical Wesley*, pp. 80-83, 95-96; Donald F. Durnbaugh, *The Believers' Church: The History and Character of Radical Protestantism* (New York: Macmillan, 1968), pp. 123-24, 212-16; Franklin H. Littell, *The Origins of Sectarian Protestantism* (New York: Macmillan, 1964), pp. 46-78.

[6]Quoted in Norris Magnuson, *Salvation in the Slums: Evangelical Social Work, 1865-1920* (Metuchen, N.J.: Scarecrow Press, 1977), p. 44. These groups and movements are merely representative of many that might be cited over the period of many centuries.

[7]Benjamin Titus Roberts, "The Law of Christ," *The Earnest Christian* (June 1870), p. 187.

[8]Benjamin Titus Roberts, "The Rich," *The Earnest Christian* (January 1870).

7 The Church as Witness

[1]The point of this chapter is to deal particularly with the question of evangelism, since little has been said specifically about this so far in the book and since it is of such vital concern among evangelicals. I recognize, however, that this focus does not exhaust the meaning of witness for the church and that other aspects of Kingdom witness also deserve to be discussed. I have, however, touched on this broader sense of witness repeatedly through the course of the book.

[2]Toby Druin, "Whence Cometh Our Strength?" *Home Missions* (November 1978), pp. 5-10.

[3]James F. Engel, *Contemporary Christian Communications: Its Theory and Practice* (Nashville: Thomas Nelson, 1979), pp. 21-22. See also C. Peter Wagner, "Who Found It?" *Eternity* (September 1977), pp. 13-19.

[4]Quoted by Druin in "Whence Cometh Our Strength."

[5]Win Arn, "A Church Growth Look at Here's Life America," *Church Growth: America* 3:1 (January/February 1977), pp. 4-7, 9, 14-15, 27, 30.

[6]George Peters, *Saturation Evangelism* (Grand Rapids: Zondervan, 1970), pp. 76-77; C. Peter Wagner, *Frontiers in Missionary Strategy* (Chicago: Moody, 1971), pp. 153-60. This is not to deny that much good has been done by Evangelism in Depth and by its more recent and better designed offshoots, nor to gloss over the significant differences between these various efforts.

[7]This is a repeated theme in Augustine. For example: "Thither accordingly, where Christ preceded us, are we on our way: and Christ is still journeying whither He has gone before; for Christ went before us in the Head, Christ follows in the Body: ... Still Christ is here in want, Christ here

still journeys, Christ here is sick, Christ here is in bonds. In saying this we should wrong Him, had He not told us this truth in His own words, 'I was hungered, and ye gave Me meat.' " *Expositions on the Book of Psalms*, 6 vols. (Oxford: John Henry Parker, 1847-57), 4:218-19.

[8]See Engel's analysis in *Contemporary Christian Communications*. Engel shows the value and proper use of the mass media, recognizing what they can and cannot be expected to do in genuine Christian communication. Our focus should be on using the media redemptively, based on a vital experience of church.

[9]NAE *Profile* 11, no. 6 (December 1978):1.

[10]As is true with *pastor* and other New Testament terms, we should be careful not to read contemporary meanings and connotations back into Scripture. Judging by the New Testament use of the verb form, *evangelist* did not have the rather specific and restricted sense it has today. An evangelist was one who proclaimed the good news of Jesus Christ and the Kingdom of God. If we keep this somewhat broader and more basic meaning in mind, the listing of evangelists in Ephesians 4:11 makes more sense.

[11]C. Peter Wagner, *Your Church Can Grow* (Glendale, Calif.: Regal, 1976), pp. 75-77. This is a suggestive observation, but certainly not a prescription or limitation. The point is that at least *some* believers in each congregation may be expected to have the gift of evangelism.

[12]See Snyder, *Community of the King*, pp. 121-32.

[13]The very architecture of any building we erect says to the surrounding community, "Some of you will feel welcome here. Others of you will not." Usually it is the poor and dispossessed we (unwittingly?) put off. On the other hand, there is no excuse for shoddy or ugly church buildings. We need structures combining simplicity, functionality and beauty that say, "All are welcome; there is love and grace here!" But even more, we need to invite people to Christian *community* (to the real church), not to "Christian" architecture. (See Snyder, *Problem of Wineskins*, pp. 69-79.)

[14]One of the more controversial proposals offered in *The Problem of Wineskins* was that the church would likely be more healthy without her reliance on church buildings. Has this point been overstated? I think not. As I travel around and see how preoccupied most churches are with property and real estate, and with related financial and staffing questions, the more convinced I am that here is one horrendous blind spot in the church's vision.

8 The Ministry of All Believers

[1]See Snyder, *Problem of Wineskins*, chapter ten, and *Community of the King*, pp. 57-68.

[2]*Johann Arndt: True Christianity*, trans. Peter Erb (New York: Paulist, 1979),

p. 261.

[3]While nearly all the gifts are seen in Jesus Christ, we have no record that he ever spoke in tongues. Little can be concluded from this, except that apparently tongues-speaking isn't important enough for Christ to have left us an example or teaching on the matter. Whether or not he spoke in tongues, we simply do not know. It would be a mistake to argue either for or against tongues-speaking (or any particular variety thereof) from the example of Christ. Those who wish to stress tongues would, of course, point to what Jesus said about the Spirit's outpouring.

9 The Liberation of Theology

[1]Peter's Pentecost sermon (Acts 2) specifically refers to Old Testament Scriptures ("this is what was spoken by the prophet Joel"; "David said . . ."), the events of Jesus' life, death and resurrection, and the birth of the church in the Pentecostal outpouring itself ("these men are not drunk"; "what you now see and hear").

[2]John Howard Yoder, "The Fullness of Christ, Perspectives on Ministries in Renewal," *Concern* 17 (February 1969):33-93.

[3]A number of people have been exploring biography and story, especially, as modes of doing theology. See, for example, James McClendon, Jr., *Biography as Theology* (Nashville: Abingdon, 1974); John S. Dunne, *Time and Myth* (Notre Dame, Ind.: University of Notre Dame Press, 1975) and other books; Frederick Buechner, *Telling the Truth: The Gospel as Tragedy, Comedy and Fairy Tale* (New York: Harper & Row, 1977). Related are the growing popularity of C. S. Lewis, Tolkien and other imaginative writers, and recent attempts by some theologians to use insights from such writers in their own work. A related fundamental concern is the importance of the category of history for theology. My concern is not only that such promising attempts be carried out with biblical fidelity, but that they grow out of the life experience (the story and history!) of Christian life together.

[4]J. A. Bengel, *Gnomon of the New Testament,* trans. Charlton T. Lewis and Marvin R. Vincent, 2 vols. (Philadelphia: Perkinpine and Higgins, 1884), 1:xii.

[5]This is not to deny the human element in Scripture. God used fallen and fallible human beings in giving us the Bible, and their humanity shows up on every page. But the church confesses that God speaks uniquely through Scripture. Through the agency of the Holy Spirit the Scriptures faithfully record God's will and testify to God's action in history and, supremely, in Jesus Christ.

[6]Clark Pinnock, "Evangelical Theology—Conservative and Contemporary," expanded manuscript of McMaster Divinity College Day Lecture, October 25, 1977, p. 14 (TSF Study Paper).

[7]Jacques Ellul, *False Presence of the Kingdom,* trans. C. Edward Hopkin (New York: Seabury Press, 1972), p. 209.

[8]Consider, for example, the fascination with utopian communities and the considerable literature on this topic. One good summary for North America is Mark Holloway, *Heavens on Earth: Utopian Communities in America, 1680-1880,* 2nd ed. (New York: Dover Publications, 1966).

10 The Book of the Covenant

[1]Donald G. Bloesch, *Essentials of Evangelical Theology,* 2 vols. (New York: Harper & Row, 1979), 2:274. See also Robert K. Johnston, *Evangelicals at an Impasse: Biblical Authority in Practice* (Atlanta: John Knox Press, 1979).

[2]Bloesch, *Essentials,* 2:270-71. As representatives of the scholastic view Bloesch cites B. B. Warfield, Gordon Clark, Francis Schaeffer, Carl Henry and John W. Montgomery, among others.

[3]Ibid., p. 275. To acknowledge this is not to introduce an element of irrationality or pure existentialist subjectivism. It is rather to allow space for the suprarational and nonrational aspects of God and of creation which in God's plan are not irrational but are fully compatible with reason. The ecology of God's plan is broader than reason but not irrational.

[4]Ibid., pp. 272-73.

[5]Ibid., p. 274.

[6]Ibid. Another important recent contribution to an evangelical doctrine of biblical authority is William J. Abraham, *The Divine Inspiration of Holy Scripture* (Oxford: Oxford University Press, 1981). Against a rigid inerrantist view, Abraham insists on the importance of distinguishing between divine inspiration and divine speaking. Against liberal views he shows that divine acting must include divine speaking. Some of Abraham's language evokes a sacramental understanding of Scripture, and his position falls into the sacramental rather than liberal-modernist or scholastic category.

[7]There are, it is true, various theories about the nature of a sacrament, so that a sacramental understanding of Scripture could be interpreted in somewhat different ways. Still, the fundamental category of sacrament seems helpful in maintaining the authority and mystery, the human and divine aspects, of Scripture.

[8]Bengel, *Gnomon,* 1:xii.

[9]Ibid.

[10]Such splits have occurred more than once in church history—for example, in later Pietism in its controversy with Lutheran orthodoxy and in the twentieth-century American fundamentalist-modernist debate, where fundamentalism maintained many essential doctrines (mixed with nonessential dispensationalist theories) while it lost an understanding of church life and its present relationship to the Kingdom of God. From this

perspective, modern fundamentalism has more in common with seventeenth- and eighteenth-century Lutheran scholasticism than with the evangelical Pietism of that era.

11 The Lifestyle of the Kingdom

[1]"The Lausanne Covenant," in *Let the Earth Hear His Voice*, ed. J. D. Douglas (Minneapolis: World Wide Publications, 1975), p. 6.

[2]John Wesley, Sermon, "The Witness of Our Own Spirit," *The Works of the Rev. John Wesley, A.M.*, 3rd ed. (London: John Mason, 1829-31), V, p. 139.

[3]B. T. Roberts, "Free Churches," *The Earnest Christian*, 1, no. 1 (January 1860):7.

[4]Jim Wallis, *The Call to Conversion* (San Francisco: Harper & Row, 1981), p. 63.

[5]Ibid., pp. 71, 68.

[6]Foster, *Celebration of Discipline*, p. 72.

[7]Ibid., pp. 72-73.

[8]Eller, *Thy Kingdom Come: A Blumhardt Reader*, p. 95.

[9]Ibid., p. 5.

[10]C. Peter Wagner, *Church Growth and the Whole Gospel: A Biblical Mandate* (San Francisco: Harper & Row, 1981), p. 17. Note Wagner's important discussion of the signs of the Kingdom, pp. 15-23. I believe Wagner is on target in warning against overlooking "signs and wonders" as legitimate and important manifestations of the inbreaking of the Kingdom. While his division of the signs of the Kingdom into "Category A" (more general, longer-range and less obviously miraculous) and "Category B" (specific, immediate acts of power, such as healings) may be useful for analytical purposes, it runs the danger of dividing up or dichotomizing the Kingdom in an unbiblical way.

[11]A significant literature on Christian lifestyle has developed over the past few years. See especially (in addition to other books cited in this chapter): Ronald J. Sider, ed., *Living More Simply* (Downers Grove, Ill.: InterVarsity Press, 1980); Richard Foster, *Freedom of Simplicity* (San Francisco: Harper & Row, 1981); John V. Taylor, *Enough Is Enough* (London: SCM Press, 1975); Doris Jantzen Longacre, *Living More with Less* (Scottdale, Pa.: Herald Press, 1980). There are also many secular books now on simple lifestyle and related issues, such as Johnson, *Muddling toward Frugality*, and Duane Elgin, *Voluntary Simplicity* (New York: William Morrow, 1981). See also Philip Amerson, "Lifestyle Research: A Review of Resources," *Review of Religious Research*, 20 (Summer 1979):350-56.

[12]Sider, *Rich Christians*, pp. 175-78.

[13]On the dismal record of the United States in nonmilitary foreign aid, see Sider, *Rich Christians*, pp. 50-56. Also Adam D. Finnerty, *No More Plastic*

Jesus: Global Justice and Christian Lifestyle (Maryknoll, N.Y.: Orbis, 1977), pp. 56-70, where we are reminded that U.S. "aid" goes almost exclusively to assist friendly elites in countries where the U.S. has economic interests and to expand markets for U.S. products.

[14]Doris Jantzen Longacre, *The More-With-Less Cookbook* (Scottdale, Pa.: Herald Press, 1976).

[15]Orlando E. Costas, "Conversion as a Complex Experience—A Personal Case Study," in *Down to Earth: Studies in Christianity and Culture,* ed. John R. W. Stott and Robert Coote (Grand Rapids: Eerdmans, 1980), p. 181.

12 "Laymen": Free to Minister

[1]Carl Wilson, *With Christ in the School of Disciple Building* (Grand Rapids: Zondervan, 1976), p. 19.

13 Women: Free to Lead

[1]Benjamin Titus Roberts, *Ordaining Women* (Rochester, N. Y.: Earnest Christian Publishing House, 1891), p. 10. Roberts was the principal founder of the Free Methodist Church.

[2]It is clear that Jesus' disciples included at least a dozen women. While we know the names and identities of only a few of these women, they apparently included Mary Magdalene, two or three other Marys, Joanna, Susanna, Salome and possibly Lazarus's two sisters, Mary and Martha. See especially Lk 8:1-3; 23:49; 24:10; Mt 27:55-56; Mk 16:1.

[3]Melanie Morrison is right: "The biblical defense of hierarchy in male-female relationships is built on a select number of Pauline passages, while the Gospels and the book of Acts are often ignored." "Jesus and Women," *Sojourners* 9, no. 7 (July 1980):11.

[4]Stephen B. Clark, *Man and Woman in Christ: An Examination of the Roles of Men and Women in Light of Scripture and the Social Sciences* (Ann Arbor, Mich.: Servant Books, 1980) gives a different interpretation to Genesis 1:26-28. He tends to see biological reproduction as the major purpose of sexual differentiation, arguing that "God made them that way . . . so that they could have children and increase and multiply." He does not wish to include woman in the commission to rule. Thus he ascribes different meanings to "them" in verse 26 and "them" in verse 27. When verse 26 says "let them rule," the reference (says Clark) is plural because it indicates "the whole human race," not just "the first human being." But in verse 27 "them" does refer to the male and the female. Thus women are included in the first "them" only in a general, generic sense, and in fact are practically excluded. With no apparent exegetical support, Clark thus gives this interpretation to the passage: "God created the human race in his own image so that it could have dominion over living things. *Moreover,* he created the human race male and female so that the race could increase

and fill the earth" (pp. 12-14; emphasis Clark's). This makes sexual differentiation unimportant except for biological reasons, giving it little or no spiritual and psychological meaning; thus it tends to reinforce the view of women as utilitarian sex objects.

[5]See Barth, *Church Dogmatics,* III/1, pp. 194-250, and Paul K. Jewett, *Man as Male and Female* (Grand Rapids: Eerdmans, 1975), pp. 33-48, where Barth's view is discussed. In *Man and Woman in Christ,* Stephen Clark takes issue with this interpretation on the basis that it is insufficiently exegetical and "has not been one normally held by scripture scholars" (p. 14). He has, however, no solid exegetical argument against it. Hal Miller in *Christian Community: Biblical or Optional?* does a good job of showing the significance of the image of God for human and Christian community but does not deal at length with sexuality in this connection. Nonetheless, in the relational interpretation which he gives to the divine image, Miller is closer to Barth and Jewett than to Clark.

[6]It is interesting that those who argue for male dominance generally put the argument in terms of women submitting rather than of men dominating. When the matter is put in the balder, starker form of male domination, we sense more fully the inconsistency of arguing for sexual equality and female subordination at the same time.

[7]This is expressed nicely in the NIV and in the *Anchor Bible* by printing these two verses as poetry.

[8]E. A. Speiser, *The Anchor Bible: Genesis* (Garden City, N.Y.: Doubleday, 1964), p. 17.

[9]Clark argues, on the contrary, that Genesis 2 clearly portrays woman as subordinate to man for three reasons: (1) the man, not the woman, is the center of the narrative; (2) the man, not the woman, "is called 'Man' or 'Human' "; and (3) man is created before woman (*Man and Woman in Christ,* pp. 23-28). But Clark's argument is not convincing. First, the center of the narrative in reality is neither the man nor the woman but the complementarity of their relationship, as suggested by the climactic passage, verses 21-24. Second, the word *adam,* "man," is applied to both man and woman in Gen 1:27. Third, while woman's creation after man's could indicate a certain priority *either* for the man or for the woman, depending on how the movement of chapter two is understood, the real point is not priority but complementarity. Regarding the more substantive argument that Paul bases woman's subordination on her being created second, the contexts of the two passages involved (1 Tim 2:12-13; 1 Cor 11:8-9) do not suggest that Paul's views here are to be understood as being transculturally normative for the church.

In arguing for complementarity, I specifically reject androgyny or the "androgynous ideal" championed by some feminists in which the male-female polarity is merged or lost. Creation and revelation show this is not God's way.

Donald Bloesch also argues for complementarity but maintains a more dominant "headship" role for the man then I feel is biblically warranted. See Donald G. Bloesch, *Is the Bible Sexist? Beyond Feminism and Patriarchalism* (Westchester, Ill.: Crossway Books, 1982), pp. 20, 31, 35.

[10]A man may be a "wife" and a woman a "husband" to the degree that these labels describe culturally prescribed social roles. This in no way, however, opens the door to a homosexual understanding of marriage. The normal pattern is husband-wife (not husband-husband or wife-wife) just as it is male-female (not male-male or female-female). The view of complementarity rules out homosexuality as an accepted norm in the church or in society. It may be true that both men and women share "masculine" and "feminine" characteristics in varying degrees, depending on how these terms are defined. The problem today is that the sexual obsession of modern society has produced serious sexual identity confusion in many people. Such people need compassion, understanding and acceptance in the church, but homosexuality should never be condoned nor homosexual practice be considered acceptable Christian behavior.

[11]See Donald W. Dayton, *Discovering an Evangelical Heritage* (New York: Harper & Row, 1976), pp. 85-90.

[12]Clark, p. 158.

[13]The two fundamental points in this whole discussion appear to be (1) what God's "original" intention at creation was and (2) the degree to which we may expect to see that intention fulfilled now, in the present order, on the basis of Christ's victory. This is, of course, another way of asking to what degree the Kingdom is, or can be, present now.

Based on the whole tenor of Scripture, my view is that God's intention at creation was full and complete equality, complementarity and mutual service/submission between man and woman, rather than unilateral subordination of the woman to the man, and that the power of God's grace in Christ is sufficient to see this relationship restored in a real and significant, if not total, way now as a sign of the new age of the Kingdom.

This view in no way ignores, tries to deny or is bothered by empirical differences between men and women; rather it glories in them as testifying to the wisdom of God, the beauty and diversity of creation and the full meaning of the image of God as grounded in the triune nature of God. This view does insist on the importance, however, of distinguishing between (or at least being sensitive to) those male-female differences which are based primarily in cultural differences and those which are based more fundamentally in the created image of God. Since full discernment in this area is impossible because of the subtle mix of heredity and environment in every person, we have little basis for dogmatism in advocating particular patterns of men-women relationships—including patterns which are seen in Scripture but not necessarily prescribed there.

Regarding the two basic points mentioned above, I am in most fundamental disagreement with Clark over the first. He sees subordination of woman to man as intended and prescribed in the creation; I see equality, complementarity and mutual (not unilateral) submission there. While exegetically either interpretation may perhaps be possible (with reference at least to Genesis 1—3), it seems to me that a full biblical theology supports the equality/mutual submission view.

Regarding the second point (the fulfillment of God's intention now), I believe my view is more "optimistic" than Clark's, but here the main disagreements trace back to differences on the first point. I agree with Clark that "God's creation 'at the beginning' was an ideal pattern for men, women, and the whole human race." But I disagree with him as to what that pattern was. It seems to me the pattern pointed to (though not fully elaborated) in Genesis 1—3 is a human community of mutual respect and submission under the sovereignty of God, with sexual differentiation greatly enriching these relationships but indicating no hierarchical arrangement.

Fundamentally, I have no trouble agreeing with much that Clark says about differences between men and women. Clearly there are significant differences, although most of these are in varying degrees culturally conditioned. I would, however, draw the opposite inference from Clark regarding these differences. Precisely because women *are* different from men in certain ways, their leadership is needed in the church. The church has suffered in part because its leadership has been almost totally masculine and insufficiently feminine.

Clark's analysis seems to presuppose quite a conservative view of tradition. It is interesting that he can say that "a consideration from tradition does not significantly modify the results of a consideration from scripture" (p. xii). This is precisely the point I would contest, on this as on several fundamental issues of ecclesiology. Frequently argument from Scripture fails to "significantly modify" traditional positions only if one already believes that tradition and Scripture cannot be in conflict.

[14]The intention here is to present a biblical feminist position. I emphasize, however, that feminism must really be biblical, or it ceases to be redemptive and helpful for the Kingdom. If it comes to a showdown between biblical authority and feminist idealism, it is feminism which must give

way, not Scripture. Otherwise Scripture ceases to be the "norming norm," and some other source of authority (reason, experience or some combination of the two) is placed over Scripture. In that case, feminism itself ultimately loses, for unless feminism can be grounded in Scripture on a hermeneutically sound basis, it is vulnerable to the subjective counterclaims of other people's reason and experience. The fundamental question is what Scripture really teaches, not whether the Bible can be made to support feminism.

[15]Both Clark and some of the more extreme feminists tend to see sexual differences too exclusively in terms of reproduction. I see them as being more fundamentally based. While I would not want to take this significance as far as did Carl Jung, nor to posit masculinity and femininity as eternal principles, I do think sexual differentiation is psychologically and spiritually significant in ways that both reinforce male-female distinctiveness and support full equality—not on the basis of sameness but on the basis of mutually necessary complementarity.

I realize that this is a primarily philosophical and psychological argument, not a biblical one. But (1) philosophical reasoning is always mixed with one's biblical interpretation; it's just not usually made explicit. And (2) this reasoning seems fully consistent with the biblical material and (in my own case, at least) is open to modification on the basis of a fuller understanding of Scripture.

The equality/complementarity model seems more consistent with Scripture and the social sciences, as well as with an ecological approach to the world, than does the male dominance model. It is certainly true that in Scripture God is at times depicted through feminine imagery—most strikingly, perhaps, when described as or represented by wisdom. (See Carl G. Jung, *Answer to Job,* 2nd ed., trans. R. F. C. Hull [Princeton, N.J.: Princeton University Press, 1969], pp. 24-29. From a completely different perspective, see Evangeline Booth, *Toward a Better World* [Garden City, N.Y.: Doubleday, Doran and Company, 1928], pp. 198-214, where Christ is pictured "As a Mother.")

The significant thing about the true God is that he is pictured biblically as exclusively or essentially neither male nor female, but as transcending and incorporating both the masculine and the feminine. In contrast, pagan mythology not only moves to polytheism but also to sexual differentiation among the gods, and, in effect, to an eternal (or primordial) masculine/feminine duality (which Jung also does with his animus-anima theory).

It should be noted, in this regard, that there is nothing biblically offensive in describing God as "she" as well as "he."

[16]"Letters," *Light and Life* 114, no. 5 (May 1981):28.

[17]Roberts, *Ordaining Women*, p. 117.

[18]The argument here is for the freedom of women to participate in the ministry of all God's people, not just in pastoral ministry. This chapter is not intended primarily as an argument for women's ordination, because ordination is a secondary question which needs to be treated and re-evaluated separately.

14 The Poor: Free to Decide

[1]The Bible is clear on these points, although only in the past decade or so has this perspective been recovered in the church—in part through the influence of liberation theology. From an evangelical perspective, see especially Sider, *Rich Christians*, pp. 59-130; Snyder, *Problem of Wineskins*, pp. 37-53; John R. W. Stott, "Who, Then, Are the Poor?" *Christianity Today* 25, no. 9 (May 8, 1981):54-55.

[2]Stott, "Who, Then, Are the Poor?" pp. 54-55. From a somewhat different perspective, R. C. Sproul distinguishes four categories of "the poor" in Scripture: (1) the poor because of slothfulness; (2) the poor because of disease, famine or other catastrophe; (3) the poor because of exploitation; and (4) the voluntary poor for righteousness' sake. R. C. Sproul, "Biblical Economics: Equity or Equality?" *Christianity Today* 26, no. 5 (March 5, 1982):94.

[3]While it may be useful for purposes of analysis to distinguish between the slothful poor and the exploited poor, we must avoid assigning people to these categories as a matter of social analysis, or as a means of deciding who is "deserving" or "undeserving" of aid. When one is unaware of, or unwilling to face, the fact of economic and social oppression, it is all too easy to see poverty as primarily the fault of the poor.

[4]See Piero Gheddo, *Why Is the Third World Poor?* trans. Kathryn Sullivan (Maryknoll, N.Y.: Orbis, 1973).

[5]See Gross, *Friendly Fascism*, pp. 32-43.

[6]See Dayton, *Discovering an Evangelical Heritage;* Magnuson, *Salvation in the Slums;* Carroll Smith Rosenberg, *Religion and the Rise of the American City: The New York City Mission Movement, 1812-1870* (Ithaca: Cornell University Press, 1971); David O. Moberg, *The Great Reversal: Evangelism and Social Concern,* rev. ed. (Philadelphia: J. B. Lippincott, 1977).

[7]Herzog, *Justice Church*, p. 133.

[8]Bread for the World, 32 Union Square East, New York, NY 10003; Evangelicals for Social Action, 300 W. Apsley Street, Philadelphia, PA 19144; Association for Public Justice, Box 56348, Washington, DC 20011; Sojourners Fellowship, 1309 L Street NW, Washington, DC 20005.

[9]Adolf Deissmann, "Christianity and the Lower Classes," *Expositor* 7

(1909):224. Quoted in Herzog, *Justice Church,* p. 132.

[10]This is not to slight the fact that dynamic renewal movements sometimes are born among, or draw their leadership from, more well-to-do segments of society. It appears, however, that even in these cases the most dynamic movements are those which profoundly identify with the poor. One may think of Francis of Assisi and Count Zinzendorf as two examples of leaders who, though they were rich, became poor for the sake of the Kingdom.

[11]Herzog, *Justice Church,* p. 136.

[12]Deuteronomy 15:11 says, "There will always be poor people in the land." But in this charge to God's people we also read that economic justice is to be done, and thus "there should be no poor among you, for in the land the LORD your God is giving you to possess as your inheritance, he will richly bless you, if only you fully obey the LORD your God and are careful to follow all these commands" (Deut 15:4-5).

15 Pastors: Free to Disciple

[1]Henri J. M. Nouwen, *The Way of the Heart: Desert Spirituality and Contemporary Ministry* (New York: Seabury, 1981), p. 22.

[2]Revelation 2—3 (the "angels" of the seven churches) is no exception. First, it is not at all clear that the "angels" or "messengers" represent human leaders. More important, the seven churches addressed were not single local congregations but probably networks of house fellowships over which there was no single human leader. With time, of course, a primary overseer or bishop emerged in each major city.

[3]It is clear from Acts 20:17-28 that plural leadership, rather than just one pastor, was the pattern in the church at Ephesus. The group of elders together were "overseers" (*episkopoi,* "bishops"). The Ephesian elders seem to have been fairly numerous; even if there were several congregations or house fellowships in Ephesus, it is clear the situation was not one pastor per congregation. A group of leaders, all of whom exercised spiritual leadership and none of whom was *the* pastor over the others was the pattern of leadership.

[4]The New Testament attests to plural leadership in local fellowships, and often these leaders were called "elders." It is important today that plural leadership be practiced and that those who exercise spiritual leadership within the congregation meet the biblical standards for such leadership (for example, those found in Titus 1:6-16). Local churches need elders, though it is not essential, it seems to me, that any one form of eldership or the precise term of *elder* be employed. Churches need the *functional equivalent* of eldership, and this can often be provided within the framework of existing and familiar official structures if the pastoral leadership will take seriously Ephesians 4:11-12.

INDEX